{ THE }

# SIMPLICITY PRIMER

{ THE }

# SIMPLICITY PRIMER

365 Ideas

*for Making Life*

*More Livable*

PATRICE LEWIS

WND Books

The Simplicity Primer

WND Books

Published by WorldNetDaily

Washington, D.C.

WND Books are distributed to the trade by:
Midpoint Trade Books
27 West 20th Street, Suite 1102
New York, NY 10011

WND Books are available at special discounts for bulk purchases. WND Books, Inc. also publishes books in electronic formats. For more information call (541) 474-1776 or visit www.wndbooks.com.

First Edition

ISBN 13 Digit: 978-1-936488-28-5

Library of Congress information available

Printed in the United States of America

10 9 8 7 6 5 4 3 2 1

To God, for my many blessings;
To my parents, who raised me;
To my children, who inspire me;
To my publisher, who believed in me;
And to my husband, who has spent the last twenty years
treating me in the manner to which I have become
happily, nay blissfully, accustomed.

# CONTENTS

## ACKNOWLEDGMENTS

SO MANY PEOPLE were instrumental in writing this book that it's hard to know who to thank first.

My children were far more patient with me than I probably deserved, displaying unusual maturity and understanding for the hours I spent hunched over the keyboard. I heard few complaints beyond an occasional wistful, "When will your book be done, mom?"

My husband was an absolute paragon of patience, love, and support throughout the entire procedure. He was my sounding board, my idea supplier when I ran dry, my shoulder to cry on, and my biggest cheerleader. Is it any wonder why I'm crazy about this guy?

My parents applauded when they heard I had a book coming out. To them I can attribute much of the wisdom found in these pages. In their fifty-plus years of marriage, they embody so many principles of a simple life that all I had to do was harvest their insight. Mom and Dad, I love you.

To our pastor, David "Spike" Shine, whose wisdom, staunch guidance, fabulous sermons, and general all-around niceness (and occasional ice-cream treats) has aided our family in spiritual growth on an exponential scale. Spike, don't ever retire.

To my writers' groups—what fabulous gatherings of lovers of the written word! I thank you all so much for your support.

To my friends Debra, Patty, and Wendy. My goodness, ladies, for how many years have you been urging me on my way? You've given me friendship, support, ideas, critiques, and inspiration. I'd be lost without you. I love you all to pieces.

To my agent, Sammie Justesen, who held my hand and listened to me whimper more times than I should have. Some people think that literary agents lead lives of glamour, but I'm here to tell you that they have to put up with a lot of whiny, insecure writers for clients. Thanks, Sammie, for doing your job so well.

Last but not least, to the Lord above for everything I have.

## INTRODUCTION

FOR A LOT of people, there comes a moment of truth when we realize our lives are too complex. Mine came in a traffic jam. There was a terrible accident on the highway during the morning commute. What was normally a half hour's drive turned into two hours.

I arrived at work exhausted and irritable and very late. I wasn't at all ready for an eight-hour day and the commute home. My job had lost its sparkle. The city had lost its excitement. The days were too full, the weekends crammed with what couldn't get done during the rest of the week. It was time for a change.

My husband and I were newly wed and ready to get out. We wanted a simpler life. We started assessing our jobs, where we lived, what we did. We took a leap of faith and left California. We moved to semi-rural Oregon where I went to graduate school, and my husband looked for a job. Life would be simple, we thought.

So there we were, unemployed and living in a house that could only charitably be called a shack (it's what newlyweds could afford). But it was on four acres, and we thought we were living in paradise. However, if we imagined our lives would be simpler as a result of leaving California, we were gravely mistaken.

Unable to find work, my husband started a home woodcraft business. It took five months before he was ready to start selling. Five months of no paycheck. Five months of me accruing expenses in full-time grad school. Five months of gnawing our fingernails and praying we could make our business succeed. Because if it didn't, it was back to the commute again.

It took a long, long time, but it worked. Eighteen years later we're still in business. We have two children, live on a twenty-acre homestead, work at home, and are living a truly simple life. Along the way, we learned what simplicity is and what it isn't.

To some people, you can't live simply without reverting to the lifestyle of the pioneers, complete with a hand pump on the well and kerosene lamps (though I don't see a rush to embrace corsets). Others feel you must engage in chanting (to raise your "consciousness"), eating a family meal in utter silence (so you can "connect" with each other on an "inner level"), beating the tar out of your pillows (after first bowing gently to your "inner self" and to "the universe"), or otherwise contemplating your navel.

But I believe simplicity is . . . well, simpler than that. Simplicity is merely *making good choices*. That's it.

As the years went by and the economy around us boomed and then went bust, we realized a secondary benefit to simplicity: it has allowed us to stay stable and calm in a chaotic, complicated economy and culture.

This book is *not* about our journey, though I use examples from our lives. Rather, it is about some of the practical and simplifying things we've learned on the trip. It is written with families in mind, and geared toward women (though men will certainly benefit from the advice).

If you hope that the contents of this book will give you fast and easy answers to your complex life, you'll be mistaken. Scaling down and making your life simple is not easy. It is, however, worth it.

If there's one thing with which I have no patience, it's "simplicity" advice that borders on new-age psychobabble and impractical nonsense. Juice fasts and tree hugging will not appreciably simplify your life. Getting out of debt and strengthening your marriage will.

This book is intensely practical. Yon won't find suggestions to get in touch with your inner-whatever. Instead you'll find advice on being frugal, cutting the clutter, and strengthening your family relationships.

This book is called *The Simplicity Primer: 365 Ideas for Making Life More Livable* because it's a primer for doing practical, sensible things to simplify your life. It addresses not just the mechanics of living simply, but the mind-set: Dealing with modes of thought and behavior that can help you reach your goal of simplifying your life.

Simplifying your life doesn't necessarily mean your life will be less busy. You might be working hard, but you'll be enjoying it more.

You will find that many of the suggestions require a change in your behavior. Many require a change in attitude. Some of these suggestions will be difficult or may even seem offensive. However, *all* of them will make your life less stressful, more joyous, and above all, simpler.

Those who seek a simpler life come from all backgrounds and are heading in many different directions. But the goal of everyone should be the same: a calmness of spirit, a joy in your work, and a peace that comes from knowing you are doing your part to be independent and responsible.

Simplicity allows you to be prepared. I believe hard times are here, and harder times are coming. We've seen an apparently endless recession that is keeping people unemployed. We've seen an ever-more intrusive government trying to increase its control by spending money it doesn't have on "fixes" that do not work.

Simplifying your life *now*, before things get worse, is a whole lot easier than trying to cope with a complex life as well as a failing economy. Only by embracing a calm, prepared life can you face the coming changes with greater serenity. When you are ready physically, mentally, and spiritually to handle the times to come, then you have achieved simplicity.

This book is laid out in twelve sections of about thirty tips each. Some of these suggestions are step-off-the-fast-track, old-fashioned ideas. Some of these ideas are of the pare-down, move-to-a-cabin-in-the-woods type. Others can be done no matter where you live.

My husband and I have lived a simpler, happier life for many years now. It hasn't always been easy, but it has always been worth it. We take pleasure in knowing that our two daughters (currently thirteen and fifteen) are growing up with sound values, family security, and with minimal commercial influences. While our lives are far from perfect, we are busy, happy, and peaceful. We can testify that these tips aren't just "nice ideas"—they work.

Good luck on your journey.

*Patrice Lewis*

Be not greedy for a cubit of land,
And trespass not on the boundary of the widow . . .
Plough the fields that thou mayest find thy needs,
And receive thy bread from thine own threshing floor.
Better is a bushel which God giveth to thee
Than five thousand gained by transgression . . .
Better is poverty in the hand of God
Than riches in the storehouse;
And better are loaves when the heart is joyous
Than riches in unhappiness . . .

*The Wisdom of Amenemope*
*Circa 950 B.C.*

{ THE }
# SIMPLICITY
# PRIMER

# Getting Personal

▼

To a greater or lesser extent, simplicity is within everyone's grasp. Most of us are capable of making good and honorable choices. Remember, the only thing you can change is YOU. Your attitude, your behavior, and your habits will all contribute toward the ultimate goal of simplicity. In a worsening economy, attitude and choices may be the difference between surviving and thriving.

# .1.

## LIFE 101

Of all the different aspects that are examined in this book, it is probably issues in your personal life that are the most in your control. *You* and only you have the power to make changes in yourself. You may not be able to change anyone else, or make rapid changes in your job, or your finances, or even your health. But you can make all kinds of changes within yourself . . . *and* you can do many of these changes quickly.

There are so many ways to simplify your personal life. Many of the following tips are to get you to realize that simplicity is frequently a product of *attitude*. By learning to control the myriad of selfish behaviors to which humans are prone, we can make amazing improvements. What if we taught ourselves to put aside ego? Pride? Arrogance? Gossip? What if we cultivated virtues that have been lauded since before Christ—humility, kindness, politeness, honesty, forbearance, and patience? Believe it or not, these virtues have been proven through millennia to simplify your life in astounding ways.

By simplifying your personal life, you will acquire the strength and ammunition to handle stresses in other areas—your job, your finances, even your family. You'll find benefits that you never imagined.

These are the external things that affect you. But gaining control over your personal life will also help you gain control over the internal stresses such as your health, your peace of mind, your virtues, and even your faith. In the brave new world we're facing, those who can keep their heads while all others are losing theirs have the best chance of surviving and thriving.

Welcome to Life 101 and the road to simplicity.

# . 2 .

## THE CHOICES WE MAKE

If I had to summarize what it takes to achieve a simpler life in three words or less, it would be these: *make good choices.* Where we are in life is largely an accumulation of the choices we've made. This concept is going to ruffle a lot of feathers because it implies responsibility for those choices.

Are you the CEO of a bank? You're there because you *chose* to work hard, obtain an education, and climb the corporate ladder. Are you happily married? You *chose* a good spouse and *chose* to work hard on the marriage. Unhappily married? You *chose* either a bad match for a spouse and/or *chose* not to do the work necessary to keep your marriage strong. If this sounds harsh, so be it. It's so hard to assume responsibility for our choices—it's much easier to play the victim.

Unemployed? Perhaps this is not a choice you made. But are you sitting on your rear end collecting unemployment or are you willing to take work, no matter what kind? Your choice tells others a lot about you, and it tells you a lot about yourself.

A friend's husband recently passed away after a lengthy illness. It was, obviously, devastating for her and their two young children. Clearly she didn't *choose* to have to deal with such a life-altering tragedy. But—here's a concept—because she *chose* to treat her husband with love and affection and respect through the nineteen years of their marriage, she is at peace that her husband left this world knowing he was married to a woman who was the envy of all his friends. And she is left with the legacy of what a good father she provided for her children.

So make smart, intelligent choices that you *can* control, because you never know when something will occur that is *out* of your control.

# . 3 .

## A CHOICE TOWARD SIMPLICITY

I'd like to hold up my mother as an example of how making good choices can lead toward a simpler life.

My mother grew up with about the worst childhood you can imagine—a brutal drunken father who frequently sexually molested some of her twelve siblings, an indifferent mother, starvation as a child . . . the stories I've grown up with would curl your hair.

My mother chose to leave that environment, educate herself in nursing, and become a professional. Good start.

Then she began dating a doctor. She was madly in love with him, she relates. But this doctor—like my grandfather—drank. One evening after a date, the doctor escorted my mother back to her apartment, threw up in her kitchen sink, and passed out on the sofa. As my mother cleaned up the mess, she thought to herself, "If I marry this man, I'll be cleaning up his vomit for the rest of my life." She told him she never wanted to see him again.

Two months later she met the man who would become my father. They married a year later. My parents still hold hands after more than fifty happy years.

See how it works? My mother had the foresight to look ahead, down the long path of life, and consciously *choose* not to marry a man like her father. Instead, she chose carefully the one who would become her life's partner.

I tell my daughters this story as an example of how our good choices impact our lives.

# .4.

## NOT JUST LUCK

People often tell us how "lucky" my husband and I are that we lead such simple lives. They are partly right—we're healthy, and we thank God for that. But mostly they are wrong. We aren't *lucky* . . . we (usually) made sensible choices, and then worked hard to make our choices succeed.

My husband had a rather wild, destructive adolescence. He chose to join the Navy, straighten himself out, and then go to college and get his education.

We chose to marry each other because we each recognized that the other person would make a balanced life mate and a good parent. We chose to be good to one another. We chose to simplify our lives. We chose to raise our children with strong morals and discipline and love and laughter. We chose to start a home business so we could always be together. Choices, choices, choices. Most of these choices weren't easy. Good choices require work to maintain and follow through.

I don't mean to toot my own horn here, but with the exception of our health—which is out of our hands, except what we do to maintain it—most of our many blessings are because we've made smart choices.

So can you. No, you can't do anything about illness, accidents, natural disasters, or economic catastrophes (the list goes on). But there are so many things *within* our control that can influence how simple or how complex our lives are. Many of those earlier choices can affect how we will weather those crises that occur *outside* of our control.

# .5.

## GET OVER YOUR EGO

It's hard to imagine just how much our ego is tied up in what we do and what we own (or want to own). Stop and think about it. So many of us imagine that we *are* where we live or what we drive.

Imagine that you must drive a 1983 two-door sedan with a crumpled fender. That's your only vehicle. It's reliable, it gets you from Point A to Point B, but it's ugly as sin. Are you embarrassed to be seen driving it?

I know I am, and I'm speaking from experience. We bought a cheap 1983 Oldsmobile Toronado (I called it the "Pimpmobile") as a backup vehicle against the day when our reliable little 1993 Ford Escort would bite the dust.

Well, my husband got into a car accident on a snowy road and totaled the Escort (and yes, thank you, my dear husband is okay). So we were—ahem—reduced to driving the Pimpmobile. And I was embarrassed. I never, ever thought my ego would be tied to a vehicle—a hunk of sheetmetal, for crying out loud—but to my surprise it was. What an eye opener. We couldn't afford to buy a new (used) vehicle, so we drove the Pimpmobile for as long as it lasted. Nothing like forced humility.

And you know what I learned? *No one cared.* No one thought less of me or treated me any differently because of what I drove. Being embarrassed was just a product of my own ego.

# . 6 .

## YOU AREN'T WHAT YOU OWN

Many of us grew up thinking that our possessions defined us. It's back to that ego thing again. Our ego is tied up in our cars, our clothes, our houses, our jobs, our education . . . nearly everything we spend money on. And yet, a lesson I've learned is that no one really cares what you own.

We used to live in a home built in 1874. It was, to put it charitably, a "fixer-upper" plagued with every interior decorating disaster spanning the last five decades: fake wood paneling, avocado-green patterned linoleum in the kitchen, stained ceilings from a leaking roof, walls painted a dingy snot color, two-toned green shag carpeting . . . the list went on and on.

With two babies and a start-up home business, there was no possible way we had the cash to remodel. Whenever people came to dinner, I found myself apologizing for everything. Again and again.

Finally a friend stopped me. "You know, when someone comes over for the first time, they might notice all these faults you keep pointing out. But we always have such a good time visiting that after the initial impression, no one notices anything but the company."

I learned a valuable lesson that day. First, to keep my mouth shut (about the house, that is) and quit apologizing over something over which we had no control. Second, your friends—your true friends, who are the only people you should care about "impressing"—aren't interested in your possessions. Truly, they're not.

What a simplifying concept.

# .7.

## WHAT DO YOUR FRIENDS THINK?

When you start letting go of your ego-induced need to impress, you become freer. Learn to cultivate your personality to survive such bruises to your ego as driving an old car or eating off glued-together plates or getting caught in sweatpants with holes in the knees. Anyone who is turned off, or on, because of your possessions probably isn't worth knowing.

Egos can be so huge, so bloated, that they can take over our every waking thought and dictate nearly everything we spend our money on. A simple life is a life of appropriate choices and balances. There is little room for ego. Pop that bubble.

Instead of feeding that ego, recapture your time. Find those days that had been lost to stroking your ego . . . days that could be spent watching your children grow, days with your parents before they leave you. Days with your spouse walking, talking, loving, and dreaming together.

Once we recognize that much of our life (and for some, this includes our career) is tied up with our ego, we can start to let things go. You can keep your car a bit longer without trading it in for the newest model. You can downscale your home and have a less staggering mortgage. You can stop longing for the big screen TV. You can even change careers.

And perhaps you can even get caught Saturday morning at the grocery store in old sweatpants with the holes in the knees and not care.

# .8.

## DON'T BREAK THE LAW

Yeah, yeah, I know that there are so many laws on the books that, in the words of Jane Austin, " . . . we are all offending every moment of our lives." But what I mean is, don't break the obvious ones, because the consequences can make your life so complex that it can take years to untangle the effects.

Sometimes people break the law and then act so *surprised* when they are caught and punished. What else did they expect? Did they think people wouldn't *mind* if they robbed a convenience store?

I should point out that there are two types of laws. *Mala in se* (meaning "evil in itself") are laws against behavior universally regarded as criminal, such as murder, rape, and arson. *Mala prohibita* means laws that are criminal only because society defines it as such, e.g., gambling or wearing a loud plaid jacket on Sundays.

There might come a time when you feel, for moral or ethical reasons, that you must break a *mala prohibita* law (like those who helped slaves escape through the Underground Railroad). If you do, recognize that you are still going to be held responsible for the consequences, which may not simplify your life.

So don't drink and drive. Don't do drugs. Don't rob a bank. Don't murder or needlessly injure someone. Don't abuse your kids. Don't shoplift. You get the idea.

This relates to #2, The Choices We Make. If you choose to break the law, whether *mala in se* or *mala prohibita*, you can expect to pay the consequences . . . and the consequences are not simple.

# . 9 .

## BE HUMBLE

How can being humble simplify your life? A humble person is generally thought of as being unpretentious and modest, someone who doesn't think he or she is better or more important than others. It's easy to look down at someone else and not even realize you're unconsciously comparing yourself to him, and recognizing that you're "better." Maybe you are, maybe you aren't.

One of the happiest, most contented men I ever met was a janitor. He cleaned the offices where I used to work. We'd chat occasionally, and he would spend the time describing in glowing details how wonderful his wife was, how proud he was of his children. By many of our modern standards, this man wasn't "successful." But because of the smile on his face, the love in his heart, and the pride in his family . . . how much more "successful" can anyone be?

Everyone has a story to tell. The person living on the streets, addicted to drugs, has one, too. You can be grateful you aren't in his shoes, but it would be foolish to think you're "better" than he is in the eyes of God. Maybe you are, maybe you aren't.

Remember the Ghost of Christmas Present in Charles Dickens' *A Christmas Carol?* He told Scrooge, "It may be, that in the sight of Heaven, you are more worthless and less fit to live than millions like this poor man's child."

At the pearly gates, are you so sure that you will weigh greater in the balance than a happy janitor?

So be humble. No one likes arrogance.

# . 10 .

## BE CONTENT

One of the principles I try to impart to my children is "Grateful, not greedy." Another good one is "Gratitude is an attitude." Think about it. If your spouse impulsively picks a daisy for you, do you wish it were long-stem roses? Why? Enjoy the moment. Be content.

Life is full of little things that fill us with discontent. Someone was rude to you on the street. You have a run in your last good pair of stockings. The waiter forgot the bread rolls. Your cell phone coverage fades in and out. Your husband put an empty mayonnaise jar back in the fridge, *again*. Your favorite sporting event was rained out. Your husband's favorite sporting event wasn't. You got a flat tire on the way to work.

Sometimes it takes facing something cataclysmic—a brush with death, the loss of a job, a natural disaster—to make all these little things suddenly become unimportant. I remember hearing that there was an enormous drop in the number of divorce filings after the 9/11 attacks. Why? Because suddenly the trivial problems *we all face* were just that—trivial. In light of larger calamities, we were able to stop focusing on the minutiae and recall all the many, many blessings in our life: our health, our way of life, our freedoms, and our loved ones.

If you have a bed to sleep in, a roof over your head, food on your table, and employment, then you're better than a large percentage of the earth's population.

Be grateful. Be content.

# . 11 .

## IF NECESSARY, PRETEND

Sometimes it's hard to put up with stuff. Sometimes you want to leave your spouse for doing something silly, like dropping dirty socks on the floor or forgetting your birthday.

Stop. Take a deep breath. Now let it out.

Sometimes we have to pretend. Sometimes when our thoughts and emotions are not in sync with reality, we have to *pretend* we're feeling something we're not.

Pretend you're still madly in love with your spouse. How would you behave if you were? Give him unexpected hugs, drop love notes in his lunchbox, make his favorite meal.

Pretend you're happy in your dead-end job. Smile at your coworkers, get your reports in on time, whistle in the hallways.

Pretend you're happy with the house you're living in. Hang a picture over the crack in the wall. Put an area rug over the horrible stain in the carpet. Plant some flowers along the edge of the muddy, ugly yard.

Catch my drift? *Pretend* you're happy with something that normally dissatisfies you, and the *emotion may follow the action.*

The times to pretend—pay attention now—are *when you can't do anything about it.* Make the best of it. Practice forbearance. You can't change anything, so deal with it. What's the alternative? You'll be miserable. And who would *choose* to be miserable?

It's worth a try. At the very least, going through life with a smile on your face instead of a scowl causes fewer wrinkles.

# . 12 .

## DON'T WORRY WHAT OTHERS THINK

We spend a lot of time worrying about what others think of us. To some extent, this is good. It keeps us in check and doesn't allow us to indulge in behavior that is too outrageous for the norms of where we live or work.

But when obsessive worrying about what others think influences what we do or where we live, or when it adversely affects our relationships with our family and friends, then our lives become complex. Did you become a lawyer instead of a car mechanic because you could hold your head higher at your high school class reunion even though you hate an office environment and love to work on cars? Do you live in an elegant condo downtown instead of a suburban house because you want people to think you're successful, even though you'd love to have a little yard of your own? Did you major in engineering and become a software designer instead of a teacher because your parents wanted you to, even though you love teaching kids? Did you stop seeing your grade school buddy who became a stay-at-home mom because she doesn't fit in with your hip, happenin' crowd of career friends?

How many of the major decisions in your life are based on what others might think? And who are you hurting in an effort to please someone else?

If you can cultivate the ability to disregard the unimportant opinions of others, within reason, then your life becomes simpler.

# . 13 .

## MARCH TO THE BEAT OF YOUR OWN DRUM

When I was pregnant with our first child, I went to the wedding of a college friend. At the time, my husband and I were starting our home business and finances were extremely tight.

Suddenly I was mingling with old and dear friends, all of whom had achieved a level of success. As we chatted, it became apparent that I was the oddball, and not just because I was wearing a second-hand maternity dress (remember, money was tight). No, I was the odd one out because we were the only ones struggling financially. The *only* ones . . . or so it seemed by my friends' descriptions of their careers. It was embarrassing to admit that we had money woes when everyone else did not.

Ready for the ironic twist of fate? My friends continued to rise in their careers. My husband and I continued to build our home business and eventually moved to a twenty-acre homestead. We still don't make a lot of money, but we get by. And now, everyone is envious of us—us!—because we are living a "fantasy" life in the country and working at home, especially since a lot of my friends are now concerned about their continued employment.

I didn't realize how unique our lifestyle was until the messages on the Christmas cards came in year after year: how I envy you, how lucky you are, how I wish we could live the way you do . . .

So march to the beat of your own drum. As long as you're doing things ethically and morally, don't worry about the opinion of others. Life is simpler that way.

# .14.

## DON'T BOTHER JUSTIFYING
## YOUR CHOICES

Whatever decisions you make to simplify your life shouldn't require justification. If you decide to change careers into a field of work that makes you happier (and you're not risking the security of your family—see #222), then ignore the dire predictions or envious sniping of those who don't have the courage to do the same.

If you decide to move to a less expensive house so that one of you can stay home with the kids, ignore the dire predictions or envious sniping of those who don't have the courage to do the same.

If you decide to downscale your consumerism so that you can save money and not be a slave to debt, ignore the...well, you know the rest.

Those who protest about any changes you make to simplify your life usually protest because you're showing them it can be done. Often the protesters don't have the courage to realize they can do it, too.

It takes guts to be the first in a group to do something. If you announce that you're going to downscale, people may look at you funny and may even try to talk you out of it. Just smile and keep going. You may even have some friends who decide to give it a try, too.

Actions speak louder than words. You don't have to justify your reasons for simplifying; your happier and calmer lifestyle will speak for itself.

The good decisions you make in your life shouldn't require justification. The bad ones . . . can't be justified.

# .15.

## PUT READING MATERIAL IN THE BATHROOM

Sounds stupid to address such a private time, doesn't it? Yet taking the opportunity to spend a few minutes reading on the throne is an indication that you're willing to . . . well, I won't use the expression "stop and smell the roses," but you get my drift.

Besides, it can be informative. My brother once showed me a very lengthy, densely printed book. On the inside front cover was written two dates about a year apart. This book, he told me proudly, was read entirely while sitting on the throne over the course of the year.

The book was the Bible. Whatever works, I guess.

# .16.

## DON'T GOSSIP

Gossiping is fun. It's entertaining. It's easy.

It's also damaging, destructive, and sinful. (Remember the verse about not bearing false witness?)

Some people are wonderful at keeping secrets (what a warm and comforting thing). Others blab the moment they hear anything juicy. What kind of person would *you* rather be?

The old Golden Rule might apply here: do unto others and all that. Do you really want friends and strangers picking apart your every move? Then have the courtesy to not do that to others.

Along the same vein, remember the old adage, "If you can't find something nice to say about someone, don't say anything at all." Maybe it's time to revive that. Besides, it seems that every time I gossip maliciously (and I do on occasion), it comes back to bite me. I remember once, while sitting in the audience watching a man receive an award, I said something spiteful about the award recipient to a friend sitting next to me. A woman in the row ahead turned around and gave me a look of loathing. Turns out she was the man's sister. Oops.

Ironically, similar incidences happened *three times* in the next two weeks. Three times. I would say something gossipy and "witchy," only to find it coming back to haunt me. I'm a slow learner, but I finally had what I call a "duh" moment: gossip hurts. Not only does it hurt the target, *it hurts me.*

So I learned to shut up (mostly) and life got simpler.

# .17.

## BE NICE TO PEOPLE

This seems so obvious, yet the busier we are, the less nice we can be. We're rushed, we're hectic, we're tired. We have too many demands on our time, our energy, and our money. The last thing we feel like doing is smiling at the doorman and asking how his family is doing.

Oddly, however, it's little niceties like this that blossom back ten-fold. The doorman smiles back, says that his son got the cast off his leg last week, thanks for asking, and concludes that you're about the nicest person in the building. And you walk away feeling a little warmer and less rushed.

Niceness tends to spread. If you do something nice for someone, then they're inclined to do something nice for someone else. Remember the old trick of paying the toll for the car behind you, who then pays for the car behind it, etc.? No one really "doesn't" pay—each car pays for the car behind—but how much brighter is your day because the first person in line took the time to pay a double toll?

Besides, there's an old saying that the best way to know what someone is like is to watch how they treat others who can offer them no benefit.

So smile and thank the waitress. Tip the mechanic. Hold the door for someone whose arms are full of packages. Help the little old lady across the street. Feel those warm fuzzies build up inside you.

That's kind of what it's all about, isn't it?

# .18.

## MAKE LEMONADE

When life hands you lemons, make lemonade . . . or at least squeeze the juice and freeze it for later.

We aren't all equally blessed in life. Some of us have physical challenges, some have emotional difficulties, some have family-related problems. But often the people we admire the most are those who have taken their lemons and made lemonade.

I have a friend confined to a wheelchair from a degenerative disease (lemons). She and her husband adore each other (lemonade). They have a ten-year-old daughter who got a cancerous brain tumor last year (*big* lemons). While she isn't out of danger, she's doing okay (lemonade), and has made many friends in the community through the hospital and cancer awareness groups (more lemonade).

My friend could be sitting there feeling sorry for herself, and probably does on occasion. But as much as possible, she has also created a happy and peaceful atmosphere in her home. She says it's because she never knows how long she'll have it. Whatever the future holds for them—and I dearly hope it holds *health*—she won't have regrets about how she is leading her life or how she is treating her husband and daughter.

I think about my friend whenever I'm inclined to gripe about something. How trivial all my little troubles seem when I look at how happy and at peace this woman is!

So the next time your husband leaves the empty mayonnaise jar in the refrigerator, don't explode. Simply smile, think about my friend, and put the jar in the recycling bin.

# .19.

## DON'T CHEAT

Don't cheat on your taxes, don't cheat in your workplace, and don't cheat your friends. Life is simpler when people know you're honest, dependable, and that you keep your word.

I forgot my wallet one day while buying a few things at our local grocery store. I discovered this *after* the clerk had rung up my purchases. I prepared to put the items back, scarlet-cheeked, but the clerk stopped me. To my amazement, he pulled out his wallet, paid for my groceries, and waved me out the door.

Yes it helps that we live near a small town and the clerk sees me frequently. But you can bet your bottom dollar I got there first thing the next morning to repay and re-thank the clerk. Had I not done so, he would have written me off as a cheat. Instead, what could have been a complicated transaction turned into something simple and beautiful.

Keep your promises or, if you can't (stuff happens), apologize and explain why. Be dependable. Show up when you say you will. Pay your bills on time. Don't make personal calls at the office. Don't write the Great American Novel at work. If you see a discrepancy on your grocery receipt, make it good (boy, won't the store clerks be surprised!).

These are all little things that your children see and emulate, your neighbors will notice and appreciate, and your employer will note and remember (and which may help determine who keeps a job during the next wave of layoffs).

The result from not cheating? Trust . . . which is a very nice simplifying thing to have.

# .20.

## APPRECIATE THE SIMPLE GIFTS

A few years back, we moved from our happy rural home in Oregon to a twenty-acre farm in Idaho. Though we love it here, there was much sadness in leaving behind the place where our children were born, where we had worked so hard to start our business, and even in leaving behind some pets that were buried in our yard. One of those pets was an Alaskan malamute, Tundra, who was my beloved companion for ten years. When she died, I grieved deeply over her loss.

After we arrived in Idaho, our new home was piled with boxes. I was feeling overwhelmed at the chaos and the amount of work facing us. Were we crazy to move away from our cozy little home in Oregon, leaving behind everything we loved, to start all over again? Had we done the right thing?

Suddenly my husband turned and handed me a canning jar with clear plastic tape over the top. The jar was full of dirt. "What's this?" I asked.

"Dirt from Tundra's grave," he replied. "I thought you might like to take a little bit of her with you."

I burst into tears.

Should my husband ever have the sudden urge to buy me diamonds, I still wouldn't prize it higher than that jar of dirt. It was, without question, the loveliest present he ever gave me.

Appreciate the simple gifts. They are by far the best.

# .21.

## DON'T SPREAD MISERY

Why is it that when someone is miserable, they want to make sure everyone else is miserable too? I don't mean they're miserable with a head cold; I mean they're miserable in life.

When I was pregnant with our first child, my husband and I spent a weekend as vendors at a craft show. In my excitement about the baby, I mentioned to many people that I was pregnant.

Toward the end of the day, the woman in the next booth turned to me and said, "So, I hear you're pregnant."

"Yes," I replied proudly. "The baby is due in December."

"You're going to hate it," she said flatly.

Startled, I replied, "Excuse me?"

"You'll hate it. Believe me, I have six kids, and I hate them all."

For the next half hour, as I slumped lower in my chair, she poured poison into my ear about how awful motherhood is. By the time she was done, I was crying.

What is it about miserable people wanting to spread misery? Did it make this woman feel *better* to tell me I would hate my child?

If you're miserable, a lot of it is because you have *decided* to be miserable. Personally I think you can change that, but maybe I'm wrong. But you sure don't have the right to make everyone else around you miserable. Keep your misery to yourself.

If necessary, *pretend* to be happy (see #11). Who knows, you might end up spreading cheer instead of misery. Wouldn't that be simpler?

# . 22 .

## ACCEPT WHAT YOU MUST DO

When faced with a difficult decision, most people *know* what they must do. They just *don't* do it, or don't *want* to do it, or don't have the *courage* to do it.

Sometimes this is because they just need affirmation that their decision is the right one (otherwise known as a kick in the pants). A counselor once said, "Most people know what they need to do; they just need somebody to help them accept it."

Look deep within yourself to help you decide the right thing to do. Try not to look at the immediate "convenience" of the moment. Will this be a decision you would be proud of ten years down the road? Twenty? Thirty?

As an example, I once met an older woman who told me she had given up an infant son for adoption thirty years before. The out-of-wedlock pregnancy had shamed and humiliated her family at a time when premarital babies were not as common as today. It would have been a much easier, quicker, less embarrassing decision to abort the baby.

But she didn't. And now, thirty years later, she told me this story with her eyes shining with pride. She had not given in to the "immediacy" of the moment and aborted her son. Instead she gave him life and made a married couple very happy. Not a bad choice.

The right choice for a difficult decision is not always easy—or simple. But many years in the future, be sure your choice is one that will make you proud. Then accept what you must do.

# .23.

## STOP BLEEDING

I once heard some advice on how to swim with sharks: don't bleed.

Sharks, as everyone knows, circle a wounded fish and then go into a feeding frenzy at the smell of blood. They will rip and tear and chew and chomp without mercy.

Likewise, bullies pick on you because they smell blood. Are you being ridiculed, belittled, or teased? It's because in some way, the sharks smell blood. They sense that you will wilt under the onslaught. They will start to circle and then go into a feeding frenzy of ripping and tearing and chomping without mercy.

"Bleeding" might be crying, complaining to the boss, getting angry, cursing, stomping away, getting into a physical altercation, or quitting your job. These are all understandable and perfectly human reactions. Unfortunately when you bleed, the bullies know they've won. Bullies like to get a reaction (blood)— that's what gives them power. It's tough to do, but you have to learn not to bleed.

So how can you stop bleeding? Stop thinking of yourself as a victim (because everyone will know it). Develop a firm shell. *Act* confident, and the *feeling* of confidence will follow. Believe, truly believe, that sticks and stone may break your bones but words will never hurt you. Yes I know, words *do* hurt . . . but you must *act* as if they don't. Don't rise to the bait. Act indifferent. Laugh with them.

Not bleeding might help simplify your work or school environment. After all, life is a lot simpler without a bunch of sharks circling around you.

# . 24 .

## ACQUIRE COMMON SENSE

My mother has always lamented the lack of common sense in people, and now that I'm all grown up I can see her point. A lack of common sense is the only thing I can attribute to why people make foolish choices in life—marrying someone who is an alcoholic (because you think love will "cure" him), buying a house with a mortgage much too big, or indulging in habits that destroy health or relationships. Fortunately, common sense can be acquired by thinking things through (forethought) and doing what you know is *right* (rather than what's *easy*).

When you're faced with a problem, try applying common sense and see where it gets you. What is the most logical solution? What is the moral solution? What solution is best in the long term? What is the solution that will give you the most satisfaction or pride years in the future?

Although people have the most amazing ability to disregard sensible habits, sensible solutions, behaviors, and choices, probably the single major reason people disregard common sense is because they *don't like the answer it gives*. Common sense may not provide a quick, painless answer to a problem, but it's likely to provide the *correct* answer. It takes intestinal fortitude to apply common sense. It takes responsibility to follow through. It takes self-control.

The benefits? A lot fewer problems later on.

The lynchpin of a simple life is making good choices. Apply common sense and see where it takes you.

# .25.

## YOU ARE WHAT YOU DO

It was Aristotle who said, "We are what we repeatedly do. Excellence, then, is not an act, but a habit." No matter what you say to the contrary, your actions reflect what you're truly like inside. We can try all we want to justify whatever bad choices we make, but until we own up to the fact that our actions speak louder than our words, we won't be able to truly simplify our lives.

It does no good to lecture your children that stealing is wrong as you swipe that stapler from the office storeroom and bring it home because you need a stapler and hey, the office manager will never notice.

It does no good to say you're a moral person while having an affair because hey, your spouse (pick one) nags / doesn't understand you / isn't affectionate, and don't you deserve some happiness?

It does no good to claim you want to protect the environment when you're living in a 10,000-square-foot home that sucks up more resources than a whole neighborhood.

How do you determine what a person is like? Do you go by what they *tell* you they're like, or by what you *see* them doing? What kinds of friends do they have? Do they treat others as they demand to be treated themselves?

Ralph Waldo Emerson said, "What you are shouts so loudly in my ears I cannot hear what you say." Make sure that what you're "shouting" is something you want people to hear.

# . 26 .

## DITCH THE SELF-ESTEEM

"Self-esteem" is a buzzword that should have been dropped a decade ago. I confess it's also a bit of a pet peeve of mine when someone complains that they don't have any self-esteem. What I want to ask them is, *Why should you? What have you done to earn it?*

Yes, *earn.* Self-esteem is not something that is bestowed upon you at birth or by peppy slogans or happy posters on the wall. It is something you earn. Did Mother Teresa ever worry about her self-esteem? Of course not. She was too busy helping others to be concerned about some mythical, mystical self-worth issue.

If you find yourself suffering from a lack of self-esteem, for cryin' out loud, get off your duff and *do* something for someone else. Volunteer at a homeless shelter. Visit someone who is ill. Help a little old lady across the street. You'll come away feeling great about yourself.

When you do things that get the focus off you and benefit others instead, you'll find that your self-esteem has miraculously increased because you're no longer being selfish. It's not about *you*, it's about what you contribute to *others* that increases your own worth. Helping others is a wonderful way to boost self-esteem.

When you set goals and then take concrete steps toward those goals, your self-esteem increases because you are achieving something rather than sitting around complaining.

Yes, life is simpler if your self-esteem is high. No question about it. So again I'll ask: What are you doing to *earn* it?

# .27.

## FEELINGS ARE NOT GODS

It's become popular to think that how an individual *feels* is far more important than what he actually *does*. Hurting someone's *feelings* these days is tantamount to a crime of the highest degree.

The result of this god-like elevation of *feelings* is that we tiptoe around, held hostage by the fragile egos of a bunch of whiners. Feelings come complete with a whole retinue of entitlements and levels of selfishness that must be catered to.

It doesn't matter who gets hurt or what gets damaged in this quest to balm somebody's feelings. If you *feel* like having an affair, too bad for your spouse or kids. If you *feel* like drinking too much, tough luck for your family. If you *feel* like buying a new car, who cares if you're already deeply in debt?

The most amazing part of the "feeling" revolution is how one-way it is. My feelings are the only ones that count. *Your* feelings aren't important, and if you don't agree then you're "intolerant." Wives do this to husbands all the time. Certain political activists are fond of this technique. Schools don't dare let a child's feelings get hurt so "everyone" wins a blue ribbon, or gets a trophy, or gets advanced to the next grade.

The trouble with this god-like elevation of feelings is that any attempt to have standards (honesty, cleanliness, decent language, etc.) is by definition intolerant, and someone's feelings get hurt. We can't have that.

Rise above your feelings. Your feelings might still get hurt, but that's reality.

# .28.

## STOP IT!

I once caught a Bob Newhart comedic skit in which he played his usual role as a psychologist. A woman came to him with a myriad of problems because she'd heard he could cure her in five minutes. She poured out one dilemma after another and then asked for his advice.

His reply? The sum total of his advice for all her problems? "STOP IT!"

The skit was hilariously funny simply because it was Bob Newhart, but underneath the humor there was some merit to his advice. Sometimes we just need to stop it. Stop living beyond your means. Stop overeating. Stop nagging. Stop driving too fast. Stop drinking so much. Stop smoking. Stop gossiping. You get the idea.

If we could just magically "stop it," life would be simpler. Now our job is to make those "stops" come true. This isn't rocket science. If you're doing something that makes your life too complex . . . STOP IT!

# .29.

## YOU'RE NOT ENTITLED

One of the joys of a simpler life is taking responsibility for making good decisions and choices, as well as developing a better attitude.

You will also experience a growing awareness that nobody *owes* you anything. You're not entitled to anything at all—except (in theory) the basic rights guaranteed by the Constitution. You're not entitled to a job, or a car, or a house, or healthcare, or an education, or anything else in this country that is not specified in the documents of the Founding Fathers.

But especially with younger adults, a sense of entitlement seems to permeate their lives. They don't want to wait long years and work their way up in the world. They want the things and the perks *now* that their parents and their employers have worked long decades to achieve.

Entitlements go beyond things. We feel that our children are *entitled* to an "A" in math, despite the fact that they didn't study for the tests. We have a baby out of wedlock and then feel *entitled* to government assistance. We don't take care of ourselves (we eat too much, never exercise, smoke, drink, etc.) and then demand that someone else pay for our medical care. When we lose our job we feel entitled to nearly endless unemployment benefits paid for by someone else.

Face it: *you're not entitled.* Once you are a competent adult, don't expect anyone else to take responsibility for providing you with the things you want. Find a way to do it yourself.

Once you lose the feeling of entitlement, you've taken a step toward independence, an important facet of a simpler life.

# . 30 .

## JUST DO IT

Okay, today is the day to start cultivating changes in your personal life. Start the day by greeting your spouse and kids in a loving, smiling fashion. Will your husband or wife be surprised when you give them a good-morning hug? If so, you're not hugging enough. If they push you away, at least you're being the "bigger" person. Don't give up. It may take them awhile to appreciate the "new" you.

Dress for work in clothes that don't flaunt wealth or status. As you prepare for the day, think about the things that you do which reflect your ego—are you snotty to the doorman? Are you lofty and supercilious with the waitress? Are you condescending to the taxi driver? Well, stop it. These people are working every bit as hard as you are for their daily bread. They don't need any attitude from you.

Is something beyond your control making you see red? The traffic jam, the bad weather, your favorite sports team losing the game? Instead of yelling, clenching your fists, swearing, and otherwise raising your blood pressure, gracefully accept the fact that there is nothing you can do about it and counter each annoyance with thoughts of one of your many blessings.

As you go through the day, you'll begin to notice how many of life's hassles can be minimized or accepted with a mere change of attitude on your part, or perhaps a determination to make improvements and changes within you. Things will seem brighter.

Nice and simple to have such control, isn't it?

# .31.

## YOUR PERSONAL LIFE IN
## A DOWN ECONOMY

It's nice to be in control of your personal life. A recurrent theme in this book is to take control of the things you *can* in order to weather the things over which you have *no* control, such as the economy.

A change in attitude and behavior, which is the only thing you *can* change, works wonders when handling whatever bad news the economy hands you. *Making good choices* is the key toward a simpler life, and it's never more true than when you're facing struggles.

Times are tight and getting tighter. Therefore, you should tighten up as well: Get tight with your friends and family, tight with your money, and tight with your Creator. In bad times, it's the loner and the exalted individualist who suffers the most. It's those with the networks and connections who weather bad times best. Since the most stable networks and connections are those composed of folks who value honesty, compassion, charity, forbearance, and faith . . . you should take stock of your own levels of these attributes and work to make yourself a good fit and valued member of your network.

A side benefit is that you may find yourself more valuable in the job market. If your personal life is clean, stable, and honest, then you may be given preference over someone whose personal life is chaotic, messy, and dishonest. Just a thought.

# Getting Along

▼

Your relationships with the people in your life—spouse, children, friends, relatives, neighbors, and coworkers—is one of the single biggest factors toward simplicity. Strong, healthy relationships can help you weather just about any nastiness the future can hold. In bad times, these relationships may be the rocks that keep you from drowning. Remember, no man is an island. We need people. Here are some ways to get along.

# . 32 .

## LOVE YOUR SPOUSE

It was the Reverend Theodore Hesburgh who said, "The most important thing a father can do for his children is to love their mother." How true it is.

Think of the sense of security and happiness you give your children when you love your spouse. You say you no longer love your spouse? He or she no longer sets butterflies to flight in your stomach? Then, and especially if you have children, just *pretend* you're still in love (see #11).

Loving your spouse reduces the likelihood that you'll divorce. Besides the death of your spouse, I can think of few things that will complicate your life more than the death of your *marriage*, especially if there are children involved.

You can't change another person, but you *can* change yourself. Are *you* the kind of person your spouse would want to come home to? If not, now is the time to make yourself more loveable. Make your thoughts and actions and behavior kind and loving. Make sure you give and give and give some more. You'll find that you and your spouse may rekindle something special.

It goes without saying that if you've picked a bad spouse—heavy on the addictions, inclined toward violence, that kind of thing—you've got problems. A huge part of a simple life is making good choices, and choosing the right spouse to begin with is a plus.

But if your spouse is pretty much an average person, then recall the reasons why you got married in the first place. Capture those feelings again. Love your spouse.

# . 33 .

## DON'T CONTRADICT YOUR SPOUSE

In front of your children, that is. On matters of authority or discipline, even if you feel your spouse is wrong, don't contradict him or her. Bite your lip until you can discuss it in private. Anytime you countermand the authority of your spouse in front of your kids, they'll see it and use it to their advantage. That's just the way kids are. That's why parents must always present a unified front.

An example of this: my husband does not want our girls wearing fingernail polish (he feels that it's pre-sexualizing the girls). Personally, I couldn't care less, *nor do I especially agree.* However, I support his position, and I tell the kids that. "Your father doesn't want you wearing nail polish, so that's the end of the matter." They respect and accept this decision.

On the other hand, I don't want my girls to have pierced ears until they're in their middle teens. You might call it just one of my personal hang-ups. My husband doesn't especially agree, but he respects and supports my position.

In both these examples, since the opposing spouse couldn't show any benefits to wearing nail polish or earrings, then the nay-sayer's opinion prevails.

By not contradicting each other, my husband and I not only show respect to each other, but we demonstrate to our children that they need to respect their parents. The kids know we are unified, and they are relieved to have clear boundaries and expectations of behavior. This makes home life *much* simpler.

# .34.

## DON'T CHEAT ON YOUR SPOUSE

There are few things that can make your life more complex than cheating on your spouse.

Is it worth the momentary pleasure of a separate love life to know that you're destroying your marriage and threatening your children's security? Is it worth the guilt-ridden, clandestine sneaking around, and the temporary strokes to your ego? Is it worth earning the scorn and disrespect and contempt from friends, family, and church when (not if, but *when*) it's discovered what you're doing?

Are you treating your spouse so well that he or she isn't *inclined* to cheat?

Stop and read that last question again, because it's important. Many people cheat not because they are serial adulterers but because they're not getting what they need at home.

Are you a nag? Are you negative? Do you withhold sex? Are you insulting? Do you forget to stroke your spouse's ego? Do you forget to do little, loving things for your spouse? While there is no *excuse* for an affair, sometimes there is a *reason* for it.

Obviously this ties into loving your spouse (#32). People who are happy with their spouses—and love them well—are not inclined to cheat. But even if your home life is less than ideal, *your life will not be simplified* if you break your marital vows and cheat on your spouse.

Be the bigger person. Rise to the occasion. Honor your vows. Love your spouse and don't cheat. Keep your life simple.

# .35.

## LOVE AND LEARN

If you don't feel loving toward your spouse at the moment because he or she never remembers to rinse the tub, then *pretend* you love your spouse (see #11). See if the *actions* of loving don't lead to a return of the *act* of loving.

A home without strife—without fights, yelling, or throwing things—is automatically a simpler, happier home. A happy home life makes it possible to deal with *all sorts of other complicating things* that might be out of your control, such as long commutes, bankruptcy, unemployment, or illness. A happy home is a refuge. A happy home makes for better-behaved kids. A happy home is a pleasure to come home to.

Loving your spouse, and being loved in return, is obviously the key to this. No matter what problems my husband and I have faced over the years—and there have been many—we love each other and solve problems as a team.

How can you achieve that level of marital happiness?

As a start, read *The Proper Care and Feeding of Husbands* by Dr. Laura Schlessinger. This book is *excellent* for improving relations with your spouse. It can literally change your life. That's a big claim, but it's true. So before you gripe, try reading the book and see if it doesn't make sense—and see if practicing its recommendations doesn't simplify your life.

Loving your spouse and being loved in return makes life so much simpler.

# .36.

## PAY ATTENTION TO RED FLAGS

Red flags are the pricks to our conscience that indicate something is wrong. Red flags can apply to everything from avoiding that scary vacant lot to marrying the wrong person.

Is your latest relationship making you uneasy? Why? Could it be that you're ignoring some red flags that are waving in your face? Remember, God gives us those little red flags *now* so we can avoid big problems *later*.

A long time ago, I dated a man who was fascinating, attractive, and debonair. He was also jealous, domineering, and bigoted. He even hit me once, an occasion I managed to explain away in my mind. He tried to turn me away from friends. He also asked me to marry him within weeks of meeting.

Oddly, it wasn't until he insulted my best friend's ethnicity that I finally saw the light and dumped him. Later, I read an article that listed common traits of wife-beaters, and he fit the bill perfectly. I broke out into a cold sweat, thinking what a close call I'd had.

I know someone who married his first wife even though she told him she never wanted children. Being young, he was sure she would change her mind once they finished school. She never did. They divorced, and he is now happily married to another woman and is the father of three kids.

The purpose of dating is to see if you're compatible with someone. Paying attention to red flags means your future will be simpler because you won't have to deal with the after-effect of a major screw-up.

# .37.

## DON'T BADMOUTH YOUR SPOUSE

Get any group of women together and within a short period of time they will start griping about their husbands. Women can spend *hours* doing this. To listen, it would seem that no man has any redeeming qualities whatsoever. Makes one wonder why these women got married in the first place.

In our society, it has become culturally acceptable for a woman to complain about her husband. That doesn't sound like a recipe for a happy marriage to me. When you badmouth your husband, especially in public, your thoughts become negative and your spousal commitment weakens. Nothing—not one thing—good ever comes from badmouthing your spouse.

To be perfectly fair, men also "badmouth" their wives when they get together. However, I am assured by my husband that the bulk of their complaints is how they don't understand women in general . . . then talk diverts to sports or cars or other manly subjects.

So here's a concept: Don't badmouth your spouse. Ever. Resist. If the people around you are complaining about their spouses, stay quiet (or leave). If they ask you your opinion, *say something positive instead.* Boy, that ought to shut them down.

Try an experiment in which nothing but praise and compliments escape your lips. See if those *actions* (talking nicely) don't bring about the *emotions* (feeling more tender toward your spouse).

Your spouse is not a burden. Your spouse is a treasure, the person whom you vowed before God and family to love and honor and cherish. Now act like it. Your life will be simpler and happier.

# .38.

## SHUT UP

Do you realize how much simpler your life and the lives of those around you would be if you just shut up once in awhile? Now before you take offense, understand I'm referring primarily to the times when the urge to complain is overwhelming. Instead, try shutting up. What I mean is, don't verbalize *everything*. Not everything needs to be said out loud.

Like most females with hormones, there are certain times of the month when I have a tendency to want to bite off everyone's head. Doubtless (male or female) you, too, have days where everything seems bleak, where you're depressed, where nothing seems to be going right, and everyone's normal everyday quirks are amplified and far more annoying than usual.

Now shut up. Keep those biting, snapping remarks to yourself because—here's the thing—you'll wake up the next morning feeling *much* better and life will seem sunny again . . . *except* for those people whose heads you snapped off the previous day during your hissy fit.

The acid you unthinkingly spread during your ugly mood of the day before may not be painful to *you* (after all, aren't you entitled to express your *feelings?*), but everyone around you is still smarting from the sting. The momentary release you got by biting produces ugly ripples that continue to spread long after your mood has improved. People will feel compelled to tiptoe around or avoid you, all because you couldn't keep your mouth shut and your temporary moods under a lid. Do this too much and you may lose friends, and none of us has so many friends that we can afford to lose some.

So shut up. Your life will be simpler—and for those around you as well.

# .39.

## WHEN SHUTTING UP WORKS

Recently a friend had her first book published, and I spent the day helping with her booksigning. My kids were with friends for the day, leaving my husband home alone.

When I finally tottered home twelve hours later, I found the kitchen just as messy as when I left that morning. We put the kids to bed and I tackled the kitchen while my husband started a writing project on the computer.

As I stood there washing dishes, I fumed. And fumed. And fumed. Silently I wondered why on earth he couldn't wash a few dishes while I was gone.

Then I stopped and thought it through. What did I do all day? I had fun with my friend and celebrated a milestone with her. And what did my husband do all day? Split wood. Worked on some business orders. Did *my* barn chores.

Fortunately my unspoken criticisms were just that—unspoken. I finished washing the last dish and suddenly everything was all better.

If I had verbalized my annoyance, I would have destroyed some of the harmony between us. I would have *taken away my husband's dignity* by indicating that the work he did wasn't worth as much as a few dirty dishes. How stupid is that?

I went to bed in a peaceful frame of mind because I did *not* verbalize my ridiculous complains over so minor a thing as a messy kitchen.

So shut up about little things. Bite your tongue. Fume in your mind if you must, then *let it go.* Your life will be simpler.

# .40.

## WHY MEN AND WOMEN SEE CHORES DIFFERENTLY

I'll bet most of the women reading this book wonder why, if a man is home alone all day long, he won't take it upon himself to clean up a messy kitchen, or pick up the dirty clothes, or dust the furniture? It's because he doesn't "see" the dirty dishes or soiled laundry or dusty surfaces. Most men don't, frankly. It's a guy thing.

Just as men and women have different strengths (i.e., men are physical, women are verbal), the genders also perceive household things differently. There are very few men who will notice the cobwebs dangling from the ceiling, but the cobwebs will drive a woman nuts until she gets a broom and swipes them away. To a man, the cobwebs do not interfere with the "function" of the room, so it doesn't matter if the cobwebs are there or not. That's how a man's mind works. They're linear thinkers.

A messy kitchen is *my* hang-up, not my husband's. To criticize him for not cleaning it up is (to him) an irrational criticism . . . since he didn't notice that it needed cleaning.

Understanding this different perspective can *vastly* simplify your life. This isn't to say that men won't or shouldn't do a household task. On the contrary, when *nicely asked* (please re-read that last part), most men are happy to help out. But you have to *ask*. Men aren't mind-readers. If I had asked my husband to tidy the kitchen, he would have done so immediately.

And then, irrationally, I would have felt guilty for leaving the dishes to him.

# . 41 .

## WHY MEN DRIVE WOMEN CRAZY
## (WELL, ONE OF THE REASONS)

If you ask any woman what her biggest complaint is about men, near the top of the list would be that they don't do household chores. And it's true. As noted in #40 (Why Men and Women See Chores Differently), it's because men just don't "see" what needs to be done to keep a house clean.

Men are linear, big-picture thinkers. Women are detail-oriented. Supposedly that's what makes us mesh together well. But when a woman expects her man to not only be a mind-reader, but also to completely re-arrange his brain's wiring in order to notice that there is laundry to fold, then things start to break down in a relationship.

And the funny thing is, most men are happy to help with household chores because they want to please their wives. My husband has never told me "no" when I've nicely asked him to do something around the house.

But—and this is a *big* but—this desire to please their wives *only* happens if the wife is pleasant. Frankly, ladies, if you're a nag, your man is less likely to feel like making you happy. If you explode with anger because he didn't take it upon himself to fold the laundry, then he'll be a *lot* less likely to happily fold the laundry next time.

You catch more flies with honey than vinegar. A sweet and loving wife gets a lot more household help than a nagger and a complainer. And everyone knows that a harmonious home (and a tidy one!) means a simpler home life.

# .42.

## BE THE FIRST TO APOLOGIZE

*Must* you be right *all* the time? Must you *always* get the last word in? Wounds over silly (or even not-so-silly) arguments can fester for years, all because some people are too stubborn to apologize first.

People are reluctant to apologize because somehow they think they'll be "lessened" if they do. They'll lose power. They'll lose face. They'll lose status.

Actually, the opposite is true. Apologizing for something doesn't (necessarily) mean you're wrong about the issue, it merely means you're sorry to have caused pain between you and the other person. Rather than making you lose power, an apology actually *empowers* you. Suddenly, *you're* the person who is more gracious, more selfless, and more courteous.

Obviously not every argument or estrangement deserves an apology. Bad behavior on the part of someone else does not deserve an apology from you. I'm referring more to the types of problems that arise when small things get blown out of proportion and then fester because both parties are too proud and stubborn to make the first move. After all, why should *you* apologize? *You're* the one who was right!

Be the bigger person. Try calling, e-mailing, or writing to the person whose estrangement pains you, and apologize. Break the ice. Amazingly, the other person will melt and become like putty in your hands. Warm feelings will blossom again.

And if the other person refuses to accept your apology? Then you are right—you *are* the bigger person. It becomes their problem, not yours. Your conscience is clear.

How simple is that?

# . 43 .

## CELEBRATE THE DIFFERENCES

"Mom," my then five-year-old daughter asked me one day. "Why are boys so mean?"

We were on our way back from a playgroup, and she had just had an encounter with a boy who pushed her down.

I explained how boys have a chemical in their bodies called testosterone, and it makes boys aggressive and strong. I told her it is because ultimately a boy's job is to grow up to become a man, and a man's job—his biological programming—is to protect women and children. I explained that it is a father's duty to teach boys how to harness their aggression into proper channels so they don't go around pushing down little girls.

It was quite the conversation to have with a five-year-old, and she understood most of it. It's a conversation that we've had over and over again through the years as my daughters have grown—understanding the importance of men.

The trend in the last thirty years or so is to feminize men. I call it emasculation. Men are made the way they are for a reason and it goes against nature, against their brain's wiring, and against chemistry to try to make them think, act, and behave like a woman.

Besides, it's insulting. What if the whole class of men thought it was the "in" thing to make women more like men? How insulted would we be?

Accept men for what they are. If you don't like a man's behavior, leave the room. It's much simpler in the end.

# . 44 .

## WHY I LOVE MEN

I love men. Maybe it's because I was raised with three brothers and no sisters. Maybe it's because my father is wonderful. Maybe it's because I have the world's greatest husband. But whatever the reason, I love men because they're men.

I love their protective instinct. Yes, men can be aggressive and violent, but there is also a time and place for that, too. If a burglar is in my house, I would far rather have my husband defend me than cower behind the sofa (as I would be doing).

I love how men are sensible and no-nonsense. I love the way their minds churn out practical, obvious solutions to problems that completely escape me.

I love it when a man opens a door for me. Occasionally a man will tip his hat (fabulous!) and even better, stand up when I enter a room. It makes me feel so special, so respected, so feminine. Don't you just *love* that?

So celebrate the differences. Men are civilized by women, and women are protected by men. We are not and never will be a uni-sex society—that's not the way it's supposed to be. Yes, of course, there are jerky men out there (jerky women too, for that matter). But my point is that my strengths are my husband's weaknesses, and my weaknesses are my husband's strengths. And so it goes throughout the world: men and women compliment and balance each other.

It simplifies your life when you don't try to fight biology. Instead, celebrate the differences.

# .45.

## BE POLITE

How much more simple would our lives be if we were polite?

Your mother-in-law says something snarky to you at Christmas dinner. You lose your temper, defend yourself, and an argument starts. Everyone else gets involved, and before you know it, people are storming out of the house, never to speak to each other again until the following year's Christmas dinner.

But what if, instead of losing it when your mother-in-law is rude, you were just . . . polite? (It has the added advantage of completely throwing her off, too, since she was expecting to get a rise out of you.)

Some people are hard to get along with. They're rude, they're arrogant, they're unpleasant, and they're a general pain in the keister. Naturally there are times and places to take a stand. But sometimes—just as an experiment—trying merely being polite and see what happens.

Politeness is the lubricant of society, without which we become crude, vulgar, and offensive. Politeness is fairly easy to dispense when someone does something nice for you (such as holding a door). But it's harder to do when, for the sake of peace, you just bite your tongue and say something nice instead.

Next Christmas dinner when your mother-in-law says something rude, smile instead and sidestep the issue by mentioning how lovely her hair looks. This has an added advantage of making *you* the bigger person. Your life becomes simpler when you are at peace because you know you behaved politely.

# . 46 .

## WHY POLITENESS IS . . . NICE

Politeness is a dying art in our modern society. Children are no longer taught basic manners. Adults no longer feel compelled to thank someone for holding a door (if anyone holds a door to begin with). Tempers are short. People are stressed.

Yet it's precisely when tempers are short or people are stressed that a simple act of politeness can light up someone's day. When your arms are full of packages and someone holds a door for you, don't you just think that's wonderful? The least you can do is thank them.

In the mid-1980s, at the height of the feminists' war against men, my office had an older man with delightful manners who visited on business. Afterward I dropped him at the airport. While walking, he took my elbow as we stepped off a curb in a courteous and old-fashioned gesture of protection.

I was charmed.

I need help stepping off a curb about as much as you do, but that didn't matter. He was being a gentleman. The least I could do was be a lady about it.

As we parted, he actually thanked me for allowing him to express his manners. "I was taught to help a lady up and down a curb," he said, adding in some bewilderment, "But nowadays women don't seem to like that."

I've remembered that incident for over twenty years. To spurn someone for an act of politeness baffles me. So please, folks, be ladies and gentlemen. Life is so much simpler when we're all polite.

# . 47 .

## MAKE LIFE SIMPLER FOR MEN

Ladies, here's a thought. When you begin to simplify your own life, it makes sense to try and simplify life for your husband, right? Then here's an idea: let your man off the hook for Valentine's Day. And your birthday. And your anniversary. And whatever other "special event" you think deserves presents, chocolates, or other indications of affection.

The reason I suggest this is because men don't "think" that way. Your husband assumedly demonstrates he loves you 364 days of the year but if he doesn't buy flowers or jewelry on Valentine's Day, then does everything else he does become negated?

The pressure put on men to, ahem, "perform" for these Special Events can be rough. Men don't understand us at the best of times, but when put under pressure to read our minds about what gift would please us most, they're lost.

For example, you've wanted a new vacuum cleaner for a long time. Yet when your husband responds to this desire by purchasing you a new vacuum as a gift, you're mad. To a man, that's an illogical reaction . . . and men are logical creatures.

So go easy on the guys. Make life simpler for your husband. Appreciate all he does for you *without* expecting him to do something that goes against his character. Life is simpler that way. Besides, he'll love you for it. You might even get some flowers some time . . . just because.

# .48.

## WOMEN TALK, MEN ACT

Women are verbal. Men are physical. Yet women get bent out of shape when men don't act like women and lavish them with verbal affection.

Men do a lot of things that women don't notice. We become so focused on the minutiae of life (cobwebs on the ceiling, dust in the corners) that when our man shovels the sidewalk or puts gas in your car, we just accept it because . . . that's what men do.

Does your man mow the lawn? Change the oil? Take out the garbage? Fix a leaking pipe? Unclog the toilet? Give the kids a bath? Paint the kitchen? Work every day at a job he hates to pay the bills?

Men show they love us by doing all the nasty, cold, disgusting, or otherwise dirty jobs that would chip our nails and snag our pantyhose. And yet so few of us appreciate them for what they do.

Understand that men *do* know what love is. They also understand the meaning of duty and obligation. Those two concepts are extremely important because those are the ways that men indicate respect, demonstrate friendship, and show love.

If your man isn't doing these things for you, then it's possible you chose the wrong man. Or, more likely, you *did* choose a good man but you aren't treating him like the man he is.

So recognize that when your husband is out there in ten-degree weather scraping the ice off your windshield, he's announcing, "I love you!" to the whole neighborhood, while you get to stay inside, warm and dry. It's nice to be loved, isn't it?

# . 49 .

## AN EXAMPLE OF LOVE

When my oldest daughter was nine, I mentioned to her how her father shows he loves me. "Men don't like to talk about stuff like that," I told her. "So your father shows me how much he loves me by *doing* things instead. See those bookshelves over there? He built those for me because he knew I wanted some shelves, and *that's* how he shows me he loves me."

It was a fairly short conversation, and I didn't think much about it.

Fast-forward two weeks. At the time, we were "dog sitting" for a neighbor while she was working. Her dog was great except he didn't like cats, and we have a cat.

So when Buddy was in the house, we put up a fireplace screen across a doorway to limit him to one room. The floppy fireplace screen was a real hassle.

One day I asked my husband if he could put a nail in the wall to hold up one end of the screen so it wouldn't flop over as much. He said sure, then disappeared into his shop. Two hours later he came into the house carrying a swinging gate, which he'd just made. I couldn't believe it. I fluttered around, delighted, beaming, thrilled!

Later I noticed my daughter looking rather dazed. "What's the matter?" I asked.

She pointed to the gate and said in a wondering voice, "You're right. Daddy really *does* show you he loves you by doing things!"

Out of the mouth of babes.

# . 50 .

## CHOOSE WISELY, TREAT KINDLY

During the writing of this book, and during the years that led to its inception, I've read just about every book published on the subject of simplicity. Recently, while re-reading some of them, I had a revelation. The authors came from a wide range of backgrounds, with different lifestyles, political opinions, religious affiliations, etc. Yet the *one thing* they all had in common was a happy marriage. This is what permits people—myself included— to look at life with a happier, simpler frame of mind.

A happy marriage is one of the major keys of a simpler life. It allows the couple to handle all of the stresses, misfortunes, difficulties, and bad luck that life throws their way. It has the added advantage of improving attitude and behavior, another key factor in simplifying one's life.

Those of us with happy marriages *did not* win the lottery. We didn't just randomly pick a guy, get married, and gosh darn it our spouse happened to turn out terrific. No, we chose well. Then we worked hard to keep our spouse happy. Read that last line again: we *chose well*. We *worked hard* to keep our spouse happy.

Once you choose a good spouse and then work hard to keep that spouse happy, it staggers the mind how much simpler your life can become. Your children are more secure and less likely to cause strife as they mature. And, pragmatically, a happy spouse will work harder to keep you happy as well. See how it works?

# .51.

## HOW TO CHOOSE WISELY AND TREAT KINDLY

Choosing your spouse is probably the single biggest decision of your life. Matrimony is not something to be entered lightly, though some people actually enter a marriage with a pre-arranged "out" already in place. Go figure.

The first part of the equation, choosing well, means choosing someone with whom you can share the rest of your life. You have similar goals; you have compatible tastes; you have similar religious views. Your spouse should be free of addictions that can doom any home (drugs, alcohol, pornography, whatever). Your spouse should be free of any emotional problems that would prevent him or her from building a happy, healthy home life with you.

The second part of the equation, working hard to keep your spouse happy, is frequently misunderstood. You should not enter into the bonds of matrimony to *get*; you should enter to *give*. By giving, you get. Very simple.

The nice thing about this is that it's within your grasp, too. No, you don't have to change spouses (unless you're married to a psychopath, in which case you didn't choose wisely to begin with). But assuming you chose wisely—you voluntarily chose to join your life with your spouse and took vows to that affect—then the next step (treat kindly) is *entirely within your power*.

You can't change your spouse, but you *can* change yourself. If you're a hard person to live with, change that.

Treating one's spouse with kindness and love and appreciation is the key to a happy marriage and therefore to a simpler life.

# .52.

## DON'T NAG

Women nag. This tendency is universal and ancient. Sources as diverse as Buddha and Confucius and Proverbs all talk about wives who nag. It's also the most common complaint men have about women. It must be built into our DNA or something.

Women tend to think that if something isn't done right away, it must be because the person didn't hear us. So we nag until they do the task just to shut us up. Then we'll mutter something uncomplimentary like, "Why couldn't you have done that sooner?" That really works to inspire people, doesn't it?

"Nag resistance"—the ability for someone to completely ignore your nagging—can also be the other person's form of control. They don't want to be pushed around, and ignoring you has the added advantage of driving you nuts.

Instead, try using humor to get something done. Try letting your husband accomplish the task on his schedule, not yours. Resist the urge to micromanage ("No! You don't wash the pot *that* way, you wash it *this* way!").

If something simply isn't getting done, calmly and gently present the issue to your husband as a problem to solve (see #150). Be sure to make it clear the problem isn't *him*, it's the *unfinished task* (i.e., the unwashed dishes).

Think how much happier and calmer—dare I say simpler— your home life will be if you stopped nagging. And the good news is that it's completely within your control.

# . 53 .

## IT TAKES TWO TO FIGHT

Human relationships are such complicated things, aren't they? Marriage is complicated; relations with one's parents are complicated; relations with our children are complicated. It's so easy to get into fights with these complicated relations.

But always remember this: it takes two to fight. Fights and arguments undermine the security of the family unit. How much simpler would your family life be if you stopped fighting?

If your spouse picks a fight with you, you have the *choice* not to rise to the bait. You have the choice of excusing yourself and leaving the room. You have the choice of not arguing back. Believe me, most people can't argue with someone who refuses to argue back. There's no point. They can't accomplish anything.

People who pick fights are trying to make you react. Every time you are involved in a fight or argument, you must accept the fact that some of the responsibility lies with you. You have chosen to do battle. Therefore, you have the power to *not* fight as well. (And of course, I'm assuming that *you* never pick fights.)

Arguments often tread the same path over and over again. The very fact that the other person knows what buttons to push can help us handle things better.

This does not mean that there is never a time to fight. Nor does it mean you "stop" fighting by giving the silent treatment, responding as a martyr, or other similarly annoying and destructive behaviors. But remember, a simple life is not a life of arguments and strife. Take responsibility for your part, and stop arguing.

# .54.

## A MAN'S PERSPECTIVE ON BEING A MAN:
## A TIP FROM MY HUSBAND

Men, so far maybe you think you've been given a pass. "This lady is so right!" you announce. "My wife needs to be much nicer to me and give me more love and respect. Meanwhile, I'll just prop my feet on the couch and wait for her to bring me a beer." Good plan!

*Not.*

A successful, loving relationship is not a "give and take." It's a "give and give." Men are simple, yes; but *simple* does not mean any less *profound.*

A man provides, protects, and loves his wife and children. Very simple. And very profound. As a man, you must live up to the vows you took on the altar, and those vows do *not* include expecting servile service from your wife.

Rather, look for ways to make your wife happy. (It goes without saying that she should be doing the same for you as well.) The most important thing to contribute to your wife's security and happiness is to act like a man of honor.

A man works hard at his job to provide for his family. A man keeps his word (if you promise to do the dishes, then *do* them!). If you want love and respect from your wife, it is your responsibility to *earn* it. Earning it includes being honorable and performing your duties as a man.

So rather than propping up your feet and telling your wife to bring you a beer, how about instead you tell your wife to go prop her feet up and bring her a glass of wine. You might find the results . . . interesting.

# .55.

## DON'T CORRECT OR CRITICIZE YOUR SPOUSE IN PUBLIC

It's one thing to gently correct your spouse in public if they're making a serious factual error *and it makes a difference* (i.e., you're directing a police officer to a burning home and telling them the wrong street). It's another thing to correct or criticize because your spouse mispronounced a word or couldn't remember whether Belfast or Dublin is the capital of Northern Ireland.

Let's face it, we all have egos. Some of us have egos that can take more abuse than others, but that's beside the point. For a smoother and simpler relationship with your spouse, it behooves you to preserve your spouse's dignity in public.

For example, I'm one of those people who can't tell a joke worth beans. That doesn't keep me from trying, though. It drives my husband nuts to listen to me mangle the punch line, but he never jumps in to correct me or criticize me for this flaw. The important thing is not that the joke gets told correctly; the important thing is that he preserves my dignity while telling it.

My husband, on the other hand, occasionally will pontificate the same old joke or story to the same group of people over and over. I never tell him that everyone's heard it. Why bother? What will it do, except damage my husband's dignity and hurt his ego? The listeners are always polite and laugh even if they've heard it before.

The ability to keep your spouse's dignity intact will go far in keeping your relationship sound and happy.

# .56.

## MEN AREN'T MIND READERS

Women are excellent and instinctive communicators. If one of our friends is down, we know just by the subtle, non-verbal cues: the drooping shoulders, the flat tone of voice. We will immediately dive in to offer a sympathetic shoulder. The trouble comes when a woman expects her man to have those same skills in communication. If she is feeling down, why the heck can't he just *know?*

A woman expects her husband to read her mind. Of *course* he should just "know" when you want something done, or that you're in the mood for Chinese food instead of Italian, or that you expect him to remember it's his night to do the dishes.

Wrong. Wrong, wrong, wrong.

Men are very, very bad at picking up subtle cues or guessing what's on someone's mind or even remembering details. Men like things in simple, concrete terms rather than vague innuendo. If you want something—a hug or sympathy or the garbage taken out—you need to tell him. This doesn't mean you nag or criticize. You just "tell."

"Honey, would you mind taking out the garbage?" "I'm in the mood for potstickers. Let's go to Ling's Restaurant tonight." "Would you like me to make you some coffee while you do the dishes?"

If it's his night to do dishes, then offering him coffee and perhaps lingering in the kitchen to admire his muscles while he scrubs pots will make him a happy man.

This simple understanding—that men aren't mind-readers— can work wonders for simplifying your relationship.

# . 57 .

## MARRIAGE IS NOT INDEPENDENT
## OF YOUR EFFORTS

Sometimes people seem to think that no effort is necessary once the marital knot is tied. Couples make no attempt to please their other half. Love is enough to carry you through all the tough times.

Then life happens. Kids are born and add strain to your relationships. Jobs are stressful. The commute is awful. Bills pile up. A job is lost. And somehow, love seems to fade.

We come to see love as something that can only be recaptured if the other person works harder to make you happy. And if you're not happy, then you're entitled to make the other person's life a living hell. Divorce begins to look like an attractive option. But it doesn't have to be that way. *Marriage does not exist outside your efforts.*

Happily married couples don't approach their relationship with the idea that the other person is there to serve them and make them happy. Rather, they approach the relationship with the idea that they will give and give and give some more.

But for some reason, this is a difficult concept to grasp. Women especially are conditioned to think that any "giving" on their part is a sign of weakness and inequality. Nothing could be farther from the truth. A happy couple is a couple that has established their own separate roles within the marriage.

Find your role in the marriage and work to make your spouse happy. Give and give and give some more. Ideally your spouse will give back. Then you'll find that your marriage will improve because of *your* efforts.

# .58.

## SEEK FRIENDS WHO SUPPORT YOU

My parents recently retired and moved to a smaller house in a new town. In seeking a new hairdresser, my mother went to a beauty salon that came highly recommended. She wasn't five minutes in the salon chair before the hairdresser started bad-mouthing her husband. Being a captive audience, my mother grew more and more uncomfortable as the woman snipped and cut and griped and complained.

At last, my mother's hair was done. The new hairdo was quite lovely, but Mom told me she would never return to that shop. "How could that woman complain so much?" she wondered. "She didn't have a single good word to say about her husband."

My mother, let it be known, has been happily married to my father since 1958. The key word here is "happily." And, as the experience with the hairdresser demonstrates, Mom prefers not to associate with women who belittle their husbands. She knows that doing so will only undermine her own marriage.

If your friends are in cahoots to sabotage your relationship with your spouse, then seek different friends. Find friends who will uphold your marital vows, not tear them down. Find friends who support you in your efforts to improve your marriage, not those who think a divorce is the answer to all your problems. Find friends who can offer constructive help toward improving relations with your spouse, not just be sounding boards for your complaints.

A support group can be an invaluable thing. Just make sure that it's supporting the *right* thing.

# .59.

## YOUR RELATIONSHIPS IN
## A DOWN ECONOMY

If ever there is a time to cultivate supportive relationships, it's during stressful times. For married couples, the primary relationship that will buoy you is that with your spouse. Get out of the mindset that your spouse is a detriment to your happiness (ladies, this applies specifically to *you*). Cultivated properly, a solid, stable relationship with your husband or wife will carry you through whatever bad things a down economy can throw at you.

Be tender toward each other if a financial blow hits your family. Men especially are impacted by a job loss, because for them it goes beyond mere money. It affects their ego, their sense of manhood, even their interest in physical intimacy. Men are genetically programmed to provide for their family, and when that is interrupted, the mental blow can be devastating. This is the time to hold a man up, not berate him when he's down.

It's the same with friends. Cultivate healthy friendships, not friendships that drag you down or encourage bad behavior. If you have friends undercutting your marriage or urging you toward profligate spending or ridiculing your efforts to prepare for hard times or encouraging you to do something contrary to your beliefs or ethics, for Pete's sake, cut the ties and find friends who aren't destructive.

Solid, stable relationships are the foundation for a simple life. Like a house built on rock instead of sand, solid relationships will help you weather the worst storms life can throw.

# Teach Your Children Well

▼

Kids can either bring immeasurable joy into your life, or immeasurable pain. They can make your life simpler, or vastly more complicated. We owe it to future generations to raise children who will learn to keep their own lives simple by making good choices of their own. It will be our choices, good or bad, that will be their greatest education—particularly those choices made in the face of adversity. And so the cycle continues . . .

# . 60 .

## SIMPLE KIDS

If your home is the physical center of your life, your family should be the emotional center. Your spouse and your children are the truly important things . . . or they should be. But as with so much else, we tend to push our family aside, to put them last, to expect them to understand how busy we are, to consider our job to be the most important (or at least the most energy-sucking) thing we do.

But, as someone once remarked, at the end of our life we aren't going to regret not having spent more time at the office. No, we'll regret not having spent more time with our family.

Family life is something I feel passionate about. Providing my husband and children with a happy home is both a calling and a duty, but it has the added advantage of providing me with a tremendous amount of simplicity. A family life centered around simple things is hard to beat.

But families can also cause great pain and sorrow. Undisciplined children, rampant peer-pressure, and divorced households can make any home life rough. It's your job as a parent to minimize the forces that mess your kids up.

Simple joys—eating dinner together, reading to your kids, and otherwise spending time as a family—are seldom found in this hustle-bustle world we've created. Maybe it's time to recapture those moments before they're gone forever.

Remember, you are training your children to become adults. Train them right. It isn't easy, but it's much simpler in the end.

# .61.

## RAISE YOUR CHILDREN IN
## A BENEVOLENT DICTATORSHIP

Your household should not be a democracy. Your household should be a benevolent dictatorship. Your word is law, your authority absolute. When kids learn this, they are more secure and better behaved because they know and respect the boundaries you've set up.

Remember the "other" Golden Rule? Whoever has the gold makes the rules. As long as you, the parent, have the money, the power, and (more importantly) the *responsibility*, then you get to make the rules. Children are dependent on their parents. They have no responsibilities (except the chores you assign and the behavior you expect), no power, and therefore no say on the rules. Does this sound cruel? Unjust? Unfair? Only if you want chaos in your house. And only if you want disrespect and whining and lies and backtalk.

In our house, disrespect isn't allowed and whining *never* works. (In fact, whining is likely to produce the exact opposite effect: the request will be instantly denied, no questions asked, merely on the basis of principle.)

Remember, you are your children's parents. *You are not their friends.* Someday you may be friends, but not until your children are grown and have learned the lessons of self-discipline that is *your* responsibility to teach them.

Children crave structure and authority, and will often push their limits in an effort to find a boundary. By being a benevolent dictator, you set up the boundaries that give children a sense of security and the knowledge of how to behave.

And *that* makes for a vastly simpler home life.

# .62.

## WHO'S THE BOSS?

If your children are the bosses in your household, your home life will be chaos.

Kids who rule a house often do so because the parents make the mistake of wanting to be "friends" with their kids instead of the authority figure. The parents don't want their children upset with them, so they give in from anything to toys and candy, to providing alcohol and birth control. Unbelievable.

Stop it. Learn to be the boss.

We are friendly, loving, and affectionate with our children, but we are not their friends. We are their *parents*. We cannot become their "friends" until they are adults. Friends approach each other from positions of relative equality. Friends don't discipline each other—they support each other.

Children don't need parents who are their buddies—they need teachers and protectors. They need guidance, discipline, and a benevolent dictatorship.

This kind of dynamic will simplify your family life. We have the happiest home life imaginable: charming, loving kids who know the rules, abide by them, and are happy because they have safe and firm limits. They have parents who love each other and them, and who are consistent in matters of authority. Even in her snarky teen phase, our oldest daughter doesn't step over the boundaries of our household rules because she knows it won't be permitted.

While the boundaries will change as our children become capable of handling additional responsibilities, those boundaries will still be firm, well-defined, carefully surveyed . . . and simple to understand and follow.

# .63.

## DISCIPLINE YOUR KIDS

It isn't politically correct to discipline your kids these days because it might interfere with their budding little self-esteems. Yet studies have shown that children do best with clear-cut boundaries, expectations, and responsibilities.

Have you ever noticed how traffic flows smoothly when all the drivers obey the consistent rules of the road? Well, similarly, a household flows smoothly when all the children obey the consistent rules of the parents. Easy as pie.

The question is, how do you discipline your children? That's something you'll have to figure out for yourself according to your personality, your child's personality, and your morals and values. Contrary to a lot of modern thought, disciplining your children is *not* punishment. It does *not* mean beatings and abuse. We spanked our children (sparingly) when they were young. We no longer have to.

Horrified? Well, think about those families whose kids run amok in stores with the parents trotting behind, ineffectually saying, "No, Junior . . . Junior, don't do that . . . Junior, come here . . . ." Meanwhile, Junior is yanking clothes off racks or tumbling packages off shelves until the store manager has to step in. (Then the parents protest that Junior wasn't doing anything wrong, he was just *expressing* himself.) *That's* what happens when you don't discipline your kids. I've seen it. So have you.

Training your children when they are young to obey your authority and conform to your discipline means that your child-rearing years will be *vastly* easier. Being a parent is stressful enough without having out-of-control brats who rule the house.

Keep your home life simple. Discipline your children.

# .64.

## THE FOUR RULES OF DISCIPLINE

While everyone's discipline philosophies differ, we have four basic rules that work in our household. What is important for children is:

1. Iron-clad household rules. These rules should include never showing disrespect to you, the parents.
2. Consistency in enforcing those rules, with age-appropriate consequences.
3. A unified front between parents; never, ever, *ever* contradict your spouse in front of your kids, especially on matters of discipline. Children will pick up on the discrepancy and play you and your spouse against each other for all its worth.
4. Tons of love and affection, both between you and your spouse, and between you and your kids.

I remember an incident where my then-ten-year-old daughter said something bratty to me. I stopped what I was doing, looked her in the eye, and said very quietly, "If I ever hear you speak to me in that tone of voice again, I will [fill in the blank—I don't remember what dire punishment I promised . . . but it was ominous]." My daughter knew she had stepped over the line. She apologized and stopped the bad behavior. She did this because of her early training that you *never* disrespect your parents. She also knew that I *would* follow through on the threat, because my husband and I are consistent in our discipline.

Strong discipline for children vastly simplifies your life with kids because it teaches them self-control. If a child learns self-control while young, they will be able to control themselves as teenagers and young adults, which leads to a *much* simpler life for everyone.

# .65.

## GIVE ORDERS, NOT REQUESTS

Children do best when given "orders." This means a firm voice and as few words as possible. Men do this better than women.

A woman might say in a sweet voice, "Johnny, it's time to wash your hands for dinner, since we all have to get rid of the nasty germs before we eat. Come on, Johnny, let's go wash your hands now. Johnny, I'll give you until I count to three to go wash your hands . . . ." Johnny is likely to ignore this, especially if he's busy making mud pies.

Men, however, are likely to bark, "John, go wash your hands. *Now!*" Johnny jumps up and washes his hands. Now.

Firm control and consistency aren't "simple" things to do. However, it simplifies your life in the long run to have well-behaved, respectful children and teens who understand their limits.

It is a gift to your children—although they may disagree at first—to teach them self-control while they're young. How else will they learn to control themselves when hormones are surging through their bodies as teenagers? How will they learn to control themselves to study hard in college instead of partying? How will they learn to control themselves to work hard at their job as an adult? These are the dramatic and long-ranging results of disciplining your child when he's young. As an added bonus, there's nothing that swells your chest with pride more than a perfect stranger walking up and saying how beautifully behaved your kids are.

# .66.

## EAT DINNER TOGETHER

Sounds simple, doesn't it? Teenagers whose families do not eat dinner together are 61 *percent* more likely to use alcohol, tobacco, or illegal drugs. By contrast, teens whose families eat dinner together are less likely to have sex at an early age, get into fights, be suspended from school, or have fewer thoughts of suicide. That's a lot of benefits from simply sharing a meal.

From time immemorial, sharing meals have been used for bonding, visiting, and making connections. Nowhere is this more important than with your family. Eating together is the perfect time for family members to catch up on each others' days, to share any joys or frustrations, and to reconnect after being apart.

But what prevents us from doing this ritual? Heavy workloads, long commutes, frantic schedules, after-school activities . . . the list goes on and on. Besides, how important can it really be to take the time to have dinner together?

Think about how much *simpler* your life would be if your teenagers weren't having sex, or doing drugs, or getting in trouble with the law. Now think again about what it would take to sit down and have dinner with your kids every night. Does it still seem like it's not important?

Is the real reason you're not having a family dinner because of yours or your kids' schedules? Or is it because you're no longer comfortable speaking with your children? I'm sorry, but if the choice is between eating dinner as a family and Junior's soccer practice, ditch the soccer.

# . 67 .

## KILL YOUR TV

Get rid of all but one TV. Or, be a radical and get rid of *all* the TVs. It's staggering how many hours we waste watching the boob tube.

The average American adult watches nearly four hours of television per day. The average child between the age of two and five watches about three and a half hours per day. And the average adult over 55 watches for almost six hours a day.

To what productive use—or what kind of fun—could those hours be put instead? Reading to your kids? Reading for yourself? Yardwork? Charitable work? Enjoying the sunrise, sunset, or thunderstorm? Talking with your spouse? Taking a walk? Making a healthy dinner?

We haven't had television since 1992, and haven't missed it in the slightest. We keep abreast of the news via radio and the Internet.

And bliss—we have children who are not accustomed to plopping down and zoning out. Reducing—or better, eliminating—television viewing by your kids will proportionally reduce their desires for toys and other consumer items. Advertisers are clever about targeting their audiences, and children are no exception.

The point to remember is not that kid's television programs are bad, though they frequently are. It's that when kids are watching TV, they *aren't doing anything else*. They're not running, or playing, or reading, or dreaming, or socializing.

Children don't need better television programming. They need less time in front of the boob tube.

# .68.

## STOP TURNING YOUR KIDS INTO ZOMBIES

Recently I saw a magazine advertisement that stopped me in my tracks. The ad featured two children staring, zombie-like, at a television. In bold letters below the children was the word "HELP."

At first I thought, "Good. Someone is trying to break those poor kids loose from the grip of the stupid television." Then I read the text of the ad: "The average American child spends close to four hours a day planted in front of a television. Which is why [name of company] is happy to sponsor the [name of an "educational" television series]. Charming characters present classic, positive stories that help you guide your children through the kinds of lessons you actually want them to learn. Courage. Honesty. Responsibility. After all, what better place to reach your children than right where they already are?"

Does anyone else find this logic *sickening*? Is there no expectation that the *parents* should actually take responsibility for their own children's moral teachings? God forbid that you should have to interact with the little tykes. Instead, stick 'em in front of the TV and turn their brains to mush so you don't have to be bothered.

How are these TV shows supposed to teach responsibility (and courage and honesty) when the kids' parents aren't even willing to have the courage and honesty to take responsibility themselves? Huh?

Teach your own kids the moral lessons you want them to learn. Stop turning your kids into zombies. Turn them into people instead. Good, decent, honest, courageous, responsible people. It's much simpler in the end.

# .69.

## TEACH KIDS TO PLAY

Children who are plugged into a television set from their earliest years never learn to play. They never develop the *imagination* to play.

By not mindlessly plopping the kids in front of the TV so that I can get a "break," my children have learned to entertain themselves. We do permit them to watch an age-appropriate movie (DVD) in the evening after their chores are done, but more often than not they skip this option. We provided creative toys when they were young, which taught them to entertain themselves—blocks, train sets, Legos, dolls, crayons, craft supplies, and, of course, books by the hundreds.

It's a rule in our house that there is no movie-watching during the day. The exceptions to this are (a) the children are sick and unable to concentrate on anything; or (b) my husband and I are working on a rush order with our home business and we need the kids out of our hair (happens a few times a year).

Our days are filled with school, play, chores, reading, and the hundred-and-one odd jobs any household entails. Life is so much simpler with kids who can entertain themselves.

By the way, you want to know one of my pet peeves? Homes in which the television is left on, even when no one is watching it. How lame is that? It's distracting, it's noisy, it's wasteful, and it most certainly is not conducive to a simple life. Don't believe me? Read Marie Winn's *Unplugging the Plug-In Drug* for an eye-opening account of how television has impacted the lives of our children.

Kill your TV. You'll be better for it.

# . 70 .

## MONITOR THE INTERNET

We've all heard how pedophiles troll for victims on popular social networking websites because children—your children—are able to post photos, personal information, and even cell phone numbers. I've seen police chiefs point out how social networking sites are a dream come true for predators. Usually these perverts pose as teens themselves, make arrangements to meet their new "penpals," and *voilà!*: Sexual assault. The Internet has made pedophiles very, very happy people, because finding victims is now very, very easy.

We thought we were doing fine with our children because we only allowed them to have access to a few appropriate children's Websites. And then one day my daughter's fingers slipped on the keyboard and she typed in the wrong address. Whatever she saw, she didn't say much about it until a few days later. Then she started making comments about a "teenager" Website she had accidentally been to. ("Teenager" in our household lingo frequently means "inappropriate.") I was disturbed by her veiled comments and realized that, monitored or not, mistakes happen. We vowed to be very careful from now on, and bookmarked her favorite website so there would be no further mistakes.

So monitor your kids' Internet access. Make sure the computer is in a public room in the house, not tucked into a bedroom. Get Internet filters. Give them a time limit. Do all the common sense things necessary to protect your children . . . or your life might become far more complex than you wish.

# . 71 .

## STOP PRE-SEXUALIZING YOUR CHILDREN

As a mother of daughters, I am horrified by the constant attempts to pre-sexualize my girls.

When our kids were four and six years old, I needed to buy them sandals for summer wear. Yet every pair of sandals I found—every single pair—had high heels. High heels for a *four year old?* Why? How can a child run and play and jump wearing high heels? It took trips to literally ten different stores before we found flat sandals.

Almost everything around us tries to pre-sexualize kids, especially girls, to a shocking degree. Television, clothing, toys (have you *seen* those awful Bratz dolls?), movies . . . everywhere you turn, it seems, someone is trying to make small girls look like sexy little adults. Again I ask, why?

We won't allow it. We're teaching our daughters modest dress and behavior. Crop top shirts and low-riding pants are simply not allowed, period. Showing their navel isn't permitted.

Why would I bring up this little peeve in a book on simple living? Because I can think of few things in life more complicating than having a pregnant teenage daughter. Pre-sexualizing kids, especially girls, leaves our daughters vulnerable to this kind of temptation and trouble.

I'll spare you the usual lambaste about morals and virtues and self-esteem and all that stuff. There are many different sources to confirm whatever your opinion is on the topic. But if you avoid pre-sexualizing your children and just let them be *kids* rather than miniature adults, your lives will be simpler. And so will theirs.

# .72.

## PRE-SEXUALIZATION
## IS YOUR FAULT

So how can you stop pre-sexualizing your kids? And who is at fault? Sure, we can blame a lot of things. Society. The fashion industry. Hollywood. The schools. Pick one. But what it boils down to is *you*, the parent, allowing it.

I've heard some parents say they can't "stop" this pre-sexualization because kids will learn it in school or from their peers. Parents prefer to feel victimized, swept helplessly along the tide of society and doing nothing to stop it.

C'mon, parents, *stop being so damned helpless.*

Edmund Burke (1729–1797) said that all that is necessary for evil to triumph is for good men to do nothing. Stop doing nothing. Tell your kids that from this day on you will only permit appropriate clothing, music, movies, and other products. Ignore their protests. Remember this is *your* home and *you* are the authority figure.

Then follow through. Stop buying your children inappropriate clothes or toys. Forbid any posters or music or DVDs that you find offensive. Don't permit them to watch movies or television shows that celebrate immorality. Be intolerant. Openly show your disgust for inappropriate products and behaviors. Make sure your children understand your feelings on the matter.

Yank them out of public schools, if need be. Yes, this is drastic; but is it any less drastic to have your fifteen-year-old daughter turn up pregnant? Or your fifteen-year-old son become a father?

Be a parent, not a friend. Resume authority. Life is simpler when your children stay on track.

# .73.

## A GENERATION GAP BRIDGED

Every generation thinks they have it tougher than the previous generation. In some regards, I think this time we may be right.

I had been telling my mother for many years about how horrible girls' fashions are. Because of the inappropriate nature of many clothes, we often shopped in the boys' department to get clothes for my daughters.

Like many of the older generation, my mother thought I was exaggerating about this complaint until the day she took my girls clothes shopping. She came home hours later, shaken. "You're right," she said. "Almost everything we looked at was bad. We ended up in the boys' departments."

Mom even decided that it might be better to sew the girls some clothes (she loves to sew), so they went to a fabric store and looked at patterns. "Even the patterns were trashy," she related in wonder. "The *patterns!*"

My mother ended up finding some old girls' patterns in a thrift store for pennies, and bought an armful. She is a talented seamstress and was able to modernize the patterns for the kids.

Now that her eyes were opened, my mother wonders how we can raise our daughters to be virtuous and decent young women. "No problem," I tell her. "We just teach them to use the tools. When they become adults, we hand them the toolbox."

Teach your children the tools of morality, decency, honor, and (what the heck) chastity. When they become adults, hand them the toolbox and wish them good luck. It's all we can do.

# .74.

## EXERT VETO POWER

We've raised our children to understand that everything—everything!—that comes into our home is subject to what we call "veto" power. This includes things our kids buy with their own money. Remember, your home is *your* home. You're the benevolent dictators. You call the shots.

In our case, we want our home to be free of what we see as destructive materialistic or commercial influences. For example, our children's bedroom walls are covered with pictures and posters of space, the planets, dragons, Lord of the Rings, and rocks (their current interests). Beats the heck out of Britney Spears posters. There will *never* be Britney Spears posters on the walls of their rooms.

Remember, your home is *your* home. This is *not* your children's home, per se. They didn't pay for it, and they don't have the responsibility to maintain it. It is *your* home. If you don't want a Britney Spears poster on the wall, even in their room, even if they paid for it, then don't allow it.

This applies to music, clothing, and even hairstyles you don't like.

Obviously as our children mature, their interests will change, but *we* will still decide what will be allowed into our home.

Think I'm living in a pipe dream here? If you think that, then it's possible that you're not disciplining your children enough, giving adequate punishment, or you're more interested in being a friend than a parent. Don't fall down on the job. Your kids need you to be strong and consistent..

Vetoing inappropriate things simplifies your home life. Trust me.

# . 75 .

## COOK WITH YOUR CHILDREN

One of the saddest television advertisements I ever saw went like this. A couple of pre-teen siblings got off a school bus in front of a beautiful, elegant house in an upscale neighborhood. They went up the walkway toward the front door slowly, hesitantly. "It *looks* like our house . . . " one said.

"But it *can't* be," said the other.

"Something isn't right."

Why were the children so concerned? What caused them to hesitate?

It was the smell of baking cookies wafting through the air.

"Could it be . . . *cookies?*" wondered the girl.

"Can't be," countered the boy. "Mom doesn't *make* cookies."

The camera panned to the mother standing in the doorway. She was attired in a snappy business suit and held a spatula in her hands. She crossed her arms, smiled smugly at her bewildered offspring, and said, "Scary, isn't it?"

The ad was for slice 'n bake pre-made cookie dough. While I have no particular objection to pre-made cookie dough, the advertisement made me want to cry. The kids were ten and twelve years old, and *they had never smelled baking cookies before?* How sad is that?

Imagine the happy memories your kids will have by making messes in the kitchen with you. Flour on the floor, dough sneaked off the beaters into sticky mouths, learning how not to touch hot pans that just came out of the oven.

Give your kids some memories. Happy, warm, floury, messy memories. They'll be sure to pass this on to *their* kids . . . and thank you.

# . 76 .

## TEACH YOUR CHILDREN
## TO DO CHORES

So few parents require their children to do chores these days. So much for developing a work ethic.

A family is like a miniature business, and like all businesses, the employees must work for their wages. Parents are obliged to provide the basics of life for their children (food, shelter, medicine, love, education). But within the context of a "business," your children's wages are toys, activities, and other treats. But employees need training. Children need to be taught what to do.

Young kids like to imitate their parents. They want to help. The time to start training them is when they are young. Later, kids get caught up in other things. School. Friends. Hobbies. And it takes some training and some reminding to get them to do their chores.

But keep at it. Give the kids assignments to do. Some of these chores can be money-earners, and some should just be part of their "job" as family members. Give consequences when the jobs aren't performed. Keep an assignment sheet on the refrigerator if you need to, and remove privileges for undone chores.

Sharing family responsibilities makes a child part of the whole. Family work should never be thought of as punishment; it is an indication of respect . . . but respect must be earned.

Responsibilities for children, such as chores, breed superior attitudes in young men and women. So give your kids some work. Train them to do it to your standards. Then sit back and enjoy the wonderful children that result.

## . 77 .

## STOP GIFTING YOUR CHILDREN

It was Henry Home (1696–1782) who said, "An infallible way to make your child miserable is to satisfy all his demands."

Modern kids are absolutely swimming in material possessions. All the electronic goodies, computers, cell phones, portable CD and DVD players, fashions, even cars. The list is endless.

Why do we *do* this? Even the most affluent among us know that drowning our kids in material possessions is wrong. Yet we do it anyway. Why?

The reasons are complex, of course. Guilt. A desire to give our kids what we "missed" when we were children. Keeping up with the Joneses. Keeping up with their classmates. Peer pressure. Buying love. Or worst of all, distracting them so that they don't bother us while we play with our own "toys."

Are our children happier for it? No. Of course not.

Kids are naturally acquisitive—given a choice, they'll take the latest whiz-bang goodie. But if you stop giving them goodies and instead give them lots of time and attention, you might be startled and amazed by some of the changes in them—less whining, less clinging, less misbehaving, more imagination, more inventiveness, and more real pleasure.

If your child wants something badly enough, have him work for it instead. He'll value it more.

Children are wired and programmed to love and trust their parents above all else. But if that love and trust is not repaid with time, attention, and consistency, kids will accept the next best (available) thing: stuff. *Love* for children is simple. *Stuff* is not.

# . 78 .

## AS THE TWIG IS BENT . . .

As the twig is bent, so grows the tree, according to the old proverb. One of the most useful things you can do to simplify your kids is to model simplicity yourself. Your kids are watching.

Do you yell at other drivers in traffic? Do you yell at your spouse? Do you yell at your kids? Well, don't be surprised when—not if, but *when*—your kids start yelling, too. After all, they had good teachers.

When my husband and I first married, we rented a house next to a small apartment complex whose occupants tended to "live on their doorstep," meaning that everyone could watch their life dramas. One mother, who had three young children, used to punish them by grabbing their hair at the top of the scalp and yanking so hard the kids shrieked. It was interesting to watch how the older children learned to do this to the youngest child whenever things weren't going their way.

Those kids are grown now. I'll bet they do the same thing to their kids. As the twig is bent . . .

As any mother does, I sometimes speculate into the future and wonder who my daughters will marry. Naturally, I pray that their future husbands will be good, kind, decent men. But how will I know whether my girls will have as good a marriage as I do?

I no longer worry. How good a marriage is often depends on how well a wife treats her husband. My girls are watching and learning. As the twig is bent . . .

# .79.

## DISARM THE VERBAL BULLIES

"Mom," asked my nine-year-old daughter one day. "How do I deal with someone who says my hair is a funny color?"

My daughter, let it be known, has lovely hair. But that's not the point. The point was, someone was trying to get her goat by telling her she had funny hair. It didn't have to be her hair, of course. It could have been her eyes, her nose, her clothes, or her fourth left toe. My daughter was dealing with a verbal bully.

Maybe this is more of a "girl" problem (boy bullies tend to intimidate you physically), but how do you handle someone who harasses and teases you?

Agree with them. It disarms them.

Bullies thrive on a sense of power. Their purpose is to make you feel bad, insecure, vulnerable, or otherwise crummy. What bullies don't expect is for their victims to not only remain unruffled, but to agree with their pronouncement.

So my daughter and I did some role-playing. "I'll be the bully, and you be you," I said. "Ready? Hey! Your hair looks funny!"

After a bit of practice, my daughter came back with, "You're right. It does. Maybe I should dye it pink—what do you think?"

Try role playing and practicing with your kids until they are able to verbally disarm a bully. And by the way, this technique is also useful as an adult.

# . 80 .

## DEPRIVE THE KIDS

Some people argue that you'll deprive little Johnny of the best you can give him if you scale back and simplify your life. I say, full steam ahead! Deprive the little tykes. They'll be happier for it.

Kids thrive on the simple things in life: walks with their parents, lots of books, baking cookies, having dinner every night as a family. They blossom when they have time to dream, play, read, and interact with you.

Their lives are *not* simple if you pack every available minute with lessons, classes, sports, activities, and other frenzied accomplishments. Nor are their lives simple if you load little Johnny with every electronic gadget known to man.

Catch the drift here? They need *time* with you, not things. They need *time* with you, not activities. They *time* with themselves in order to figure out this crazy world and their own unique place in it.

Often kids are loaded with material things or extracurricular activities in an attempt to fill a void within ourselves (giving them chances *we* never had) or to fulfill our own egos. Depriving our children of *our* over-reaching expectations will give them back the one true currency in the world—time to be themselves.

Besides, if your child has a particular skill (music or dance or sports), then reducing other distractions such as too much stuff or too many things to do will allow them more time to cultivate their gift.

So deprive your kids. They'll be happier for it.

# . 81 .

## IT'S THE QUANTITY, STUPID

A myth that developed during the nineties was the idea that children didn't need *quantity* time, they needed *quality* time.

What a stupid idea.

If you showed up at your job for oh, say, three hours a week—but you did *quality* work during that time—do you think your boss would be satisfied? Of course not. Your job performance depends on how many hours a week you show up, as well as how well you do.

It's the same with parenting. It does no good to see your kids for oh, say, three hours a day and still say you're parenting them. No matter how concentrated the "quality" of your time is during these hours, it's not enough. If you're not there to parent your children, someone or something else will. (Think of television, peers, gangs, sexual relationships, etc.)

We'd better define "quality," too. Is "quality" time running like mad from one event (ballet, sports, theater, art shows, or music lessons) to another? Or is "quality" time spent playing on the floor with blocks or reading books? Don't misunderstand, sports and music and the arts are important to a child's well-rounded development. But you can't do it all and be anything but tired, cranky, and stressed. That kind of "quality" time won't be of very high quality.

So go for the quantity. Do something crazy, and go for quantity *and* quality. Why the heck not? The more hours per week that kids interact with their parents, the more likely they are to stay out of trouble. That simplifies things.

# .82.

## READ TO YOUR KIDS

There is nothing sadder than a home with no books. Children who watch television are less likely to read. See a connection here? The more you read to your kids, the more likely they are to do better in school.

Children's books can be bought cheaply. You can easily stock a children's library with many excellent selections for a bargain. For the cost of one DVD of the latest hit movie, you can provide weeks of entertainment by visiting your local thrift store, used bookstore, or library sale and stocking up. And while the kids may not remember *Happy Feet* any longer than it took them to watch it, Tom Sawyer or Laura Ingalls will be a friend for life. And unlike the passive entertainment of watching TV or movies, reading fosters brainpower and boosts imagination.

But of course, children will become better readers if they see their parents enjoying books. So turn off the TV and pick up a novel.

One of my husband's greatest daily pleasures is his bedtime reading of classic books to our kids. He reads the books in installments (chapters or partial chapters). Both kids read very well, but they love to listen, too. This ritual is also calming and centering for my husband, and it makes him feel that he's still "daddy" even though the kids are getting older.

Besides, once children learn to read—and learn to love it—there is no finer method of keeping them occupied when you need a break.

# .83.

## MAKE YOUR KIDS MAD AT YOU

It baffles me how many parents are afraid of doing something that will make their kids "mad" at them. Let them be mad! You're the parent, the ultimate authority figure. You're not their best friend who will approve of anything because you're friends. If you're being a responsible parent and setting appropriate limits, then don't worry about your kids being mad at you.

Children and teens respond best to strong authority figures who set limits and parameters. When parents do not consistently enforce house rules and decent behavior—maybe because the parents are afraid the kids won't "like" them anymore—then trouble begins.

If your nine-year-old has a temper tantrum and says you're mean because you won't let her hang around the mall with her friends, smile and agree. You're behaving the way a parent should.

If your teenager says he hates your guts because you won't let him stay out late, your chest should swell with pride. It means you're doing something right.

You've heard over and over how adult children will thank their parents for being so "mean" while they were growing up, and how they plan to be just as "mean" to their own kids. Woo-hoo!

You don't have to plan for this. If you're parenting correctly, it will occur, believe me. So make your kids mad. They're less likely to get in trouble. And nothing will make your life with children simpler than having kids who are decent and respectful.

# . 84 .

## BALANCE COMPLEXITY AND SIMPLICITY

When you're trying to simplify your children's lives, it may be necessary to "complexify" your own life for awhile, at first. Balance is needed.

The goal of any rational parent is to raise decent children. But if you're trying to make changes toward a simpler life *and* trying to force those changes on your children at the same time, try not to add the "simpler" things *on top of* the complexity they already face.

For example, you might think life would be *lots* simpler if you quit your job so you could spend more time with your children. Sure, your kids would see lots more of you . . . but you would soon be stressed because you couldn't pay the bills. Your life would be out of balance.

Nor can you assume that you're going to do all sorts of new "family togetherness" things like hikes and picnics and stuff on top of complicated extra-curricular school activities like sports, music, and karate. You would be stressing your children because they would have less time for homework and down time.

It's up to you to decide what simplicity factors will work for your family and what won't. It really isn't rocket science; it's just a balance. If it adds to the "wholeness" of the family, it's good. If it subtracts, it's bad. So get rid of one bad thing and replace it with one good thing. It's your job to find that balance and then tilt it toward a less stressful life for you and your children.

# .85.

## LET YOUR KIDS BE BORED

Our kids are never bored. Or if they are, they don't dare admit it because a typical conversation would go like this:

"Mom, I'm bored."

"Okay, so go clean your closet."

My husband and I can *always* find something for bored children to do, and it's almost always something they won't enjoy. By using this simple strategy, the kids will never admit it when they're bored.

I'll bet you could do this in no time flat in your house. What do you normally do if your kids say they're bored? Let them watch TV, drive them to the mall, buy them a new toy? What about, instead, you made them clean their bedroom? Sort the recycling? Do laundry? Wash dishes? Mow the grass? Help cook dinner? My goodness, your kids would *never* admit to being bored again.

I can tell when my oldest daughter is bored because she practices the piano more than usual. Or she might decide that the cranny behind the couch will make a great reading nook, and she begins to furnish it. Or she'll do a craft project. My youngest daughter will draw pictures or read or sort through her rock collection. I can deal with that.

If your kids were bored, what might they do? Make a cave out of couch cushions? Make a city out of blocks and railroad tracks? Build a fort in the yard? Boredom can actually lead to some amazingly creative play. Don't mess it up by catering to it.

# .86.

## DON'T COMPETE WITH YOUR SPOUSE

I once attended a birthday party at a friend's house where the mother and the father presented separate presents to their three-year-old son. Each tried to "top" the other in terms of what they gave the boy. It was pretty sad. Rather than presenting a unified front, the adults competed with each other for the fanciest present and, by extension, for the boy's affection.

Being a canny and intelligent child, the boy picked up on this spirit of competition as he grew older. He began to play one parent against the other. He grew more out of control in terms of discipline, while the parents took to quarreling. The marriage didn't last.

I'm not saying that separate gifts will lead to divorce, but the individual gift-giving was a sign of a fundamental problem in the marriage. Unity was lost.

When parents compete with each other for their children's affection, bad things happen. Parents lose authority. Children learn to control the house. Divorce is more common, after which there is even *less* control over the child, who grows into *more* of a discipline problem.

Moms and dads are different, but presumably they love their children in equal amounts. And children love their parents equally, but in different ways. By competing with your spouse, you stress not only your marriage but your child as well. No child should have to "choose" which parent he loves best.

Be simple. Be unified.

# . 87 .

## DON'T BE YOUR KID'S FRIEND

What is a friend? According to the dictionary, a friend is a favored companion. A friend is your equal in terms of maturity, experience, and tastes.

Your child is *none* of these. Your child is utterly dependent upon you, the parent, to provide his physical, emotional, and spiritual needs. He requires appropriate boundaries, discipline, and love. When you only apply *one* of these needs—love—your child suffers.

When a child only gets love, he is cut adrift. He has no boundaries and no expectations of behavior, so he "makes it up" as he goes along. Every time he tries something new, he looks to his parents to see if it's okay or not. If the parents just shrug it off as "kids will be kids," the child learns that whatever he does is fine . . . no matter how obnoxious or evil the behavior.

I know someone with two children. She loves her kids to pieces but she has seldom disciplined them, preferring to stay their "friend." Nor will she allow her husband to discipline them. These kids have been rejected from classrooms and extracurricular activities all over the city because of their wild, unruly behavior (including taunting handicapped children). These kids are approaching adolescence now, and I shudder to think what will happen next.

Quit being pals with your kids. Be their parent instead. Naturally you can "pal" around, but in the end, your children look to you as their guide and their teacher.

Rise to the occasion. Your life will be immensely simpler with well-behaved children.

# .88.

## APPLY PHYSICS

Newton's Third Law of Physics states that for every action, there is an equal and opposite reaction. A friend suggested that Newton's Law can also be applied to raising kids: For every action a child does, there is a consequence.

Try setting the rule that if your child does something, then he'll get a consequence (either good or bad). If he makes his bed, he gets praise. If he kicks the dog, he gets punishment. The secret is that the parents must be consistent in applying the consequences to the action. This can apply to anything in your family's life. Homework. Chores. Attitude. Behavior.

If they don't do their homework, then they have to spend the weekend doing endless chores at home (this is another friend's strategy). There's nothing like scrubbing out the inside of the refrigerator, vacuuming the entire house, or washing windows to convince a kid that it's a lot easier to do his homework.

If they don't do their chores, they go without all television, computer, and phone access for a period of time.

If they develop a snippy attitude, then post a chart on the wall with all their favorite things to do. Whenever they mouth off or get sassy, you quietly walk over and cross off an activity.

This puts a lot of power into the hands of the child. It becomes *their* responsibility to control their behavior in order to retain the privilege. It's up to them.

# . 89 .

## YOUR KIDS IN A DOWN ECONOMY

I once had a conversation about the economy with a friend who has four kids ranging from 11 to 18. "I don't want them to overhear us," she cautioned, as we moved into a different room. "I don't want them to get stressed or anxious about the economy."

I don't agree with her position. My kids are always overhearing discussions between my husband and myself about the economy. They're not left to speculate and suspect the worst because their parents are sneaking around and speaking in whispers. Besides, it's all over the media. How could they help but hear what's happening?

The difference is we, as a family, have decided on various strategies to cope. Our children (presently 13 and 15) watch, listen, and participate as we take what steps we can to stabilize our family. The key here is *action*. Action always mitigates fear and uncertainty.

This is where, depending on their ages, you can solicit input from your children, as well as their cooperation. If they know daddy lost his job, it makes them feel good to ask for $3 sneakers from Goodwill instead of $120 sneakers from the mall. Doing so puts them in control of their requests and lets them contribute toward the family's strategy to weather hard times.

So don't hide some of the harsh facts of life from your children. Instead, give them something concrete and positive they can do to help. You might be pleasantly surprised by how mature and sensible some of their suggestions may be.

# Amazing Grace

▼

S tudies have shown that people with a strong faith in God are far more capable of handling stress, difficulties, and hard times than those without.

Just a thought—and a hint.

# . 90 .

## THE AMAZEMENT OF GRACE

I have always disliked the term "spirituality." Somehow it smacks of a vague, vaporous cosmic consciousness of *something* out there—a distant awareness of a deity, I guess—without having to pin one's self down to something as concrete as worship or doctrine or even a statement of beliefs. If you describe yourself as "spiritual" and nothing else, it relieves you of any duty or obligation to attend a house of worship, subscribe to a set of rules, or otherwise curtail any hedonistic behavior on your part.

So here's where I state that I'm Christian. Here's where I also state that (within limits) I'm pretty tolerant about other people's religious beliefs. I draw the absolute line at expressing violence in the name of religion (which strikes me as the ultimate violation of the Third Commandment), but otherwise I like to think I'm open-minded . . . as long as you *practice your faith.*

Those who skate through life calling themselves "spiritual" without ever demonstrating it through regular attendance at a place of worship, or without pinning down any reasons why they should constrain their behavior into moral channels, are copping out. *And missing out.* Doctrines and beliefs contribute mightily to a simpler life.

There are few things available to humans that offer more comfort and joy than a strong, active, and practicing faith in God. It is staggering what the human spirit can endure when faith is strong.

Your beliefs are your own affair, a spiritual journey strictly between you and God. My approval or disapproval won't make a whit of difference to the Almighty. But at least practice your faith. Don't be "spiritual"—be *religious.*

# .91.

## GO TO CHURCH

Organized worship soothes the soul, and there is nothing more simplifying in life than to be able to hand over your troubles to a Higher Authority.

I'm not here to preach or convert. I'm here to tell you that belief in a Deity—and organized worship of that Deity—simplifies one's life in ways that don't seem possible until you've experienced it. Organized worship calms and soothes and uplifts. The beauty of ritual, the empowerment of hymns and songs, the wisdom of a sermon all help heal and fortify you. It gives you ammunition to handle life's difficulties.

Some people resist taking this step because they don't like the restrictions or commitments that churches require. Shop around. Doubtless you'll find something that suits your temperament, beliefs, abilities, and whatever spiritual criteria you may have.

Others protest against this advice because they don't feel that "organized" worship has anything to offer. They'd rather go off on a rock by the beach and commune with nature. Trouble is, communing is a solitary activity, whereas attending church with your family brings you closer to the ones you love. It also puts you in touch with a community of people with shared morals and philosophical beliefs. In times of trouble (and we all have them), their support can make all the difference.

Besides, as I mentioned earlier, being able to dump your troubles in the lap of God can do wonders. Give it a try sometime.

# . 92 .

## COUNT YOUR BLESSINGS

If we counted our blessings as often as we counted our problems, we would be overwhelmed with gratitude. Read that line again, because it's important.

Sometimes it seems that all we do is complain. Our jobs, our spouse, our kids, our finances, our politicians (OK, I'll grant this is often justified). The economy, the weather, the traffic, the credit card bills, the car payments, the run in your hose, the ding in your car, the malfunctioning CD player, the guy who took your parking space . . .

*Stop!* Take a deep breath and *count your blessings* for once.

Your job. Your spouse. Your kids. Your money. The fact that you live in a free (mostly) country. The beautiful weather. Your health. The clean water coming from your kitchen sink. The plentiful food. A warm house in the winter. Transportation to your job (be it a bus, a bicycle, or a car). Your childrens' ability able to read and write. The fact that you have money to pay most of your bills and sometimes even go out to dinner. The fact that you are surrounded by people who love you (how cool is *that?*). The fact that you have healthcare when you need it and police protection when you require it.

You see where I'm going with this? When we complain, we forget about our blessings. I'm sure that anyone who has ever traveled to Bangladesh or the Sudan or any other troubled country will come home overwhelmed by their blessings.

I know we're facing trying times right now. For many of us, these are the worst times we've ever known. But no matter how bad things are, we still have the ability to make a difference, and we have a God who loves us.

While we have breath, we have blessings.

# . 93 .

## DON'T BLAME GOD

Bad things happen. Life is uncertain. Tragedies occur. We might be downsized out of our job. We may experience a devastating illness. A child may be born handicapped. We might lose our spouse in a car accident. We might lose our home in a natural disaster. And then we blame God for allowing this to happen. How could He *do* this to us, when we've been nothing but faithful to Him all our life?

But sometimes spiritual enlightenment can happen in the oddest places. For my husband, it came when he was at a neighbor's house, watching a pretty mediocre western movie . . . except for one gem.

The movie was about some pioneers. A man's wife had died, leaving him with a small daughter. And a woman, pregnant with her first child, lost her husband on the trail. The woman looked at the wreckage of all her hopes and dreams and blamed God for her troubles. The man took her aside and said, "I know you're mad at God. But God is not responsible for your problems." He added, "When I go for a walk with my daughter and she trips and falls, *she knows that I didn't cause her to stumble.* But she also knows that I will be there to lift her up, to minister to her hurts, to support her on our journey, and if necessary to carry her home."

I do not believe God *causes* our misfortune. But—what a wondrous concept—God is here to pick us up, minister to our hurts, support us on our journey, and when the time comes, to carry us home.

# . 94 .

## PREACH THE GOSPEL
## AT ALL TIMES

And when necessary, use words. Thus said St. Francis of Assisi somewhere around the year 1200.

I've always liked this quote because it strikes me as sensible. People are seldom converted to your viewpoint, opinion, or religion when you bang them over the head with words (sometimes literally—the term "Bible thumpers" comes to mind). Rather, the Gospel can best be spread by actions, acts of charity, decency, gentle words, and the example of a life lived by walking with God.

In some ways this is similar to one of Cicero's Six Mistakes of Man (#305), attempting to compel other persons to believe and live as we do. Even in matters as important as the Gospel, *words* do not have as much impact as *example*.

Think back to those people who have had the most profound influence on your life. Why did they have that impact? It's because of their *example*.

Who do you admire? Your parents? A sports figure? A politician? A scientist? The elderly lady down the street? Doubtless you admire them for what they have done. Perhaps they took the time to raise you right. Perhaps they helped win the Superbowl. Perhaps they instigated a national policy you admire. Perhaps they invented a cure for something. Perhaps they always have a kind word to say.

Whatever it was, I'm quite certain that what they did *not* do was back you into a corner and talk at you until you came around to their opinion. No one likes to be pushed. Something to think about.

# . 95 .

## IN MEMORIAM

How do you want to be remembered when you die?

Sorry to throw this question at you when you're likely in the prime of your life, but it's important . . . because you never know when your time will come.

We like to think we're going to be around forever, and so we don't have to worry about how we'll be remembered. Like Scarlett O'Hara, we'll think about that tomorrow. There's plenty of time to improve our attitude and behavior. Trouble is, of course, you never know when "tomorrow" will hit.

A dear friend lost her husband of nineteen years. Martin was forty-five years old, active, and in perfect health. Then he was diagnosed with a malignant brain tumor, suffered for a year, and died. He left behind a loving wife and two small kids.

But here's the thing: As tragic as Martin's death is, he is remembered with great love and fondness by everyone. He isn't remembered for the fancy house or cars or extreme toys he owned. No, he's remembered as a man who loved God and put his family first. Not a bad epitaph.

What would *your* epitaph be? "He was remembered for having three vacation homes and a boat, and was always too busy to play ball with his kids." "She was remembered for her corporate ladder-climbing and executive skills, and how she managed to give her children an entire hour of attention each night."

When it comes *your* time to join the majority, how will you be remembered?

The fortunate thing is it's never too late to change. Think about how you want your epitaph to read—and then live up to those ideals.

# . 96 .

## GROW OLD GRACEFULLY

We all know the charming older gentleman or gentlewoman with the white hair, the bright smile, and the gnarled hands with a grip so strong it crackles your bones. We also know the older man or woman with the tightly-drawn skin, a quarter-inch thick layer of makeup, and either a Speedo swimsuit (for men) or a miniskirt (for women).

When you're seventy years old, which category do *you* want to be in? What happened to the old maxim of growing old gracefully? Doesn't anyone recognize how just plain *silly* you look, trying to act like a teenager when you're fifty years old? We all age, and to do so with poise has become something of a lost art in this "Me Generation."

I have no particular objection to covering up the gray hairs for awhile, especially if you tend to gray prematurely, but please reconsider the plastic-surgery and miniskirt route. Give your children someone to admire and model when they're older—not someone trying so desperately to hang onto youth that you end up looking absurd.

So much of our ego is tied up with our appearance, especially for women. Women have been conditioned to think that if they're not attractive (read: young and sexy), then they aren't worth anything.

C'mon. This is the twenty-first century. Haven't we gotten over that yet? Quit searching for the Fountain of Youth. The myth died, or should have, with Ponce de Leon.

Grow old gracefully. Life is simpler when you accept what you cannot change and learn to appreciate the wisdom and wrinkles that come with experience.

# . 97 .

## THE SERENITY PRAYER

I remember the first time I saw the Serenity Prayer. I was in middle school, and the school nurse had a poster in the Health Office with those words. At first, seriously, I thought it was a joke. Honestly, I did. When you think about it, the prayer *does* sound rather flippant: "God grant us the serenity to accept the things we cannot change, the courage to change the things we can, and the wisdom to know the difference."

Pretty funny, eh?

But the older I got (and to give you an idea of how "old" I am, I went to middle school at a time when it wasn't illegal to post the Serenity Prayer in a public school nurse's office), the more sense it made.

Life tends to throw stuff at us that is beyond our control. We can't do anything about illness or natural disasters. When a tragedy hits, our first impulse is to lash out and blame someone, including God. But it's useless to rail against the uncontrollable.

Rather, it behooves us to rise to the occasion and behave with dignity and poise. When my friend's husband died, leaving her widowed with two small children, she was able to accept the inevitable with grace and strength because of her faith, family, and friends.

This doesn't mean she wasn't angry, grieved, or hurt. Of course she was. But what could she do? Instead, her dignity in accepting what couldn't be changed made us admire her strength.

Accepting things that cannot be changed brings serenity . . . the essence of a simple life.

# . 98 .

## LIVING WITH SERENITY

The Serenity Prayer asks God to "grant us the *serenity* (nice concept) to accept the things we cannot change." What a great idea, to accept what "is" with serenity.

I have a friend who is wheelchair-bound. Her condition has not kept her from being happily married, raising a daughter and stepdaughter, being a successful author, and generally being loved by all who know her. Sure, she could be bitter about a situation she cannot change, but she's not.

Some things cannot be changed in life. Illness, injuries, deaths, tragedies, setbacks, natural disasters . . . the list goes on. What cannot be changed must be accepted.

"The courage to change the things we can . . . " Yes, it often takes courage to make changes. The courage to change yourself into a person your spouse *loves* to come home to. The courage to discipline your children so they learn to behave respectfully. The courage to stop an addiction. The courage to speak up when you see an injustice.

"And the wisdom to know the difference." Ah, the crux of the whole deal. What is the difference between what we *can't* change, and what we *can?*

What *can* we change? Our attitude. Our behavior. How industrious we are. How kind we are. How helpful we are. How emotionally strong we are. How giving we are. What we say. What we do. How we act. How we react.

It takes courage to change these things. It takes courage to let those mental defenses down and confess that you're vulnerable or scared or wrong or addicted.

But what comes from accepting the Serenity Prayer? Simply put, peace.

# . 99 .

## LISTEN TO THAT STILL, SMALL VOICE

If your gut is trying to tell you something, *listen.*

Many years ago, I had a large dog I would exercise by riding my bike with her. One warm summer afternoon, my dog and I were running when we passed a broad vacant lot, quiet and sunny and completely deserted.

Suddenly, I got the chills. I became horribly, irrationally afraid. I looked at the vacant lot and saw nothing, absolutely nothing, to cause concern. Still, I didn't waste any time. I wheeled the bike around and urged my dog to a run to get out of there. I stopped a few hundred yards away to let her catch her breath.

I have no idea what caused that fear. I saw no one. I didn't hear or smell anything. I even kept an eye on the news for the next few days and saw nothing related to that particular spot. The only thing I had to go on was instinct, pure gut. And my gut said *run.*

I've experienced this twice more in my life, both times with no cause that I could see. But both times I listened to that still small voice.

Why? Well, I figure that humans have cultivated an amazing ability to disregard warnings. We still have instincts that we are often too "civilized" to heed. But I figure instinct is there for a reason, and that reason might be very important.

Un-cultivate the ability to disregard an instinct. Listen to that still, small voice inside you. It may be saying something important.

# . 100 .

## EXAMINE YOUR LIFE

On Sunday, April 29, 2007, I found a lump in my left breast.

There are probably few things scarier for a woman. Instantly my mind spiraled off into a myriad of worst-case scenarios, each more dire than the last. Naturally I made a doctor's appointment as soon as possible, which meant I had three days to imagine the worst. During the wee hours of the night, staring at the dark ceiling, I couldn't help but wonder about the "what ifs."

My daughters at the time were 11 and 9. If the worst-case scenario came true, then my daughters would grow up without their mother. Who would teach them the things young women needed to know? Who would direct them when it came to discussing intimate matters and growing-up issues?

Thanks be to God, it was nothing serious and my fears were abated. But the experience made me examine my life.

Was I pleased with what I was doing? How I was behaving? What was (or wasn't) I accomplishing? What should I be doing differently? It was a chance to ask some hard questions of myself and make some changes.

I have two people close to me who have breast cancer. One caught it early, and her prognosis is good. The other caught it late, and after fighting for two years, she died.

Don't wait for a disease or tragedy to examine your life. Examine it now, and make the changes needed to make your life truly simple.

# . 101 .

## KILL THEM WITH KINDNESS

Sometimes, when you least expect it, you can find something hilariously funny in the Bible. Consider Proverbs 25:21: "If your enemy is hungry, give him food to eat; if he is thirsty, give him water to drink. In doing this, you will heap burning coals on his head."

Ooooh, ain't it great? Now you can *really* piss off your snarky mother-in-law by . . . being polite (see #45).

Seriously, nothing is more annoying to someone who doesn't like you than to be kind to them. Buy them lunch. Pour them a cup of coffee. Ignore their barbs. Smile sweetly. Ask how they're doing. Inquire about their hobbies. Help them move something heavy.

Crud, *now* what can they say to complain about you? That you were too . . . nice? See what I mean? Someone back in the times of Proverbs had a wicked sense of humor. I can't think of a more fun way to mess with someone's head.

# .102.

## THE HAPPIEST PEOPLE

The happiest people don't *have* the best of everything. They just *make* the best of everything.

The following story is entitled "God's Coffee." Unfortunately the author is anonymous, so forgive me for not giving credit where credit is due.

A group of alumni, highly established in their careers, got together to visit their old university professor. Conversation soon turned into complaints about stress in work and life.

The professor went to the kitchen and returned with a large pot of coffee and an assortment of cups—porcelain, plastic, glass, crystal, some plain, some expensive, some exquisite, and told them to help themselves.

When all the students had a cup of coffee in hand, the professor said: "If you noticed, all the nice looking expensive cups were taken up, leaving behind the plain and cheap ones.

"While it is normal for you to want only the best for yourselves, that is the source of your problems and stress. The cup adds no quality to the coffee. What all of you really wanted was coffee, not the cup, but you consciously went for the best cups.... And then you began eyeing each other's cups.

"Now consider this: Life is the coffee; the jobs, money, and position in society are the cups. They are just tools to hold and contain Life, and the type of cup we have does not define or change the quality of Life we live. Sometimes, by concentrating on the cup, we fail to enjoy the coffee."

Amen.

# . 103 .

## "A" IS FOR ANGEL . . . RIGHT?

A friend sent me this quote. I have no idea who wrote it, but it struck me as profound. Ready? "If anyone speaks badly of you, live so that none will believe it."

Remember Hester Prynne in *The Scarlet Letter*? Condemned by the Puritans to live with a scarlet "A" on her bodice (for adultery), she lived such a virtuous life afterward that people forgot what the A stood for and started thinking it stood for "Angel."

There will always be malicious gossip in this world. Often it is painful, damaging, and destructive. And, all of us being fallible humans, sometimes it's even true.

We've all done things we're ashamed of. There is not one person on this planet who doesn't wish they could go back and undo something from our past. But if you live your *present* with dignity, humor, helpfulness, kindness, and other admirable qualities, how long can the nasty gossip continue?

We even hear stories about people in jail who turn their lives around and do things that are truly useful and helpful to others. People may speak badly of what is in the past, but they'll speak admirably of what's in the present.

If you start living your life in such a manner that the gossip doesn't stand up, then you, too, will be called Angel, regardless of what you may have done that warranted the gossip to begin with. And it will come to the point where the gossip backfires on the gossiper (which might teach them a lesson).

# .104.

## FORGIVE YOURSELF

There isn't one single person on this earth who hasn't done something they regret. We're only human, after all.

There comes a point, though, where wallowing in regret begins to interfere with one's life. It's at this point—when you've made whatever amends it is possible to make—that you need to ask God for forgiveness, and then forgive *yourself*.

A few years ago, I met a woman I'll call Jane. When she was younger, she had an abortion. Afterward, she was horrified by what she'd done. She spent years in remorse, unable to get over it. Friends, psychologists, and ministers tried to help her forgive herself, but she just couldn't do it.

On the advice of a minister, she held a funeral service for the baby she killed. Her remorse eased a bit, but not entirely. She was still consumed with guilt and shame.

"The trouble with you," a friend wisely told her, "is that you feel like you need a receipt from God before you can forgive yourself."

Jane realized her friend was correct. She was waiting for some divine, celestial ticker-tape receipt. Jane realized that simply by asking, she had received God's forgiveness. There was no receipt needed. Her mood lifted, and she's been able to cope since then.

I certainly hope you'll never find yourself on the horns of such intense (but understandable) guilt, but recognize that at some point you must forgive yourself. Only then can your life simplify.

## RE-READ THE TEN COMMANDMENTS

Never in the history of civilization has a more succinct, prescient, and accurate summary of the pitfalls of human nature been documented than in the Ten Commandments.

Think you don't need to bother with them? Why not? Why should the Ten Commandments apply throughout history to (theoretically) every king, every emperor, every president, every citizen, every peasant, every slave . . . but not to you?

I'm not saying the Ten Commandments are easy to follow, nor am I saying that we all succeed even when we do try to follow them. But for heaven's sake, at least we could try.

One thing's for certain: if you were to live your life doing your best to follow them, you'd find yourself living a much simpler, happier life.

# . 106 .

## KNOW WHAT YOUR HILL IS

There's an old expression that asks, "Is this the hill you want to die on?" What this means is that there are some things in life that are worth fighting and even dying for. The important thing is being able to distinguish what those things are. It is helpful to know in advance what your "hill" is.

My husband's hill is his family. There is nothing more likely to fire up his protective instincts than something that threatens us. My hill is my kids.

Too many "hills" leads to unnecessary stress, angst, and ulcers. Nobody should have more than one hill. It could be a darn big hill with a lot of stuff on it, but your "hill" should not be the guy who cuts you off in traffic, or the person with one too many items in the "ten items or less" checkout, or the fact that someone keeps forgetting to fill the ice cube trays.

If you have a mountain range of "hills" in front of you, you can't keep track of the hill that's important. If you've built a mountain range where all the peaks are the same height, then you stand in a valley where the peaks look all the same. You get so tired of climbing every single hill that by the time you get to the hill you want to die on, you're too tired to climb it. You get "peak fatigue."

This metaphor can only go so far before it starts to sound silly, but the purpose of this exercise is to recognize what's truly, truly important in your life. Know your hill.

# . 107 .

## LIVE LIFE

I once read a Maxine cartoon and found the following advice to be fabulous:

"Life should NOT be a journey to the grave with the intention of arriving safely in an attractive and well preserved body, but rather to skid in sideways, chocolate in one hand, wine in the other, body thoroughly used up, totally worn out and screaming 'WOO-HOO, what a ride!'"

I just have this vision of St. Peter at the Pearly Gates grinning over this one. I don't know how this might simplify your life, but hopefully it made you smile.

# . 108 .

## DON'T DEFINE GOD IN YOUR OWN IMAGE

Don Lewis said, "We stand in the galaxy-sized footprint of God. And we argue his existence because we can't find the marks of the crutches we've assigned him."

The human ego never ceases to amaze me, and never more so than when we try to define God within our own human limitations and parameters. The most obvious example of this is when we sneak around doing something naughty. Our spouse may not know if we're secretly having an affair . . . but someone Else does. Think you can put one over on God? Think again.

You can justify bad choices all you want, but God sees inside your heart and soul. He knows, in the words of the liturgy, your thoughts, words, and deeds, the things done and left undone.

The idea of an omniscient Deity peeking over our shoulder, watching (and judging) our every move is actually rather liberating. It makes it easy to make the right choices. Hmmm, do I yell at my husband for squeezing the toothpaste from the middle of the tube, or do I say nothing while I roll the tube up from the bottom? Which would be the more intelligent choice for family harmony? Which would God prefer?

Accepting the fact that God is not restricted to human emotions, human abilities, and human limitations really is a pretty spiffy and simplifying concept. Personally, I like knowing that I don't have to go it alone in this world. There's someone out there going to bat for me. Ain't it grand?

# . 109 .

## STOP BEING OFFENDED
## BY GOODWILL

As I write this, Christmas is just over—Christmas with its joyous expressions and cheerful spirit and exultant attitude, a time when strangers are pleased to wish each other blessings for a happy season.

But of course, not everyone celebrates Christmas. Some celebrate Hanukah. Others celebrate Kwanzaa. Yet others celebrate the winter solstice. Still others celebrate nothing at all.

As a result of this melting pot of a nation, the season is rife with people willing to take offense when wished the wrong blessing. If I say, "Merry Christmas" to my Jewish friend, am I insulting her? Of course not; not any more than I would be insulted if she wished me a "Happy Hanukah."

Why is it that people are so eager to get bent out of shape by a simple and joyous blessing, even if it doesn't correspond with our personal beliefs? How on earth is anyone to know what anyone else believes or what might insult them? Do you really think that being told "Happy Hanukah" is meant to insult you because you're Christian?

Even the intentionally bland "happy holidays" or "season's greetings" should be accepted in good faith. Presumably the wishers aren't saying this to insult you—they (hopefully) are sincere in their expression of happiness or greeting.

Our lives are simpler when we're not so quick to take offense and can accept offers of goodwill from others that may not be in accordance with our beliefs . . . because they're offered with just that: goodwill.

Instead, smile back and say, "Thanks . . . and God bless."

# .110.

## MAKE SURE YOUR ACTIONS ARE IN LINE WITH YOUR BELIEFS

It's too easy to get caught up in socially acceptable expressions of success. The right job, the right career, the right kind of house, the right neighborhood . . . these are things that should fill us with pride and happiness.

But sometimes people are miserable because, deep down, they know their actions are not in line with their beliefs.

If you feel horrific guilt every time your drop your baby off at daycare, it could be because deep down you know you should be staying home with him.

If you dread the workday because your job goes against your political or moral beliefs, then maybe you should change jobs.

If you stand silent while someone in your office makes disparaging remarks against an individual or a group of people, you should feel ashamed at your silence.

If you feel pressured to do something at odds with what you know to be right, then you feel uncomfortable.

When I was in college, I remember being asked to sign a petition for something. Quite honestly, I don't even remember what the issue was—all I remember was that I felt pressured to sign it even though I didn't believe in what the petition was addressing. It's been over twenty-five years and I *still* remember the sense of shame that came from signing that petition, even though I don't remember what it was about. Weird, eh?

So if what you do is making you uncomfortable, it's time to realize why . . . and then do something about it.

# .111.

## THANK GOD

You will simplify your life by recognizing that there is a Higher Being. Personally I don't go for all the vague "spirituality" stuff that seems to abound these days. God is God, period. Not "the universe" or "your inner self" or whatever.

Even our national holiday, Thanksgiving, is being made over to exclude the importance of the Deity. We are now supposed to be "thankful" without specifying exactly to whom our thanks are directed. The turkey? The dressing? The universe? Who knows?

So don't forget to thank God for your blessings, even if you're not sure just who God is. After all, it can't hurt and it might help.

# . 112 .

## IF YOU HEAR A CALL, LISTEN

It's become something of a cliché, but clergy often describe the sense of "Calling" that accompanies their chosen profession.

Our pastor knew he wanted to be a minister as far back as high school. He ignored the Call, and instead went to college, became an engineer, and worked in the professional world. He married and had two kids. But all that time, the Call kept nagging at him.

He finally heeded it when he was in his thirties. It was not a light decision to give up a well-paying job and move his family all the way across the country in order to attend seminary. He says it would have saved a lot of grief if he had only heeded the Call when he first got it. However, he has never regretted his decision.

It's not as profound, but I've been Called to live a rural lifestyle. Sometimes it's hard, but I've never regretted our decision to raise our kids in the country.

What's your Call? What longing have you been ignoring? Deep down inside you, what is it you want to do?

It's not easy to hear your Calling when it's cluttered up by the daily pressures to earn a living and raise your children. Sometimes the Call is not shared by your spouse, in which case you need to do what you can to listen to the Call within the context of your marital vows.

Heeding your Call can feed your soul and greatly simplify your life. Pay attention.

# .113.

## READ ECCLESIASTES

Every so often a Bible verse will smack me upside the head anew with its powerful summation of the human condition. This is what happened recently with the third chapter of Ecclesiastes.

Most people are familiar with this chapter because of The Byrds' popular song from 1965, "Turn! Turn! Turn!" (To everything, turn, turn, turn / There is a season, turn, turn, turn / And a time for every purpose under heaven . . . ).

Well, it's true. There *is* a time for everything.

For example, I take a ninety-eight-year-old woman to church every week. It's not a big deal—she's only a few blocks away from the church, and she's an absolute delight to be around. But she always apologizes for the amount of "trouble" she is. For heaven's sake, the woman is almost a century old, and she still lives independently! "Lillian," I tell her, "this is just your time to accept a little help. Don't worry about it. I hope when I'm your age there's someone around to take *me* to church."

It's Lillian's season to accept rides to church. You might say this is *my* season to take Lillian to church.

What's your season? It is your season to get married? To have babies? To work two jobs so your wife can stay home? Is it your season to mourn the loss of someone? Is it your season to fight a war? To recover from battle? To build up? To tear down?

Accepting and not fighting your "season" can greatly simplify your life. Remember, He has made everything beautiful in its time.

# .114.

## THE DREAM

My youngest daughter woke up crying after a bad dream early one morning. We snuggled on the couch in front of the wood stove, and she told me about it.

She dreamt that the world was coming to an end. Apparently God was angry because everyone was fighting. She glimpsed a scroll that predicted the future. Pretty heavy stuff for a then nine-year-old!

Trying to comfort her, I knew I couldn't tell her that the end of the world *wasn't* coming, since none of us know what tomorrow will bring. However, I said that the only thing we can do is live our life with no regrets.

It was the "no regrets" part that I took pains to explain. I said that if Daddy and I made our living by robbing banks, is that something we would be proud to explain to God? We giggled for a few minutes and made up worse and worse "jobs" until her fears abated.

We also discussed Lillian, an extremely elderly lady in our church. "She could die tomorrow," I said. "And we would all be sad, but do you think she has many regrets?"

"No," said my daughter. "She's a nice lady."

"You're right. And now she's looking forward to meeting God after a long and happy life."

I wouldn't be surprised if my daughter has forgotten all about that dream by now, but I haven't. It made me realize that I have a lot of "regrets" for which I can only hope God understands and forgives me.

How much simpler would our lives be if we lessened our regrets?

# .115.

## YOU REAP WHAT YOU SOW

This is similar to "The Choices We Make" (#2). Yet people always seem surprised when there are consequences to their actions.

I know a family who lives far, far beyond their means. They are in debt past their eyeballs. Everything—including their clothing and furniture—has a lien on it. Yet they act as if nothing is wrong. They continue to spend and spend and spend (on credit, of course). When I mention that perhaps they should scale back, they shrug and say they'll be okay.

They *won't* be okay. They are very close to losing their home. And—here's the thing—they will be totally shocked when it happens. They will think it *unfair*.

This is not a tragedy. Their financial situation was not caused by medical hardships or something similarly out of their control. No, it was caused by their poor choices. They will shortly reap what they sow.

What are *you* sowing? Are you sowing undisciplined children who will grow up to cause you pain and sorrow? Are you sowing a poor relationship with your spouse, who will then divorce you and bereft your children? Are you sowing destructive gossip? Are you sowing a bad attitude?

Or are you sowing happiness, joy, and understanding? Are you sowing children who are raised with love and discipline? Are you sowing a contented spouse who will work hard to keep the family intact? Are you sowing kind words? Are you sowing forbearance and patience?

Simplicity is understanding that we are *all* a product of our choices. We reap what we sow.

# .116.

## THE DEVIL'S BEATITUDES

I wish I could give credit to whoever wrote this because it's brilliant.

- *Blessed are those who are too tired, too busy, too distracted to spend an hour once a week with their fellow Believers—they are my best workers.*
- *Blessed are those Believers who wait to be asked and expect to be thanked—I can use them.*
- *Blessed are the touchy who stop going to church—they are my missionaries.*
- *Blessed are the troublemakers—they shall be called my children.*
- *Blessed are the complainers—I'm all ears to them.*
- *Blessed are those who are bored with the minister's mannerisms and mistakes—for they get nothing out of his sermons.*
- *Blessed is the congregation member who expects to be invited to his own congregation—for he is a part of the problem instead of the solution.*
- *Blessed are those who gossip—for they shall cause strife and divisions that please me.*
- *Blessed are those who are easily offended—for they will soon get angry and quit.*
- *Blessed are those who do not give their offering to carry on God's work—for they are my helpers.*
- *Blessed is he who professes to love God but hates his brother and sister—for he shall be with me forever.*
- *Blessed are you who, when you read this, think it is about other people and not yourself—I've got you, too!*

# . 117 .

## ADJUST YOUR EXPECTATIONS

Sometimes it takes a simple readjustment in our way of thinking before we recognize the incredible blessings we have in our lives.

Sitting in church one Sunday morning, our pastor said this in his sermon: "I'm sure there are people here this morning who feel that life has somehow cheated them, but I can guarantee you, if you lost *everything* you have *right now*, and then suddenly had it all restored, you would be one grateful person. The problem is *not* what we have, but our *expectations*."

My husband and I sat there momentarily paralyzed as we heard those words. What if we lost our health, our home, our way of life, our neighbors, our job, our voice, our children, our spouse, our food, our water . . . and then had it suddenly restored again?

Would we ever grumble about our spouse again? Would we ever complain because our home was too small or shabby? Would we ever gripe about our kids' eternal soccer games? Our parents' tendency to call too often? Our neighbors' bright pink house? The traffic jam? The interruption in your Internet service? The little old lady who drives too slow? The bad haircut?

See my point? All our petty annoyances are so *petty* in light of what it would be like to lose *everything*.

Gratitude is an important part of simplifying. Cultivate it *now* before you lose anything more.

# .118.

## CULTIVATE A HAPPY MEDIUM

Simplicity means maximum satisfaction for what you have. It is not *perfect* satisfaction because perfect isn't possible. Rather, go for maximum satisfaction.

Food is nice, but too much food makes you sick or obese, and too little means you starve.

Money is nice, but too little money means eternal deprivation and too much money can lead to debauchery.

Free time is nice, but too little free time means stress and too much free time leads to boredom.

Each of these items (and many others besides) can have an effect on your level of happiness. But don't get caught up in making the mistake that any *one thing* is all that's necessary to reach your "happiest" state.

An incredibly wealthy person isn't any more likely to be truly happy than the janitor who lives paycheck to paycheck. It's who we are and what we do with the things we have that give us our position on the happiness scale.

Are my husband and I any "happier" than Bill Gates with all his wealth? I don't know. He seems like he's pretty happy—he's got a nice wife and kids, from what I hear—but who's to say he's happier than we are, with our limited finances and our modest lifestyle? I like to think that those who are wealthy derive some satisfaction from their wealth, and strive to do good with it. I just don't know if Bill Gates leads what I would call a "simple" life.

I think the goal of simplicity is a happy medium, neither too much nor too little of something.

# .119.

## THE STARFISH

There's an old story about a father and his son walking along the beach when they come to a stretch where hundreds of starfish have been washed ashore.

Taking pity, the boy picks up a starfish and throws it back into the ocean so it will survive. The father tries to stop him. "There are too many," he says. "You can't possibly save them all."

"But I can save *some*," the boy answers, throwing another one into the sea.

Sometimes our efforts to improve things seem futile. There is so much evil in this world—so much injustice and unfairness, so much madness and mayhem, so many gangs, so many criminals, so many people in high authority who care only about themselves and not the people they purport to represent—can God really expect us to make a difference?

In a sermon one Sunday, our pastor said, "Our caring isn't enough to guarantee the safety of all the whales in the ocean, or the purity of all the water in the ground. Our caring isn't enough to change all the 'bad' into 'good.' But it's all we are asked to do. And it's enough."

Edward Everett Hale (1822–1909) said, "I am only one, but still I am one. I cannot do everything. But still I can do something. And because I cannot do everything, I will not refuse to do the something that I can do."

God doesn't expect the weight of the world's troubles to rest on *your* shoulders alone. All you can do is throw a starfish or two back into the ocean so they survive. It's all we are asked to do . . . and it's enough.

# .120.

## YOUR SPIRITUAL LIFE IN A DOWN ECONOMY

Some of the religious cynics will note that we only turn to God when we're experiencing troubles. A bad economy is no exception—I hear church attendance is up around the country. But really, is that such a bad thing?

One thing that a greater awareness and worship of God will do for you, besides comfort you in any affliction (ill health, job loss, foreclosure, bankruptcy, etc.) is also balance your sorrows with a great joy. With surrender comes peace, and worshipping God will grant enormous peace of mind and awareness that, despite our troubles, we have a great many more blessings than we're sometimes willing to admit.

Worship also gives you a church community to fall back on. Here is a group of people who believes and worships the same way you do and who are willing to extend the hand of assistance in times of trouble. Such a community also breeds generosity in you as well. You don't attend church to *get*; you attend church to *give*. Your willingness to help others in your faith community who are experiencing hardship or trouble will not go unnoticed should the day come when you yourself need help. See how it works?

I don't mean to reduce your spiritual journey to purely mercenary terms, to be thought of as just a means to an end. But I do know that faith takes *practice*, and only by worshipping on a regular basis and joining with others will that practice breed true faith. Joining those who believe as you do will help you find God's mercy and peace. And if your physical needs are met at the same time, well . . . so much the better.

# Home is Where the Heart is

O ur homes are the physical center of our lives.
If we strive to cultivate simplicity at home, the
peace that results will affect every other aspect of our
lives—our jobs, our relationships, our stress levels,
even our finances. Home is where we gather to celebrate the good, and gather our strength to weather
the bad. Make sure your home is a refuge for both
conditions.

# .121.

## A SIMPLE HOME

Our careers are merely the foundation for the castle we build, namely, our homes. I use the term "castle" loosely. Obviously our "castle" doesn't have to mean a 6,000-square-foot palace that costs $3,500 a month in mortgage payments. That's rarely a home, that's a house.

Our home should be our sanctuary and our refuge against the world. It should be a place of peace and harmony. Yet so many of us have houses, not homes. We are oozing with fancy expensive things at too high a cost, both physical and emotional. We stuff our houses with more and more things, thinking that will bring joy. The result, of course, is a living space that squeezes the "living" right out of it.

People say they admire the simplicity of Japanese or Shaker furnishings—the sparseness, the clean and efficient atmosphere. They appreciate the beauty of space and the quality of peace that surrounds a home that isn't cluttered.

Yet they turn around and keep stuffing their own corners with new things. This new Japanese-style armoire or Shaker-designed table is *just* what I need to give my home that elusive *je ne sais quoi* of simplicity. And these knickknacks! Perfect. And look, another piece to add to my collection. And so it goes.

Dump the clutter. Simplify your housework. Reduce your possessions to only the useful or the beautiful. Make your home lovely, peaceful, open, and welcoming. Because, after all, that's the whole *purpose* . . . isn't it?

# . 122 .

## SHED THE CLUTTER

Of all the people I've talked to, of all the possibilities that could exist, of all the suggestions and ideas and topics to address while writing this book, the one overwhelming agreement for helping to simplify your life was: "Get rid of the junk."

Reducing the clutter of our possessions has always been a topic of interest to me. When I was young and single, I rather prided myself on how few possessions I owned. I'd read books on voluntary simplicity and, philosophy aside, it seemed simpler not to own too much because I moved frequently.

After I got married, we were the typical startup couple with mismatched furniture and a hodge-podge of possessions from our college days. But we didn't have clutter, or so I thought.

Then as a joke for my husband (who tends to hang on to things more than I do), I purchased Don Aslett's books *Clutter's Last Stand* and *Not for Packrats Only* and my eyes were opened. Did I *really* have that much stuff cluttering us up? Old childhood papers that were no longer interesting, trinkets, hosiery with runs, socks with too many holes, wind chimes that were missing pieces, class notes from college courses taken ten years ago . . . oh man, the list went on and on. What happened to my good intentions of staying streamlined in life? I looked around at our home with new eyes, set my teeth, and got to work.

Look around you with new eyes. Dump the junk and see how much simpler your home becomes.

# .123.

## DON'T BURDEN YOUR CHILDREN

I have a friend whose parents were wealthy. When they died, Jane inherited a large amount of ornate antique furniture. It looked terrific in her parent's mansion, but it overwhelmed Jane and Jim's modest home. In addition to the furniture, Jane now had her mother's full selection of fine china (three sets), crystal, silver, gourmet kitchen implements, and other items.

Jane and Jim were unable to have children, so two years after Jane's parents died, they adopted a baby girl. Then they had to leave their little home and move temporarily to an apartment in another city in order for Jim to take a short-term job. They took only the bare necessities to the apartment, since they had plans to return to their house within a few months.

Jane and Jim felt vastly liberated in their little apartment. It was tempting to return to their cluttered house and sell off all the stuff they had inherited. Yet Jane expressed sadness that if they did, her new daughter would never know "grandmother's things."

I suggested that, since her daughter has never met Grandma, it might be better to show pictures and tell happy stores about her, rather than become weighed down with possessions that held cherished memories for Jane but not for her daughter.

Inherited possessions are some of the hardest to purge because of the memories, but you don't want to burden your children with unnecessary items. It doesn't contribute to a simple life for *them*.

# .124.

## CLUTTER ISN'T CUTE

There are few things that weigh us down as effectively as our possessions. They pack the corners of our hearts as well as the corners of our homes. They cause us to go into debt, to insure them, to care for them, to take time away from our loved ones. All this . . . for *things?*

Learn not to look at your possessions with the blank eye of habit. Try to look at your stuff and think, "Do I use this on a daily/weekly/monthly basis?"

A few years ago, I found some free magazines at the library that highlighted "country"-style decorating. The contents were so humorous that I've kept those magazines as an example of extreme cluttering. "Since *country* equals *cluttered*," claimed one article, "and *cluttered* equals *cozy* . . . ." Cozy? What kind of logic was this? The article then went on to advocate filling your "country kitchen" with junk of every imaginable variety. The photo showed a kitchen so crammed with unnecessary stuff that the countertops were overflowing. Even the curtains were so ruffled and frilled that they nearly obscured the windows. How the heck were you supposed to *cook* in a kitchen like that?

Look at photos of minimalist décor or Japanese interior design or Shaker homes. Aren't they beautiful? Look around your home and think about what it would take to clear those surfaces and get rid of unnecessary collections.

Ridding your home of frou-frou junk is an amazingly simplifying and delightful task. Your home becomes streamlined, efficient, and a joy to live in.

# . 125 .

## READY, AIM, START

"De-cluttering" is not the same as "organizing." The object is to get rid of stuff, not make it neater.

Armed with your new knowledge, get rid of the excess clothing you'll never need. Chuck the knick-knacks that do nothing but gather dust. Give away anything that you're only keeping in case you need it "someday." Sell off any duplicates of items. Keep your home and car and office environment streamlined and efficient. And yes, you can have a "country"-decorated house that isn't so full of knick-knacks that you knock things over when you walk.

About the easiest way to start is to go through your stuff, look at each item, and see what is actively used and what is not. Don't ever, ever hang into something because it might be useful "someday." Until that nebulous "someday" comes, you're stuck with shuffling the item around, dusting it, insuring it, etc. You get the picture.

What happens when you're too overwhelmed to start? Simple, start the same way you start a thousand-piece jigsaw puzzle—one piece at a time. Your house is nothing but a 2,500-square-foot, three-dimensional puzzle. Remember, one piece at a time. Much of decluttering comes down to the Nike slogan of "Just Do It."

"But," you might groan, "It will take me five years to sort through all this stuff!" So what? In five years, you'll have a de-cluttered home. Or, you could do nothing and have a junked up home for another five years. Your choice.

# . 126 .

## ONE BITE AT A TIME

Decluttering is like eating an elephant. How do you eat an elephant? One bite at a time. So pick a "bite" and get started. Let's say you pick the kitchen.

There are various techniques for decluttering something like the kitchen. If you can go through your cabinets and thin out what you know you never use, great. More power to you. But sometimes it's easier to remove the entire contents of a cabinet into a box (you might as well give the cabinet a good cleaning, too, since it's empty). Only take an item out of the box if you're going to use it. The rest stay in the box.

This works wonders. If you put the box someplace inconvenient, such as the washroom, then you have to go fetch the pots and pans or spices or pasta maker or yogurt incubator only as you need them. Anything left over in the box for a few weeks or months are likely things you don't use often enough to justify keeping. Transfer the unused stuff to the give-away box.

Or, try taking the entire contents of something and dumping it somewhere central. Only put back what you know you actively need or use. Donate the rest.

Get your kids involved. They'll probably have a blast making a mess (though it's less fun to get everything cleaned up).

This is not a one-day thing, but rather a procedure that must be done a little at a time. But getting started can give you a great feeling of accomplishment and is an essential step toward making a simpler home.

# . 127 .

## THE FOUR LAWS OF HOME SIMPLICITY

From his Website www.zenhabits.net, Leo Babauta gave me kind permission to share his ideas to simplify your home, which he distilled into four steps:

1. Collect everything in one place;
2. Choose the essential;
3. Eliminate the rest;
4. Organize the remaining stuff neatly and nicely.

It's hard to get much simpler than this.

# . 128 .

## CLEAN OFF THE SURFACES

There's something psychologically liberating about having the surfaces in your home or office clean. The drawers might be stuffed, the desk overflowing, the cabinets bursting, but as long as those surfaces are clean, life seems a lot easier. So it's routine in our house, when the girls are doing their chores, for me to remind them that any tidying activities must include cleaning off the surfaces.

Remember the "country" kitchen whose countertops were so overflowing with junk that cooking was impossible? The same goes for tabletops, cabinets, bookshelves, coffee tables, end tables, or any other horizontal surface. When a horizontal surface begins to develop layers, you know you're in trouble. When it's cluttered up with junk, *it has lost its purpose.*

Sometimes, when the housecleaning gets away from me, I'll go through and swipe every surface clean and dump everything on the kitchen table. The kitchen table is perfect for this because it *can't* remain cluttered for too long—we need it to eat dinner. Once everything is collected in one spot, I can work my way from one end of the kitchen table to the other, sorting and recycling and filing and doing whatever else needs to be done. I get the kids involved by telling them to take everything that is theirs and putting it away (*not* just pitching it in their bedroom!). My husband takes all the tools that managed to find their way into the house and returns them to the shop.

When the kitchen table is done, *voilà!* We have clean surfaces throughout the house.

# . 129 .

## REDUCE YOUR COLLECTIONS

Americans have a passion for collecting. Everything from glassware to antique doorknobs to plants to bugs to stamps to shells to figurines to pottery to baskets to tools to teapots . . . we collect and collect and collect.

Collections come and go. You might develop an interest in, say, music boxes (perhaps based on the fact that your grandmother gave you one). You begin scouring eBay. You collect twenty or thirty . . . then suddenly your attention is diverted by cowboy memorabilia. You begin to collect that, and meanwhile the music boxes gather dust and take up room.

While I wouldn't suggest you get rid of *all* your collections, I urge you to look closely at what you have and choose to keep only those collections that bring you active joy. Donate the rest.

In our home, we collect books. If there is a single "thing" in my home I prize above all else, it is our collection of books. We enjoy seeing shelves of books all over the place. We find them beautiful, useful, and interesting. To me, there is something so sterile and depressing about a home without books.

You may feel the same way about your Star Wars memorabilia. Or your CD collection. Or your Precious Moments glassware. Whatever it is, make sure you actively *enjoy* collecting, dusting, insuring, moving around, displaying, and living among your items. If not, reduce or eliminate.

Remember, the only things in your home should be what you find useful or beautiful. Get rid of the rest.

# . 130 .

## DON'T ABANDON ALL TECHNOLOGY

Some people insist that living simply isn't possible as long as we continue our fascination with technology. I disagree. Technology *can* simplify your life. My life is immeasurably easier because I have a washing machine, a laptop computer, a telephone, and a car (your choices may be different). Consider living without these items and see how "simple" it is.

Technology is not the enemy of a simpler life. It is our selective use of technology that determines whether it helps or hinders our goals.

I once read a suggestion in one of those simplicity books that we could simplify our lives by reducing the amount of laundry we create. A good start. This person supported her position by pointing out how our ancestors only did laundry once a week, and how therefore their lives were "simpler." These kinds of observations always send me into gales of laughter. Sure, our ancestors—our *women* ancestors—only did laundry once a week. That's a week of filthy farm clothes and snotty handkerchiefs washed by hand on washboards. It only took twelve or fourteen hours of backbreaking labor. How simple! Thanks, but I'll take a washing machine any day.

Technology can be good. Some Luddites (people who are opposed to modernization) feel that anything requiring a computer chip or an internal combustion engine should be dumped, but clearly this doesn't apply to most of us.

So keep what you use, and be thankful that you don't have to write letters with a quill pen, hitch up the horses whenever you need to go to town, or do laundry by hand.

# . 131 .

## BUT ABANDON THE TECHNOLOGY
## THAT CLUTTERS YOU UP

Now, of course, too many technological marvels take the "simple" out of simplifying. I see no advantage, for instance, for an electronic address book. For me, it's easier to take my address book and find the address I need. No need to fuss with an electronic gizmo, no worries about it malfunctioning, and no batteries needed.

If you couldn't live without your electronic address book, fine. I won't argue. But look around at your other technological marvels. Call waiting? Bookkeeping software? Automatic vacuums? Electronic tie racks? CD players that hold a hundred CDs? Portable GPS system? Flexible electronic keyboards? Twelve-language translators? Do these things *really* simplify your life . . . or are they just things to spend money on?

My mother grew up in a family of thirteen children. She spent much of her childhood washing dishes. Of all the household appliances in existence, the one my mother simply adores is the dishwasher. She says she would prefer to wash clothes by hand than wash dishes by hand (though if push came to shove, I doubt it!).

To me, a dishwasher is the last thing I would want cluttering up my kitchen, but then I didn't grow up with the quantity of dishes she had, either. I'm happy to wash dishes by hand.

If something truly simplifies your life, go for it. Then get rid of the rest. Be selective about the technology you allow into your house. When in doubt, apply the KISS Principle: Keep It Simple, Stupid. And remember, if you seldom or never use something, why have it at all?

# . 132 .

## PRETEND YOU'RE GOING TO MOVE

Ah, there's nothing like moving to decide what stays and what goes. Take a few hours to mentally sweep through your home with an eye toward what you would actually take with you if you moved. This might help you decide what to get rid of.

If there is no possible way for you to roughly inventory your home in that amount of time, you have too much stuff. Whatever you decide isn't worth moving, perhaps you might decide it isn't worth keeping either.

Think of all the stuff that's packed away in closets, basements, attics, and spare bedrooms. Boxes, chests, trunks, and bags. Stuffed shelves, stuffed corners, stuffed hutches, stuffed porches. Stuff stuff stuff.

You might try getting some boxes and packing away some stuff that you can move to the basement or attic for awhile. Let the boxes sit there for several months. If you can't remember what's in them, then take those boxes and move them again . . . to Goodwill.

A variation on this theme is to pack away an entire room, such as the kitchen (see #126, "One Bite At a Time"). Only remove an item from the box when you need to use it (then place it back in the kitchen). After a year, whatever is left over in the boxes are things you don't need. Get rid of them.

Author Maurice Sendak said, "There must be more to life than having everything." Don't be a slave to your possessions. Is that how you would like to be remembered—as someone who *had* the "right" stuff? Or as someone who was *made* of the right stuff?

# . 133 .

## ALLOW YOURSELF TO BE ANAL

Some simplicity advocates have suggested that you ease up on your housekeeping standards by leaving some tasks undone in an effort to free up more time. While this occasionally works— I can happily leave six loads of laundry unfolded for *days* at a time—sometimes the stress buildup isn't worth it.

I'm anal about the kitchen being clean before I go to bed. Sure, it might "simplify" my life if I didn't fuss over such a chore and simply went to bed. But knowing those darn dishes are sitting on the countertop and filling the sink keeps me awake. Rather than relaxing me, leaving the dishes undone causes me *more* stress. So even if it's late, I clean up the kitchen. Doing so gives me a feeling of accomplishment and peace of mind, which is not a bad reward for doing a few dishes.

Some household chores tend to multiply if they're not done promptly (like kitchen cleanup). If I vacuum the house, it doesn't take much longer if the gap between the last vacuuming was a week or a month. But if I don't tidy the kitchen twice a day, it's a disaster.

The ultimate purpose of this is to allow yourself to cut the stress as you simplify your life. If you have a cleaning "itch" that must be scratched, then by all means scratch it. Allow yourself a few quirks. Be anal about a few things if it ultimately gives you comfort. The trick, I believe, is not to be anal over *everything*.

# .134.

## SPAY YOUR PETS

Unless you are in the business of breeding, it is beyond me why anyone would allow their cat or dog to have a litter. There are hundreds of thousands of beautiful animals that are put down every year because people didn't get their animals spayed. I don't know about you, but I think that would be on my conscience.

Spay or neuter your pets. Keep your life simple. And theirs.

# . 135 .

## BLOOM WHERE YOU'RE PLANTED

I have a friend who experienced financial chaos for five years. Through a failed business, a series of job losses, and other mishaps, she and her husband and children moved six times in two years and finally filed for bankruptcy. The stress, as you can imagine, was incredible.

They landed smack in the middle of a large city, which was about the last place they wanted to be. They were unable to afford a home, so they rented. And there they stayed.

With no choice, my friend decided to bloom where she was planted. Sure, she could have griped and complained and moaned and made herself and her family miserable, but instead she decided to rise to the occasion and *bloom*.

A country girl at heart, she planted the small backyard with vegetables and flowers. They even got the city's permission to keep three chickens (hens) that supplied eggs and a huge dose of amusement. For three years, until they could afford to buy a home, she made a peaceful oasis for her family.

We can't all have what we want in life, right now, at this moment, under our present circumstances. We face job losses, home losses, loss of family members, and other hardships. We dream of a life in the country when we're stuck in the city. Or, we dream of life in the city when we're stuck on the farm. Whatever it is, we're never satisfied.

But things change. Set yourself some life goals (see #221) and make plans to achieve them. But meanwhile, make your home a home and bloom.

# . 136 .

## IT'S NOT WHERE YOU LIVE, IT'S HOW YOU ACT

This is related to "Bloom Where You're Planted" (#135) but it applies to not "waiting" for a change of scenery before changing your behavior. You're as likely to be miserable in a mansion or a farmhouse as you were in your suburban tract home . . . if you were miserable to begin with.

Some people are certain that once they achieve that Special Something (the nicer home, the fancier car, whatever), *then* and only then will they be happy. Meanwhile, they gripe and moan and complain and make everyone else around them miserable.

Well, knock it off. Be happy where you are. Believe me, you have a lot more blessings than you realize. Maybe it's time you made a list of them.

Remember my friend who bloomed where she was planted, even though she was renting a house in the midst of a huge city? Well, the good news is that she and her husband managed to purchase a home in a semi-rural location in a different state and are ecstatic. While I'm very happy for them, I should point out that my friend decided not to "wait" to be happy.

If you don't like where you are, then make goals to achieve what you want. But don't think that achieving the goal will make you "happy" if you are not a happy person already. Externals change. Internals don't, unless you work on them.

Change your behavior and attitude *now* and your life will be simpler. Even if you're stuck where you don't want to be.

# . 137 .

## KEEP YOUR HOME TIDY

Oh yeah, sure, right. Good one. With kids, two jobs, and no time . . . how on earth do you keep your home tidy? Most people live in a state of mild chaos that only increases the stress in an already stressful life.

For purposes of definition, let me state what I feel is "tidy." Tidy isn't perfect. No one should be forced to live in a perfect home. Kids and spouses make messes. A home should be comfortable and lived-in, not a museum replica. A home that is welcome, moderately picked-up, and comfortable for all inhabitants is "tidy."

A tidy home is accomplished in two steps. The first "step" (or epic journey, depending on your particular circumstance) is to do a massive purge. This may be done in small incremental steps, or in one humongous everyone-pitches-in weekend. The purge is to get rid of the clutter. You want to donate or recycle all the stuff that you've acquired over the years but don't use. Yes, it'll take awhile, but wow! What results!

The second part of a tidy house is daily maintenance. Daily. There's no getting around it. Bigger jobs, like vacuuming the whole house and cleaning the bathrooms, can be reserved for weekends if you wish. But it's the daily maintenance—the small incremental steps of undoing a mess—that will keep a house tidy. For me, this includes doing dishes, picking up randomly-scattered items, and making beds (your list may be different).

Keeping your home tidy—not perfect, but tidy—can make your home life simpler and easier.

# . 138 .

## THE BIG PURGE

If you open a stuffed closet and look at the compact contents, you are far more likely to simply close the door again rather than tackle cleaning it. Decluttering a closet (or drawer or cabinet or whatever) can be a massive job. So try this. *Completely empty* the closet into the center of the living room floor. Then only put back what you need.

This forces you to sort and toss. If you don't need six pairs of snow boots, why keep them all? Oh, so *that's* where little Sarah's winter coat disappeared to three years ago! Too bad it's much too small now. Skis? I'd forgotten I had them. Never did learn how to ski.

When the only things in the closet are what you use on a daily or weekly or seasonal basis, then remove the rest of the pile either to the garbage can or the Goodwill box. By having the pile somewhere central like the living room floor, this (assumedly) helps motivate you to get the job done as rapidly as possible because of the sheer inconvenience of stepping around the annoying piles.

When the job is done, I'll guarantee that you'll open the closet door occasionally just to bask in the delightful sight of a tidy, uncluttered closet.

Now repeat the same process for everything else. This may take weeks or even months to complete the entire house, but that's okay. At the end of that time you'll have a completely purged house. How cool is that?

# . 139 .

## LATHER, RINSE, REPEAT

These well-known shampoo directions can apply to your home as well.

Decluttering is not a one-time deal. Every six months or so, do it again. Stuff has a tendency to creep back in when we're not looking.

Even if you're vigilant on keeping your surfaces clean and your drawers organized, you might be surprised what you find when you do a "purge" every few months. Three pairs of hopelessly run stockings. A couple of pairs of socks with holes too big to patch. Eighteen romance novels you have no interest in reading again. Clothes or shoes the kids have outgrown. The wacky costume you assembled from Goodwill purchases but don't intend to reuse. The oversized decorative tin once filled with flavored popcorn you purchased from the Boy Scouts. The spices you bought for that gotta-try-it ethnic dinner that turned out to be iffy. The two pairs of sunglasses you accidentally sat on and keep thinking you'll try to fix. The blouse you purchased on impulse and ended up hating. The six magazines you read once and don't intend to read again. You get the idea.

The nice part about "shampooing" your house every few months is that it goes quickly. When your home is streamlined down to what you find either useful or beautiful, then things that are neither begin to stick out like a sore thumb.

So "lather" your stuff into one great big pile. "Rinse" out everything you don't need. And "repeat" every six months or so as needed.

# . 140 .

## TIDY AS YOU GO

Tidying is a constant thing. When you let things go, your house starts getting out of control. The secret is to tidy as you go. But don't worry; it's fairly painless.

Simply put, every time you walk from one part of the house to the other, *you should have something in your hands* (well, most of the time). Going to the bathroom? Scoop up the dirty socks to put in the hamper. Heading for the kids' bedroom? Grab the three stray hair bands and put them in the hair band jar. Reshelve a book or two. Put a stray dish in the sink. Hang a coat. Put a hairbrush in the bathroom. Put a toy in the toybox. Put some gloves in the appropriate cubbyhole. Put the salt-and-pepper shakers where they belong. Bring an item you've stacked downstairs, upstairs. Bring an item you've stacked upstairs, downstairs. Put a music book back in the piano bench. Bring the coffee cup by your computer back into the kitchen. Put the cereal box away. Tuck a random snow boot back under the foyer bench. Swipe the bathroom sink clean after you wash your hands.

Train your kids to do the same (good luck). Train your husband as well (fat chance).

This incremental tidy-as-you-go habit works wonders. In fact, I have found it to be a startlingly effective technique. Sure, there are still the big jobs (vacuuming, cleaning toilets) to keep a house clean, but tidying as you go keeps the daily mess from getting out of hand.

# . 141 .

## THE GIVE-AWAY BOX

We keep a "give-away" box in the washroom. Items that we no longer need are placed in the box for eventual donation to a thrift store. Once I put one of the kids' toys, clothes, or other items into the give-away box, it can only be removed by being redeemed.

Children are notorious for neglecting a possession until it is to be given or thrown away. Then suddenly it becomes precious beyond words. When you place an item in the give-away box, even if they haven't looked at it in years, there are likely to be howls of protest. But if they really want a toy back, all they need to do to redeem it from the give-away box is find five less important items to replace it with.

This works well for two reasons. One, if they *really* want something back, then they're motivated to find some less "precious" toys to replace it with (and you can bet they'll find those things immediately). And, since they placed the five toys in the box voluntarily, they're unlikely to protest that they also want those back. And two, more clutter is cleared from their rooms (on a five-to-one ratio, no less).

And if they *do* find those five other items to redeem the one, by all means let them redeem it. Chances are they'll actually use it again. For awhile, at least.

Be sure not to put things in the give-away box out of anger or punishment. If your children's room is too cluttered with toys, that's more likely *your* fault than theirs.

# . 142 .

## PICK YOUR HOUSEKEEPING BATTLES

Everyone has quirks when it comes to housework. In my case, I find nothing more depressing than a perpetually messy kitchen. Since we have no dishwasher, I try to do dishes twice a day to keep things under control. Somehow other messy spots—laundry, junk mail, coats, and boots—seem more tolerable if the dishes are done. That's just me. Pick your own battle.

What drives you nuts if it's messy? Is it the unfolded laundry? A dirty bathroom? An unvacuumed floor? The state of the kids' closet? The dusty surfaces? The cluttered desk? The toy-strewn living room? Whatever it is, pick that "battle" to keep abreast of, and don't obsess too much about the other stuff.

Once the main battle is done, your forces may be marshaled enough to fight a skirmish on the kid's closet, or attack the pile of laundry. Perhaps you need to lay siege to your chaotic pantry, or launch an assault on your under-the-bed clutter. What about riding a sortie on the washroom or making a strike on the basement? (I forgive you if you plan a strategic retreat from cleaning the toilets.)

Everyone is busy these days, so picking your housekeeping battle can simplify your home life because you don't focus on *everything*, just one (or two) things. Perhaps you can let the rest of it go until the weekend when everyone can pitch in. Then you, as the general, can rally your troops to launch a full frontal raid on the mess.

# . 143 .

## DID GRANDMA KNOW A THING OR TWO?

We have a tendency to dismiss Grandma's wisdom as not pertaining to our modern, hurried, busy life. After all, what does Grandma know about two-career families, long commutes, McMansions, and tons of after-school activities?

Well, Grandma may not have worked outside the home but that doesn't mean she didn't know a thing or two. Crack out your old copies of the Laura Ingalls Wilder books and look in Little House in the Big Woods, where she lists the work week as follows: "Wash on Monday, Iron on Tuesday, Mend on Wednesday, Churn on Thursday, Clean on Friday, Bake on Saturday, Rest on Sunday."

Anyone who has studied anything about pioneer times knows that often these chores took all day, and naturally they were piled on top of all the other daily farm chores required of women in those days.

Our ancestors utilized a work-week strategy to maximize their efficiency. Maybe we can do the same thing. Rather than farm chores, we have our office jobs, but the idea of a work week has some merit (modernized, of course).

Perhaps you can assign one "major" chore per day of the week and leave the rest until later. Laundry on Monday. Folding and putting clothes away on Tuesday. Vacuuming on Wednesday. Cleaning bathrooms on Thursday. Dust on Friday. General tidy-up on Saturday. Rest on Sunday.

This is similar to picking your housekeeping battles (#142) and may simplify the stress and frustration you feel when faced with a messy house day after day.

# . 144 .

## MY MOTHER'S COPING
## TECHNIQUE

When I was a child, my father often traveled extensively on business. My mother was required to handle the four of us kids on her own for weeks on end. Add to this a typical Buffalo winter with tons of snow, and you had the recipe for four confined squirrelly brats that could drive a mother nuts.

Doubtless we did, but Mom developed her techniques for coping. This included allowing us to leave our projects out. So when we built forts out of chairs and sheets, or twined plastic railroad tracks and block cities through the dining room chairs, or built zoos and towns with Legos and Lincoln Logs in the middle of the living room, she did not require us to put them away when we were done for the day. These types of games, she well knew, could often extend for days at a time, and so to prematurely clean everything up would interrupt the fantasies we built around our creations.

The result was that there would be a few days where we would have to carefully step over and around various structures. But that was okay. My mother's philosophy was that a house was for living, and what better expression of kid creativity than to have towns made of blocks?

Eventually, of course, the towns would be abandoned . . . and only then would she ask us to clean up.

Mom was forced to take a long view toward a tidy house. But you know what? It simplified matters for her.

# . 145 .

## A HOUSE IS FOR LIVING

I try to practice the "long view" toward scattered toys and projects with my own kids. Idaho winters can be long, and kids can get antsy being confined much of the day. We homeschool, so unless they're playing with friends, they're home more frequently. This past winter was especially harsh, too. We're two miles off-road (read: unplowed), so there have been times where we've been snowed in and unable to leave the property.

My children have every right to enjoy our home during these confined days by spreading out their toys. They like being able to plan elaborate towns or pirate islands or knights' castles without me yelling at them to clean up the mess. It makes their days better, and that makes my life simpler.

So sometimes my husband and I spend days on end stepping over toy cities or other imaginative structures which the kids will elaborate on until they finally lose interest. When I need to tidy, I tidy around the toys. Eventually they'll go onto something else, and that's when I ask them to put everything away.

I try to distinguish between just scattered random toys that aren't part of a project, and cohesive structures. Random toys get cleaned up at the end of the day, structures do not.

Remember that a home is for living. Enjoy your children's creations. (Hey, at least they're not plopped like zombies in front of the TV set!) Watch their imaginations soar. Learn what populates their minds. It's fun!

# . 146 .

## IT'S NOT DRUDGERY, IT'S PERFORMANCE ART

We all have household chores that some might call "drudgery." Dishes, laundry, vacuuming, dusting, cooking—they all need to be done. Often we think that anything required to keep a home clean, in other words, "women's work," is of so little value that women should be ashamed to perform such menial tasks.

Hogwash. Mundane chores can be a joyous thing when you look at the larger picture. I am not merely keeping my home tidy, I am conducting a piece of performance art dedicated to creating an atmosphere of love and welcoming and friendship.

There's an old story about three men moving stones. A traveler asks the first man, "What are you doing?" The first man snarls, "What does it look like I'm doing? I'm moving these stupid rocks around."

The traveler asks the second man what he is doing. The second man shrugs and replies, "What does it look like I'm doing? I'm building a wall."

The traveler asks the third man what he is doing. The third man gives him a beatific smiles, lifts up his eyes, and says, "What does it look like I'm doing? I'm building a cathedral."

We all have chores. Sometimes they're irksome, tiring, and boring. But if you look at your chores as building a cathedral instead of moving the stupid rocks around, your day will go by easier. Your life may be simpler.

Take pride while moving your stones. They have to be moved anyway, so you may as well build a cathedral with them.

# .147.

## A PROCESS, NOT AN END

A tidy house is a process, not an end. People live. Home is where they do it. You don't want to be a five-star general or a five-star nag (or both) and make your family miserable by demanding that they live up to *your* superior expectations of cleanliness. And don't make *yourself* crazy by demanding a Martha Stewart-perfect domain.

A house is not, nor should be, in "perfect" condition. You are not the curator of a museum; you are maintaining living quarters to a moderate standard of tidiness.

Housework is like performance art (#146). It's "building your cathedral," not moving the stupid rocks around. Heck, you might even get to enjoy it someday.

Because my family does so much of our living here in our home (what with homeschooling, working at home, and just living), we frequently have controlled chaos. Because our place is a fixer-upper, we are often in the midst of a project (you might say our "cathedral" is perpetually under construction).

So when sheet-rock dust is falling on a pirate's island, or the dogs have discovered that someone left a box of crackers on the floor by the pantry, or the cat decides he has to hack up a hairball on a pile of dirty laundry someone left in the closet, or the neighbor kids all come pouring in asking for hot chocolate after sledding, or the kitchen table is piled with math books, a half-finished science project, and six encyclopedias . . . we try to remember that all of these are blessings.

We're alive, safe, happy, secure, living simply, and in the loving hands of God. That's the kind of worship service we like to do here in our cathedral.

# . 148 .

## KIDS WILL BE KIDS

The things that are important to *you* may not be important to anyone else in your home. For example, I like our winter boots to be tucked under the entryway bench. My kids never remember. I must constantly remind them. But here's the thing: I *remind* them. I don't yell, I don't get frustrated, I simply ask them to tuck their boots under.

Sometimes when the kids are doing something else like studying or reading or playing with friends, I just bite the bullet and tuck the boots away myself. It's a matter of physics (the conservation of energy).

My home would be a lot more uncomfortable if I blew my top every time kids were kids. For the children, it's a lot simpler to kick off their boots when they come stomping in from outside, leaving their footwear scattered hither and yon. It's not that they're deliberately flaunting my expectations. It's that they're kids. They don't think about it.

So I remind them to tuck their boots. Day in. Day out. Week after week. Eventually, maybe, someday, they'll learn. But if they don't, I don't care. Tucked-under boots is *my* issue, not theirs. It's not life-and-death; it's just sloppy.

What's more important: a perfect home, or a happy home? Yelling over trivial issues doesn't make for happiness. So go easy on your children (or spouse) who aren't mind-readers or who don't consider *your* issues to be important to *them*. Just remind them to tuck their boots under.

# .149.

## MEN WILL BE MEN

One of the most frequent complaints women have about their men is that they don't do enough housework.

Okay, here's a surprise for women: it's because men don't think about it. They don't "see" what needs to be done. No matter what progress women have made in the last forty years, most men weren't raised to consider housework as "their" job. Deal with it.

That being said, there's no reason for a woman to do it all if both parties work outside the home (if you're a stay-at-home mom, I would expect you do more housework).

First, never *ever* discount the things your man *does* do. If he fixes the leaky faucet, caulks the windows, cleans the garage, takes out the garbage, or other "manly" tasks, then he is contributing to the household chores. He deserves thanks and recognition for that.

Most men are willing to help around the house because they want to please their wives. Therefore, don't make it hard for them to do this. Men are simple creatures, and respond best to strokes and praise.

Men are also problem-solvers, another thing women can use to their advantage. The issue isn't your husband, the issue is the household task that needs to be done. This is a wonderful thing to know, because now you can present the specific cleaning task to your husband as a problem to be solved. But remember, the whole thing falls apart if you nag or criticize. Just a warning.

# . 150 .

## HOW TO GET MEN TO
## DO HOUSEWORK

So how do you get a man to take on more responsibility for household chores? Well, if the boots in the wrong place or the soiled clothes on the floor or the dirty dishes bother you *right now*, do it yourself. But if you want long-term boot placement or clothing picked up, make it a "problem" that needs solving. Men are problem solvers. Go with their strengths.

Without yelling or nagging, present the issue as a problem. Not *his* problem, just "a" problem that needs solving. "I wish I could come up with a way to get the dishes done more frequently," you might say. "Any ideas on how best to do this?"

Being a man, of course he will! Or, if he doesn't right away, he will shortly . . . because solving problems is what men were created to do.

Perhaps he'll suggest alternate days for washing dishes. Or perhaps he'll suggest posting a schedule on the fridge. Whatever it is, once he suggests a solution, *praise him* for thinking of it (even if it's a solution you thought of years ago). Men respond well to positive reinforcement. As an added advantage, the man is now vested in proving that "his" idea couldn't possibly fail.

Sometimes men need a gentle reminder: "Hon, I think tonight's your night to do dishes." A quick glance at the schedule will show you're right. Remember to thank him afterward, because *a happy man is a willing man.*

This solution may not be perfect, but isn't it simpler than yelling and fighting?

# . 151 .

## YOUR HOME IN A
## DOWN ECONOMY

Homes, as with anything else, are to some extent a reflection of our ego. My kids always laugh (and grumble) at my insistence on cleaning the house before we have guests over. "They know we don't live this way," they complain. "So why do we have to dust, vacuum, mop, tidy, and clean toilets before they come?"

"You'll understand when you have your own home someday," I reply. "It's natural to want to put forth your best face when company is expected."

But extend that sentiment further and it can be easy to fall into the trap of using one's home to impress rather than live in and enjoy. The McMansions of the last twenty years, with the designer furnishings and landscaped-to-perfection yards, are an example of this.

When money is tight or finances are uncertain, it's time to stop thinking of your home as a vehicle to impress people and start looking to it as a physical refuge during hard times. Make your house a home. For some, this means downsizing (if it's possible during a bad housing market). For others, it means remodeling instead of upgrading to a larger home. For yet others, it means nixing the new furniture or other furnishings, dumping the clutter, and being happy with what you have.

As always, look for the simplest solution for your home, and make sure your living space reflects the calm, peaceful, simpler life toward which you are striding.

# To Your Health

▼

Few things complicate your life more than illness or poor health. That's the bad news. The good news is that, for most people, good (or at least improved) health is within our grasp. If there was ever a time to shed bad health habits and cultivate good, it's when we're facing an uncertain future.

# .152.

## SIMPLE HEALTH

Okay, this is it. Today's the day to begin a new health régime. This is the point where I put in a disclaimer like the following: *This book is not intended to replace medical advice or to be a substitute for a physician. Always seek the advice of a physician before beginning any diet or exercise program.*

Okay, that's done. I'm not a doctor so I won't pretend to be one. This section is not meant to be medical advice (consult a *real* doctor for that), but rather about the common sense things you can to do improve or maintain your health, both physical and mental. These are suggestions backed by what I believe to be sound medical evidence.

It doesn't take a doctor to tell you that you shouldn't drink too much or smoke at all or do drugs. It doesn't take a doctor to tell you that it's better to exercise than live a sedentary life. It doesn't take a doctor to repeat the news that fruits and veggies are good for you. And being overweight is not as healthy as being within a proper weight limit.

So what do you need to do to become healthier? And will you do it, or will you continue to come up with a creative batch of excuses not to? What'll it be?

A simple life is a healthy life. A healthy life is a simpler life. The two are entwined.

So have a nice salad for lunch. Go for a walk. Quit smoking. Treat your body like the temple it is, and don't put things in it that you wouldn't recommend to your children. You only have one body, and it has to serve you your whole life.

# . 153 .

## DO FOUR THINGS TO
## STAY HEALTHY

The entire health industry—all the books and organizations and doctor's advice and medicines and everything else out there—that attempt to keep us healthy can largely be reduced to four major things:

1. Don't smoke
2. Keep to a healthy weight
3. Eat five to six portions of fruits and vegetables daily
4. Exercise regularly

That's it. It's very simple. Doing these four magical things will reduce or solve the health problems of 90 percent of us. Studies have shown that people who do all these things live an average of *fourteen years longer* than people who adopt none of these behaviors. Yet surveys have shown that only 3 percent of us do all four.

It's annoying that there has to be such a massive industry dedicated to helping us stay healthy, especially since these four major things are *within our control.* But such is life. So simplify your health and do these four things.

# . 154 .

## WEAR YOUR SEATBELT

There are few things more life-complicating than a car accident that causes injuries. It's especially sad when injuries are due to a person not wearing a seatbelt. (Seatbelts reduce injuries by *sixty-five percent.*)

I read somewhere that the major excuse people give for not wearing their seatbelts is that they're too "confining." But I personally can't imagine that a seatbelt is more confining than a wheelchair.

# . 155 .

## LEARN WHAT HAUNTS YOU

My mother had a horrible childhood due to a brutal, drunken, abusive father, abusive mother, beatings, poverty, starvation . . . you name it. Until she was in her sixties, my mother bit her nails, a residue from all the childhood trauma. Her short nails were always a source of shame for her, but she was never able to break the habit until a few years ago.

But you know what? With the exception of those bitten-down nails, mom was able to overcome her past, marry a good man, and raise her children to be happy and secure.

Those of you who have had rotten childhoods will recognize what a supreme effort it took my mother to overcome her past. My mother knew what haunted her, and so she was able to choose *not* to let it influence (too much) the rest of her life.

We can't all be blessed with a secure and happy childhood. But recognizing what haunts you—and deciding you're going to overcome it—can be a major step in simplifying your life. If you are haunted by something from your upbringing, I suggest you read Dr. Laura Schlessinger's book *Bad Childhood, Good Life*. This book is superb for understanding why your adult behavior is frequently reflective of your childhood traumas.

My mother takes great pride in her lovely nails today. However, I take great pride in my mother. It's not everyday you meet someone who has risen above a bad past with such grace, and gotten on with life.

# .156.

## HOLD YOUR BABIES

It amazes me to see the sheer quantity of things out there dedicated to physically separating us from our babies. And it starts at birth. Don't carry your baby, tuck him in a stroller. Don't hold your baby, put him in a playpen. Don't entertain your baby, stick him in a wind-up swing. Don't breastfeed your baby, prop him up and give him a bottle. Don't sleep with your baby, use a crib in another part of the house.

Obviously this doesn't apply to parents who may have physical limitations. Not every mother can breastfeed. My friend who is confined to a wheelchair couldn't use a sling.

But we've been brainwashed to think that we shouldn't touch our babies too much for fear of "spoiling" them. We've swallowed the garbage that babies should learn to be "independent." Independent? *Babies?* They're not *supposed* to be independent. By definition they're *de*-pendent.

If we force a baby to go against his nature and become *independent*, by an ironic twist of fate we create a *dependent* older child—a child who is so desperate for a loving touch from his parents that he becomes clingy, whiny, and needy. Or, if the parent isn't around, children will find someone else to fulfill those needs.

What happened to carriers that allow the infant to be on your body, getting stimulation and close physical contact? What happened to sleeping with your baby? What happened to breastfeeding your baby?

Life is simpler with happy, secure children. Hold your babies and see how happy and secure they grow up.

# .157.

## OF BENEFIT TO BABIES

From the time my girls were born until they were toddlers, I wore them in a sling. I have never, ever come across a more useful device. I wore them so many hours a day that I bought a second, so I could have one handy while I washed the first. A third sling I kept tucked in the car. Slinging your baby allows you to keep an eye on them—heck, a whole *body* on them—while you go about your daily household activities. The kid is happy because he's always with mommy. You're happy because your hands are free.

The benefits of holding your baby while bottlefeeding or breastfeeding, and lots of other times besides, are indisputable. Yet so many parents prefer to raise "independent" babies, and then wonder why teenage rebellion hits like a sledgehammer.

Slings aren't just for women. My husband used one during those many nights when he paced the floor with our kids. Men might need a larger-sized sling to be comfortable, but think about how happy a baby is when tucked against daddy's chest, listening to his heartbeat.

I once heard something that struck me as profound: *needs that are not met as babies come back as adults.* If babies aren't held, stimulated, and nurtured—in other words, if they're forced to become "independent"—then as adults they may crave what they missed as infants and turn to destructive behaviors, such as indiscriminate sexual activity or drugs or alcohol.

So hold your babies. In the long run, it makes things simpler.

# .158.

## STOP USING EXCUSES

I know a woman whose babies were bottle babies, raised to be "independent," and mostly stayed in playpens. She got pregnant with her last child shortly after I got pregnant with my first.

Naturally, we compared baby notes. "You've *got* to try breast-feeding!" I enthused. "It's wonderful!" Impressed with my fervor, she decided to breastfeed her newest baby.

Well, it lasted two weeks, then she put the baby on a bottle. "Why on earth did you stop?" I asked, genuinely puzzled.

"Because it was too inconvenient," she replied.

*Inconvenient?* Next to the cost and hassle of formula and bottles?

"It wasn't just that," my friend continued. "But with breast-feeding, I couldn't prop the baby up and go do something else."

Ah. That's it, of course. The breastfeeding itself wasn't the issue. Not everyone can breastfeed. It was the fact that my friend actually had to *hold* her baby, interact with it while breastfeeding. That was "inconvenient." She far preferred to prop the infant up with a bottle and go away. This woman had created, with her husband's help, the greatest earthly gift that God can give to any human being, and she found it too trouble-some to bother with. How sad.

How many times do you consciously avoid interacting with your kids? Do you choose not to breastfeed, not to touch and cuddle, not to read to your kids? Do you prefer they occupy themselves with TV so you can have some time to yourself?

Kids need security. Provide that. Stop using excuses.

# . 159 .

## GET A CHECKUP

Routine physicals are not a doctor's way to get rich at your expense. Regular physicals are meant to catch medical problems in the early stages. Yet we come up with every excuse not to get checkups. I don't have time. I don't want to bother. I'm healthy enough. It's nothing serious. I can't afford it. I don't like doctors.

There are also some procedures that are uncomfortable or embarrassing so we avoid them. Naturally, these are critical for a clean bill of health. A Pap smear. A colonoscopy. A prostate exam. Believe me, if there's anything wrong with these organs, you *want to know*.

Modern medicine is one of the wonders of our time. We can cure diseases today that were regular killers a hundred years ago. Yet I've actually heard people claim, with a straight face, that doctors are out to "get" you, and that a minimum-wage clerk at a health food store knows more about curing your condition than someone who has spent years studying medicine. Go figure.

Just as you get your teeth checked out twice a year (you *do*, don't you?), then you should get a physical at whatever intervals your doctor suggests. It's a cheap price to pay for peace of mind.

It's a much simpler thing to catch that skin cancer early and have the spot removed. It's a lot less simple to die from something that could have been cured in half an hour. I should know. My husband is alive today because of a routine physical.

# .160.

## WHEN IN DOUBT, CHECK IT OUT

Most medical conditions are treated much more easily if caught early. It always baffles me why some people stick their heads in the sand when a scary medical issue arises. I think their logic is "What I don't know can't hurt me," but of course the opposite is true where medicine is concerned.

Take skin cancer. Detected early, it is nearly one hundred percent curable. Detected later, it can be fatal.

Going in for a routine physical one time, the doctor asked my husband to remove his shirt so he could examine some of the moles on his back. The doctor didn't like the look of one of the moles. He removed it and sent it in for a biopsy. It came back as a cancerous melanoma. Scared the bejeebers out of us.

What would have been a lot scarier is if the doctor *hadn't* caught that mole. My husband now goes in twice a year for what he calls his "strip and twirl."

A few years ago, I found a lump on my left breast. Any woman knows what this can do to your peace of mind. Fortunately, the extensive exams and mammogram found it to be a benign sebaceous cyst, and a hundred-pound weight was lifted from my shoulders.

Nothing can complicate the lives of you, your spouse, and your children more than a devastating illness. What's more devastating is when that illness could have been *prevented* by prompt medical attention. It's not hard to do. In fact, it's simple.

# . 161 .

## EASY ON THE ALTERNATIVES

I have a high regard for alternative medicines. Herbs, biofeedback, yoga—these all have sensible applications. But be reasonable about serious medical situations. I do not believe that chiropractic back adjustments can cure cancer or bring on world peace. If you have a serious issue, it behooves you to try all realistic treatments, including conventional.

I know some people who swear by alternative medicine to the exclusion of conventional. They will believe *anything* as long as it's alternative. Anecdotal evidence about a cure is proof enough. No scientific testing needed to support its claims. Yet only by applying such techniques as double-blind studies can the efficacy of a treatment be demonstrated.

Many people who turn to alternative medicine are disenchanted with conventional doctors. Perhaps they were either not helped or suffered side-effects from conventional treatments. Patients feel that alternative doctors listen more (they often do). Alternative doctors believe that the mind, body, and psyche all are factors in health (they often are). But there are quacks who feed on the hunger of the disenchanted by making medical claims that have no proof. Dress it up with fancy lingo, put together an infomercial or a book, charge a hefty price, and *voilà*: a new cure. Pretty neat, eh?

Choose alternative doctors who have a sound medical training. Treatments have either been proven to work, or they have not. Don't risk your life dipping into something unproven in the hopes that it will cure you.

Illness isn't simple. Don't complicate it further by trying something scientifically illogical.

# . 162 .

## QUIT OBSESSING OVER
## YOUR PERSONAL APPEARANCE

It is reasonable to want to put your best face forward to the world. But must you obsess about it? Narcissism is defined as "inordinate fascination with oneself." Does this describe you?

If you are overly concerned about your personal appearance, you have little energy left over for others. Everyone else has to dance around your obsession. You run late for appointments because your hair isn't perfect. You freak out when you chip a nail. Your bald spot is the center of the world. The gray which begins to lighten your sideburns makes you squirm.

Of course, most people aren't *that* bad, but I still wonder why a woman has to spend an hour putting on makeup, for example. It's like painting a portrait, don't you think? What would happen if you just went *au naturale?* It's not like people are going to run away screaming or anything. (Besides, hordes of women find bald spots sexy. I know I do.) But with all the attention on hair, clothing, and makeup . . . how much is *disguising* the real you?

I admit I tend to be at the opposite end. I have less than no interest in my personal appearance and sometimes that's just as bad. I'm certain that I would look nicer if I took the time to dress in something else besides sweatpants, and combed my hair every so often. The rare times I wear makeup, my kids stare at me in amazement.

So find a balance. It's simpler.

# . 163 .

## EVERYTHING IN MODERATION

Did you know that you can eat chocolate cake while on a diet? Did you know that drinking water can kill you? Did you know that arsenic is perfectly safe? Of course, these things only apply in moderation. A small piece of chocolate cake won't hurt your diet. Drink eight glasses of water a day, not eight gallons. And arsenic? Sure, one or two molecules are fine (any more and you'll be in trouble).

The essence of a simple life is to find the proper balance in everything. Or, as the old saying goes, everything in moderation. Focusing on work, for example, is fine until you begin to neglect your family. Decluttering your home is wonderful until you start getting rid of things you actively need and use. Giving up your job to stay home with your kids is unbeatable unless it leaves you with no source of income. Becoming thrifty so you can pay down debt is terrific until you become a miser and refuse to spend money even when it's necessary.

You can go overboard in health issues as with anything else. Exercise is great until you begin to experience joint stress and physical injury. Giving up smoking is wonderful until you begin to snatch cigarettes out of the mouth of strangers on the street and screaming that they're killing themselves. Eating lots of fruits and veggies is terrific until you become ill because you're not eating anything else and your body becomes deficient in a critical nutrient.

You probably don't take things anywhere near these extremes. Or do you? Remember, balance and moderation are good for simplicity.

# .164.

## GET REGULAR EXERCISE

Ever wonder why everyone harps on the fact that you need more exercise? It's because it's true. Our bodies were formed to require exercise to stay healthy. Our muscles need to be toned, stretched, and challenged in order to perform at peak capacity.

Of course, we argue that we have no time to exercise. Nonsense. You've all read the articles out there that tell you how to incorporate exercise into your daily routine (take the stairs, don't use a golf cart, walk around the block during your lunch hour, etc.).

In our case, we bit the bullet and purchased a second-hand elliptical trainer so I wouldn't have to spend the money on our local health club. I like it because I can do a workout whenever I wish—6 a.m. or 10 p.m. or whenever I have time. If you can promise to *use* it (besides as a place to drape clothes), purchasing a home exerciser might be a wise decision.

But it doesn't require a piece of exercise equipment or a membership to your local gym to get exercise. Housework can burn about 207 calories an hour. Anything more vigorous—energetic yardwork or cleaning the garage or helping someone move—can burn about twice that amount.

My husband and I try to take a walk together every day (it gives us a chance to connect as a couple). Our girls are active in hiking, biking, and gymnastics.

Our lives are simpler if we can stay healthy. Making sure our bodies receive the amount of exercise needed to keep our muscles toned and our lungs at full capacity contributes to that. So break out that push mower or snow shovel and get a nice workout.

# . 165 .

## EAT SIMPLY

"Tell me what you eat," said Brillat Savarin, "and I will tell you what you are."

Every so often, such as when my husband is out of town, I'll buy the kids a pre-made frozen meal for dinner. It's a big treat for them. They spend a lot of time looking over the grocery store selection, finding which option has the items they like, wondering how the mashed potatoes will taste.

The mashed potatoes will taste awful, of course. But in a weird way, that's half the fun. Afterward, my younger (and more verbal) daughter will conclude, "Can you imagine eating these *every single day?*" She says it with a tinge of pity, the little snob. Just think of the poor saps who are forced to eat like this all the time. My daughter finds this disturbing.

When trying to simplify your life, it's a natural extension to try to simplify your diet. What's healthy? What's not? Clearly food that is highly processed, pre-packaged, expensive, and full of ingredients you can't pronounce is not as healthy as making something from scratch. Also, if you really look at the cost in both money and health, why would you try to live on that stuff?

I'm not an organic freak, nor do I object to the occasional quick meal from the grocery store. But to live on this stuff, day after day, week after week, would batter me down. I think it would batter my body down, too. So eat more simply. It's good for you.

# . 166 .

## COOK FROM SCRATCH

The primary reason why people buy deli-made, or pre-packaged, highly-processed foods is to save time. But *time* is something I'm trying to help you create. By simplifying your life, you save time so that you can cook decent healthy meals from scratch.

I don't like to cook—a detriment, when you're a mother—but I have a standard selection of meals that I've mastered and whose ingredients I keep handy. I can glance at my list and think, "Oh, I haven't made pizza in awhile. Maybe I'll make that tonight." Keeps the fussing to a minimum.

If I know my afternoon will be busy, I'll throw the ingredients for navy bean soup in the crockpot first thing in the morning and forget about it for the rest of the day. I'll make some garlic bread or a salad, and dinner is done in fifteen minutes tops (except for the crock pot time).

Cooking from scratch is easier if you do two things. One, find some recipes that are fairly simple and that your family enjoys. Scratch cooking has earned a bad reputation as being time-consuming and complicated. With forethought, it doesn't have to be that way.

Second, keep your standard ingredients on hand. A scratch meal isn't made any simpler if you have to take a hasty dash to the grocery store for some forgotten item.

Ideally, a simple life is also a healthy life. One thing's for sure: if you continue to put unhealthy foods into your system, you won't be healthy forever. And that ain't simple.

# .167.

## GET RID OF THE ADDICTIONS

Addictions cover a lot of territory, including smoking, drugs, drinking, watching TV, pornography, shopping, hoarding . . . the list is endless. Stop for a moment and think how much simpler your life would be if you didn't pander to your addictions.

Don't congratulate yourself because you don't smoke while you sit glued to the television four hours each day. Don't imagine that because you drink in moderation, your seventy hours a week in the office isn't detrimental to your wellbeing.

Most addictions are destructive to your health, your wealth, your time, your relationships, and most certainly to the concept of the simple life.

A clear indication of when a behavior is becoming addictive is whether your family complains about it. Does your wife object to the hours you spend surfing the Internet? Do your children wish they could invite their friends over but the house is too cluttered with junk? Does your husband blow his top when he sees the MasterCard bill every month because of your shopping habits?

Getting rid of an addiction will instill a sense of accomplishment within you seldom found by other means. Imagine the pride you would feel if you never smoked again. Imagine the freedom of never losing control from alcohol.

The actual how-to of breaking a particular addiction is beyond the scope of this book. Depending on what your particular weakness is, there are many sources that can offer assistance. So get help. Read books. Acquire discipline. Join support groups. Remember the Nike slogan: Just do it. Your life will be simpler for it.

# . 168 .

## ACKNOWLEDGE YOUR INNER CLOCK

Is it possible to work around your inner clock? I'm not going to make any silly suggestions like "Watch the sunrise every day." Sure, it might seem virtuous and admirable to get up early enough to watch the sunrise, but it would kill my husband to do that. He's a night owl. To him, it might be better to watch the moon rise. It's a cruel requirement to ask a night owl to get up just to watch the sun come up.

It is easier to work around one's inner clock. My perfect job would start at 6 a.m. My husband's perfect job would start at 11 a.m. Since we work at home, we often do just that.

It isn't always possible to work around your inner clock. Employers are fussy about their employees showing up on time, and if that means being at your desk at 8 a.m., it's tough on the night owls. It's just as tough to be an early bird working the swing shift.

Obviously you're not going to convince your employer to work around your inner clock (though you might consider working for someone who does have flexible hours). But acknowledging you *have* an inner clock may be enough for you to understand why the first half of your workday passes in a caffeine-blurred haze.

The desire to cater to your inner clock can be a powerful tool to simplify your life. Wouldn't it be lovely to actually work during those hours when you're at your most productive?

# .169.

## WATCH THE SUNRISE

Snail, snail
Slowly slowly
Up Mt. Fuji.

*Kobayashi Issa,*
*763–1827*

If watching the sunrise means you have to get up too early, don't bother. Watch the moonrise instead. Or the sunset. Or the snowflakes. Or the raindrops. You pick.

My point is to pause every so often to watch *something*—your dogs romping in the yard, Canada geese flying overhead, your kids playing, the city skyline. Stop and smell the roses. Pause and admire something, anything. The view at this moment will *never* be repeated.

# . 170 .

## MAKE YOURSELF A CUP OF TEA

There is something about holding a steaming mug of fragrant tea that makes you pause and relax. Tea is somehow conducive to contemplation, even if it's at your desk in the office. You might grab the opportunity (while the tea is still hot) to spend a few minutes thinking about what it is you really want out of life and how to get there.

Tea is a delightful social beverage, conjuring up images of proper Victorian ladies or elegant soirées. It's helpful in breaking the ice with new acquaintances, or excellent for stimulating conversation between friends or family members. It's body-warming on a cold winter's day, and heart-warming on a summer morning.

People who hate coffee (me!) won't ever be able to find a coffee flavor that will taste good; but teas come in such a wide variety as to please any palate. My preference is for the hearty black teas (Darjeeling is my favorite), and your favorite may be a non-caffeinated herbal blend.

Besides, haven't you heard? Tea is now an official stress-reducer. In 2006, University College London researchers published a study in the journal *Psychopharmacology* that reported men who drank black tea four times a day for six weeks were found to have lower levels of the stress hormone cortisol than a control group who drank a fake tea substitute. The tea drinkers also reported a greater feeling of relaxation after performing tasks designed to raise stress levels.

So have a cup of tea and relax.

# .171.

## DON'T DO STUFF YOU DON'T WANT YOUR KIDS TO DO

Our kids are excellent barometers for keeping us in line. There's something about looking into a child's innocent face, full of admiration for his parents, to make you want to live up to his lofty expectations. But all it takes is for little James to pick up a nasty word to make us realize that everything—everything!—we do is being watched and emulated.

Do you smoke? Is every other word in your vocabulary four letters? Do you drink a six-pack every night? Do you maliciously gossip over juicy exploits? Do you yell at drivers in traffic? Do you quarrel with your spouse?

Everything you do is modeled and internalized by your children. You can preach all you want that smoking is bad and you never want to see them with a cigarette in their mouths . . . while you smoke. What will this teach them?

You can drag your kids to church every Sunday so that they'll believe in God, while you lie and cheat during the week.

You can wonder why they're sneaking alcohol from your personal stash even though you have martinis every night.

You can sermonize about protecting the environment while you drive five hundred miles to attend a save-the-whales rally.

You can swear like a sailor and then spank the kids when they let a four-letter word rip.

Follow practices that maximize your physical and mental health, as well as your peace of mind. Then it becomes easier to teach your kids to do the same. When your practices are consistent with your preaching, your life will become simpler.

# .172.

## STOP BLAMING YOUR PAST

Some of us were blessed with happy secure childhoods. Unfortunately, there are all too many people whose childhoods were not happy. Some people think this gives them license to do bad things as an adult.

At what point does your bad childhood become an excuse for your current behavior? Do you beat your kids because you were beaten as a child? Do you live beyond your means to make up for being poor as a kid? Do you refuse to read a book because you hated your fourth-grade reading teacher? Do you have sex with serial boyfriends because you're trying to make up for your father's absence when you were young? Do you "act out" and get in trouble with the law because your parents loved your brother more than you?

Well, *stop it*. Stop doing things that prevent you from having a happy, secure, simple life *today* because of what you experienced *yesterday*. You are *not* the sum of your past bad experiences. You are a rational, thinking, feeling, self-directing adult. Act like it.

Believe me, this is *not* to negate any of the pain and suffering you may have endured as a child. But you do not have the right to make your spouse and children suffer because of what *you* suffered. Break the cycle.

If you can let go of the horrors of your childhood, you gain strength to rise above. Your life becomes simpler, and so do the lives of your spouse and children.

# . 173 .

## STOP THE SILLY GUILT

Let's say I'm sitting down and reading a book, which I do occasionally during the day. Whenever my husband walks across the driveway from our shop and enters the house, I jump to my feet and start doing something. It makes no difference that he's coming in to take a break, and he'll take a break by sitting down and reading a book. The point is, I feel guilty if I'm "caught" relaxing. It's silly guilt.

This is *especially* problematic for women. Maybe it has something to do with that extra "X" chromosome or something, but women universally suffer from guilt. Silly, useless, inappropriate, unnecessary, burdensome, painful guilt.

Yet what *is* guilt? According to the Merriam-Webster Dictionary, the definition of *guilt* includes feelings of culpability, especially for imagined offenses or from a sense of inadequacy.

Imagined offenses. A sense of inadequacy. For sitting down and reading a book? It would never, ever dawn on my husband to be annoyed at me for sitting down and reading a book, any more than it would dawn on me to be annoyed at him for doing the same. We are both hard-working responsible people and deserve a break once in awhile. Yet, I still jump up and get busy when he walks through the door. Go figure.

Guilt implies that you've done something wrong. But unless you actually *have*, stop feeling guilty.

There's nothing wrong with occasionally sitting down to read a book and letting your spouse carry the load. Our lives become simpler if we can diminish the silly, inappropriate guilt.

# .174.

## GOOD GUILT VS. BAD GUILT

Now, of course, there are times when we *should* feel guilty. Silly guilt is not to be confused with serious guilt. Serious guilt is when we know darn good and well that we're doing something wrong. Neglecting our kids, forgetting to be pleasant to our spouse, brushing off an obligation, being selfish or thoughtless . . . these are things that *should* prick our conscience and make us strive to do better.

Guilt has a purpose. It tells us that we've done something wrong. It behooves us to listen to that annoying conscience of ours and figure out (a) what we did (or didn't) do to feel guilty, and (b) what we can do to remedy the situation.

Erma Bombeck called guilt the gift that keeps on giving. Chronic guilt can be debilitating to our health. Maybe now is the time to ask forgiveness from someone you've offended, or make amends for some bad behavior, or otherwise correct (to the best of our ability) whatever it is that caused the guilt to begin with.

Does this mean you confess *all* your failings and sins to your spouse or children or friends? Not if doing so will burden them or cause more damage than was caused by your original failing. However, that doesn't mean you have to continue to bear guilt. Ask God for forgiveness. Then forgive yourself. Try to repair any damage you did, and then make a promise never to repeat the mistake.

Taking the steps to reduce guilt increases your health, body and soul.

# . 175 .

## RELATIVE RISK

Back in 1972, at the height of the hippie movement, my older brother (twelve at the time) made an interesting observation about some new friends. "All their food is organic," he said. "But they don't wear seatbelts."

Which is more likely to kill you tomorrow? Non-organic food, or a car accident?

Sometimes we tend to become zealous and evangelistic about a particular practice or belief without considering its relative importance in the grand scheme of things.

If we ignore that painful lump in our breast but insist on flossing our teeth every day, the relative risk from tooth decay is far less than the risk of breast cancer.

If we're too afraid of flying (I sympathize) to get on an airplane, so we opt to drive across the country, we forget that driving is, statistically speaking, far more dangerous.

If we feel virtuous by ordering a diet soft drink along with our high-calorie, fast-food meal, we forget that it's the meal and not the soft drink that will pack on more pounds.

A simple life is a life of balance, a life in which we can look at the Big Picture and assess relative risk.

In no way am I implying that organic foods or flossing your teeth are not practices you should follow. Just keep things in perspective. If you don't wear your seatbelt while you drive to the store to purchase your organic food and dental floss, then your relative risk has shot through the roof.

# .176.

## PRACTICE PREVENTATIVE MEDICINE

Wearing your seatbelt is an excellent example of preventative medicine. We immunized our children for the same reason (though I know others who feel differently). Regular checkups and routine medical tests (such as a pap smear) are all common forms of preventative medicine.

But for some people, that prevention might need to go deeper. If you know that your family history puts you at risk for a certain medical condition—breast cancer or high blood pressure or strokes or heart attacks—then it behooves you to consult with your doctor about the most sensible ways to reduce or eliminate the risk. Pretending "it won't happen to me" is a problem waiting to happen.

It means taking responsibility for a lot of your own health management. When your doctor tells you to lose weight or you'll suffer a heart attack, don't you think it's wise to listen? If your doctor suggests that you get a colonoscopy because your father died from colon cancer, I'd follow through if I were you.

A close friend of mine has a family history of strokes. Her grandmother suffered a serious stroke. A few years ago, her mother suffered a serious stroke. She is now understandably concerned about having a stroke when she is her mother's age. Forewarned is forearmed, however, and she can now take steps to reduce the possibility.

The more we can be aware of our own personal responsibility for maintaining our health, the higher our chances for keeping our health good. Which, as I'm sure you agree, is simpler than the alternative.

# . 177 .

## GET DIRTY

We are a country obsessed with cleanliness. The shelves of any grocery store are loaded with soaps, detergents, antibacterial wipes, lotions, cleansers, spray, scrubs, and ointments, all designed to kill germs. Yet there are times when old-fashioned dirt is good for us. According to Dr. Dean Edell in his book, *Eat, Drink and Be Merry*, "People raised in too germ-free an environment are left with a weak immune system and higher rates of certain diseases such as diabetes and asthma."

Now that we can "see" those big scary germs via electron microscopes, and because the media is willing to dramatize every instance of ebola or flesh-eating bacteria (no matter how rare), we've developed an irrational fear of germs. Naturally this is compounded by instances when germs *are* a serious issue (such as *E. coli* in foods). And obviously those individuals who have compromised immune systems need to be especially vigilant.

Germs can and do cause serious illnesses, but if they were as bad as people have been led to believe, then we would be sick all the time. Yet parents often refuse to let their children rough-and-tumble about because of germs.

Be sensible where germs are concerned. Yes, I'll continue to open the door to a public restroom with a paper towel after I've washed my hands (call me fussy). But don't be paranoid to the point where you're convinced the restroom door will kill you.

And let your kids play in the dirt. It builds their immune systems. Just make sure they wash their hands before supper.

# .178.

## ACCEPT MORTALITY

One unexpected drawback from the spectacular medical advances we've experienced in the last forty years is we expect *everything* can be fixed. But it can't. No matter how healthy you are, no matter what you do to maintain your body, death happens. You could be the most balanced, healthy, and unstressed person imaginable . . . right before you get hit by a bus.

My daughter's elderly piano teacher, Julie, just lost her husband of sixty years, a charming gentleman named Bob. A few months ago, at the age of eighty-five, Bob's heart started giving out and there was nothing that could be done about it. He was on what they called "sudden death watch," meaning it could happen any minute. He made it through the Christmas holidays, he made sure he told his friends and family goodbye, and he simply . . . waited. He died in early January.

The most remarkable thing about this was how calm and at peace both Julie and Bob were as they waited for the end. I believe two reasons for this calmness were (a) their rock-solid faith, and (b) they had no regrets. Julie misses her husband horribly, of course, but she knows he's in a better place waiting for her.

No matter how shocking or unexpected a death may be, minimal regret is what can get you through the grief much more easily. If my husband died tomorrow (please God, no!), at least I would not have any regrets for the way I've treated him.

Live your life so you don't have many regrets. It's much simpler when the end comes.

# .179.

## PAY NO ATTENTION TO
## THE MAN BEHIND THE CURTAIN

Remember the old line of, "If it's in print, then it must be true"? These days, most of us don't take the headlines of the tabloids very seriously ("Two-headed Aliens Land in Guam and Present Doctors with a Cure for Cancer!"), but let any news anchor on TV tell you that hanging rabbit's feet around your neck is the latest treatment for ulcers and we're likely to believe him.

Two things must be remembered about medical claims you hear on TV or radio. One, as intelligent and knowledgeable as news anchors are, most have no scientific or medical background. This makes it hard for them to distinguish between junk and authentic medical news. Two, the media's job is to sell news. The more outrageous or extravagant or dire the claim, the more they like it . . . regardless of how sound the claim actually is.

The media tends to distort or skew medical news in favor of what will sell newspapers or get TV ratings. If a hundred studies demonstrate that drug X is harmless for pregnant women but one badly done study concludes that there is a slight risk, which study do you think the media will publicize? Not only publicize, but dramatize? Dr. Dean Edell in his book, *Eat, Drink and be Merry* says, "The media peddles you threats because threats sell ratings."

This is *not* to imply that medical news you hear on TV or the radio is not correct. What I *am* saying is that such news should be checked out with your doctor before you start hanging rabbit's feet around your neck.

# .180.

## UNDERSTAND CAUSE AND EFFECT

Did you know that one hundred percent of people who eat broccoli will die? It's true. This isn't to say that eating broccoli causes death of course. But admit it—isn't that the first conclusion that flickered through your mind?

Many people misunderstand cause and effect, especially in health issues. If I drank a new type of tea and the next day I was diagnosed with (pick your favorite disease), my first impulse is to *look for something to blame*. Since the tea was the only "new" thing I did recently, I'll blame the tea. However hundreds or thousands of other people might have drank the same tea with no ill effects. It's just a coincidence on my part that I was diagnosed with (name the disease).

Naturally there are times when things genuinely do have a true cause-and-effect relationship. If 75 percent of the people who drank that tea develop the same illness, then it behooves the tea-drinkers to look at the issue seriously. The tea needs be studied and examined.

But in today's society, we are all victims. Everything that goes wrong with us needs a cause, and sometimes the wrong thing gets picked to be at fault. I won't go into specifics, but in the past ten or fifteen years, there have been many examples of innocent treatments or procedures or prescriptions being blamed for a variety of effects *even though serious studies have shown no link*.

According to Occam's Razor, the simplest explanation is more likely the correct one. Try not to make things so complicated when looking for the cause of your concern.

# . 181 .

## YOUR DOCTOR WANTS YOU DEAD

Did you know that? Yes, the entire medical establishment is in cahoots to keep you sick, keep you dependent on their ineffective treatments, and ultimately kill you so you can't complain. At least, those are the opinions of certain extremists who go out of their way to convince you doctors are evil and want you dead. Gee, I guess all the times I've been sick and a doctor cured me must just be a fluke.

There are many, many sensible things you can do to optimize your chances of a healthy life. Those four things mentioned in #153 are a good start (don't smoke, keep to a healthy weight, eat lots of fruits and veggies, and exercise).

Your doctor is not out to kill you or withhold effective treatments. He is not part of a vast medical conspiracy to stay in business by repudiating valid, tested, studied, reproducible treatments that stand up to scientific scrutiny. Believe me, if someone came up with a simple, cheap, easily-available cure for cancer that was *scientifically proven to work*, can you honestly believe that doctors would eliminate this person so he won't mess up the conspiracy?

But let a Hollywood starlet or a self-proclaimed health guru tell you a colon cleanse will cure appendicitis, and we flock to their wisdom, despite the fact that not one thing they claim will stand up to scientific scrutiny.

The human body is a complicated thing. Keep your life simple by understanding basic science. And for Pete's sake, if you have an inflamed appendix, get it removed. Appendicitis can kill you—and it can't be cured with a colon cleanse.

# .182.

## YOUR HEALTH IN A DOWN ECONOMY

Life is complicated right now. Try not to make it more complicated by doing things that contribute to ill health. That means following the usual advice spouted by the health industry. Quit smoking (think of the money you'll save), quit excessive drinking (ditto), get more exercise (walks are free), eat more fruits and vegetables (in-season produce is cheap). See where I'm going with this?

You're already balancing enough worries about the economy and possibly your own dire personal situation (unemployment, bankruptcy, foreclosure, whatever). While it may seem like just another hassle to worry about your health at a time like this, it's important. Stress and worry add enough pressure to your health as it is. Don't compound it by doing dumb things like eating bad food, not exercising, or not wearing your seatbelt.

Looking outside of yourself also helps your health. So go to church. Help others. Take time for your family. All these things will relieve stress.

Remember, sensible practices to maintain your health are within your control. Utilize them in order to better handle those things *outside* your control.

# Your Daily Bread

▼

**M**oney. Ah, one of life's greatest blessings—and curses. Cultivating a simpler approach toward finances means simplifying life in general. In fact, you can argue that money is the crux of a simpler life . . . or the lack thereof. Our approach to money is instrumental in how we approach a future of economic uncertainty. If our ego is tied to our income, we'll have a harder time adapting to decreases in that income.

# .183.

## MONEY AND EGO

Have you ever thought how money is tied up with our ego to an enormous extent? We are termed "successful" if we bring in a certain amount of income, despite how messed-up or complicated the rest of our life is. Wouldn't you rather be termed "successful" because you lead a life mostly free of stress, worries, anxieties, and debt?

The big house, the four platinum credit cards, the designer wardrobe, the corner office, the brand-new SUV . . . how can these compare to the freedom of living modestly without owing anyone a dime?

But money is more multifaceted than that. An excessive desire for money can cause marital strife, dishonesty, illegal actions, and a myriad of other complex problems. (Remember, "For the love of money is a root of all kinds of evil.") It's not just money, but what it can buy—things, power, prestige, and ego. These things don't contribute to a simple life.

We are sensitive to the opinions of others. We want others to think well of us, and we try to ensure that by buying things we think will elevate us in their eyes. We believe that if our home, our wardrobe, and our career are up to a certain level, people will think we're successful. Likewise, if our home, wardrobe, and career don't meet our own inflated standards, we're a failure.

If someone in a designer suit looks down at me because I'm wearing old sweatpants with holes in the knee, I'll just smile. My life is simpler than theirs, and I know it.

# .184.

## BE GENEROUS

We have some friends who are living in what some might term poverty. Yet their cramped, small home (1,200 square feet for seven people!) is always open, welcoming, and gracious. In fact, *gracious* would be the best term I could find for the mother, who sets the tone for this home. I'll call her Elizabeth.

Despite their modest financial situation, Elizabeth and her husband are remarkably generous with their time and possessions. This generosity is so effortless and cheerful that it sometimes takes people aback.

As an example, one day Elizabeth received a phone call. "Good morning," said the caller. "I'm with Xyz Charity [a reputable, well known organization]. We supply necessary household items for families in need . . . "

"Of course," interrupted Elizabeth. "What do you need? We'll be happy to donate what we can."

There was an awkward pause. "Actually," said the caller at last, "we have some items we were going to give to *you* . . . "

Elizabeth declined the offer, while reiterating that they should call back if they needed donations. I think *that* is one of the highest tributes I've ever heard.

When people become focused on saving money or becoming thrifty or adopting frugality, they sometimes allow generosity to fall by the wayside. But being generous  with your time, your possessions, your empathy, and yes, sometimes your money, keeps the focus off *you* and places it on others.

Try to take Elizabeth's example and keep your generosity cheerful and effortless. It's a lovely thing to see people considering the needs of others.

# .185.

## IGNORE THE JONESES

Do you really want to keep up with the Joneses? Why? What's so great about them, and what happiness or fulfillment has it ever given you to keep up with them? It all boils down to our concern that we may not be good enough in the eyes of others if we don't own such-and-such.

I hope by now you'll understand that one of the methods of simplifying is not to be concerned about the opinions of others. Yes, maybe you can say with pride at a cocktail party that you're an attorney. Or a stockbroker. Or a bank president. But do you hold your head up just as high if someone asks you what you do for a living and you say, "I'm a mechanic," or, "I'm a stay-at-home mom," or, "I'm a gardener"? If working on cars or raising your kids or mowing lawns fulfills the Inner You—and it *can*—then who the heck cares if the attorney looks down his nose at you? Do you honestly think he's *better* than you just because he makes more money?

The Joneses live in high-end neighborhoods, drive brand-new SUVs, and put their kids in exclusive private academies. You, meanwhile, live in an ordinary suburb, drive a ten-year-old Subaru, and send your kids to the elementary school around the corner. Do you breathe a sigh of envy every time you see Mrs. Jones, in a business suit and pearls, driving little Johnny to Le Chic Academy in the SUV? Don't. The day will come when you'll realize the Joneses are deep in debt and have undisciplined kids.

Ignore the Joneses. They're not worth keeping up with.

# . 186 .

## DITCH THE DEBT

Getting out of debt is like losing weight—it can seem hopeless at the beginning. There will be two steps forward and one step backward.

So when things get tough, and when you're tempted to whip out the plastic and purchase something because you deserve it, because you've had a rotten day, because you had a fight with your spouse, because you can't resist the latest whizbang electronic gizmo, because (fill in your best excuse here), it's time to visualize.

Close your eyes and imagine yourself completely out of debt. No car payments. No student loan payments. No credit card payments. Nothing. Feel the lightness, the airiness? Feel the weight off your shoulders? Feel the sensation of flying on angel wings? Feel the freedom? That's what it's like to be out of debt.

Visualize yourself walking down the street with a spring in your step, looking around at all the people who are still so burdened down with debt that they have weights on their shoulders. Think of the sensation of airiness and lightness you will feel.

Especially in these tough economic times, debt makes you a slave. Set yourself free and get all the help you can. Two of the best books I've found on the subject are Dave Ramsey's *Total Money Makeover* (www.daveramsey.com), and Joe Dominguez and Vicki Robin's *Your Money or Your Life* (www.newroadmap.org).

Now put that credit card away.

# .187.

## STAY OUT OF DEBT

You'd think this would be a no-brainer too, but apparently not. If people are in debt, they tend to dig themselves deeper, which is obviously counterproductive. Other times, people have worked their fannies off to get out of debt, only to find themselves back *in* debt within a year or two. The problem is that they didn't change the underlying behavior that racked up the debt to start with.

*Staying* out of debt is easier than *getting* out of debt, but barely. It's hard work until you develop the right "muscles." Like anything worthwhile, you have to start with training and constant control.

Part of the problem is that people often associate frugality or thrift as deprivation. Nothing could be farther from the truth. Being debt-free frees you.

What are some of the things you could do if you stayed out of debt? Leave a hated job? Move to a prettier part of the country? Spend more time with your family?

Learn to exercise the financial "muscles" that will keep you from racking up those credit cards again. Save for a purchase rather than charging it. Buy a used car rather than a new one.

Figure out the fun of frugality. Instead of tracking your debt (no fun), track your savings (lots of fun!). Be proud of your debt-free lifestyle. Let it become second nature. Enjoy the freedom it gives you.

Stay out of debt. Life is a lot simpler when you don't owe any money.

# . 188 .

## LIVE WITHIN YOUR MEANS

This is another one of those easy things to keep your life incredibly simple: live within your means. And yet so few of us do it!

A friend emailed me in distress about a family she knows: "The father is literally dying over money problems. The stress has given him high blood pressure and put him in the highest possible risk category for stroke. He's constantly sick but has to keep pressing on because creditors are calling *every ten minutes* from 9 am to 9 pm. The power, phone, and satellite have all been shut off periodically over the last few months. The whole family is gaining weight rapidly because of stress. The scariest thing is that they don't get it. Everything they have has a lien on it—including personal items and furniture—yet they keep making bad decisions left and right. They have no health insurance, no disability insurance, and no savings. He's almost sixty-four years old and no possibility of retiring . . . And yet the wife decided that she *must* have the living room painted and new recessed lighting put in because she just can't *stand* the wall colors anymore. This is the same woman who was crying because of bills, creditors, loans, liens, lies, multiple bankruptcies, and knowing that her husband is on the verge of a stroke. Now she's looking at *paint chips?*"

Okay, I'll grant this is an extreme example. This family has lived beyond their means for many, many years, and now it's catching up to them in a horrible way.

But do you catch glimpses of yourself in this sad story? How close are you to this situation? If so, it's time to bite the bullet and stop it. Live within your means.

# . 189 .

## DON'T DO THINGS YOU CAN'T AFFORD

My husband and I decided many years ago that we would never put ourselves under the onus of car payments again. Been there, done that, didn't like it. So when we need another car, we'll save up and pay cash (we only buy used). It's not that we can't afford to make modest car payments. We can. But the trouble with monthly payments is that they add up.

Car payments. Student loan payments. Three credit card payments. Department store payments. Boat payments. Home equity loan payments. And this doesn't even include the monthly mortgage payments and utility bills. See how it adds up? Suddenly you have no money.

We, as Americans, want everything at once. We have little patience with the concept of deferred gratification. But do you remember how our parents and grandparents had to wait for the finer things in life? They didn't start out with the 6,000-square-foot home or the three SUVs in the four-car garage. No, they bought a little suburban fixer-upper and drove an old beater of a car until they could afford something better.

The trouble with us is that we want it all, and we want it all now. We are willing to burden ourselves with monthly install-ments to get it now. This leads to a complexity of life that increases stress. But the stress of trying to make those monthly payments isn't worth it. Simplify your life by deferring the "wants" until such time as you can pay for them.

# . 190 .

## WHAT IS YOUR TIME WORTH?

Let's say you went to lunch today with a friend. Your total came to $20 for the two of you. When your lunch hour is over, you go back to work where for the next hour or hour and a half (depending on your salary) you will essentially be paying off your lunch. Or it might take you four or six hours of your labor to pay for that sophisticated "impress them" lunch at an upscale restaurant.

If you do this every day—go to lunch—you're essentially reducing the number of hours you'll be getting paid. Is this *really* how you want to spend your life—paying for things that have no lasting value or are wasteful or are otherwise contrary to a simpler life?

These are the points raised in Joe Dominguez and Vicki Robin's book *Your Money or Your Life.* Our "life energy," the limited time we have on this planet, is being exchanged for stuff that is unnecessary, wasteful, or even downright stupid.

If you can rearrange your life so that you are no longer consuming as much, and therefore no longer working as much, then you are on the right road to simplicity. You will have more time for the important things in life—time with family and friends, time for hobbies and charity work, time for exercise and proper nutrition, time, time, time. You might even argue that this is the only way to *buy* time.

# .191.

## TRACK YOUR EXPENSES

Nearly every book on the subject of improving one's finances will include the advice to track your expenses. This advice is included for a reason. Tracking expenses is an amazing eye-opener. First of all, you have to be honest with yourself. You can't let the daily latté "slip" because it "doesn't count." *Everything* counts. You're not Congress, so nothing goes "off budget."

Get one of those little pocket notebooks and make a notation for purchases made with cash, checks, credit cards, debit cards, and any other monetary form of exchange. Also, keep *all* receipts. When you get that big ticker-tape receipt at the grocery store, keep it.

At the end of a period of time (a week, or two weeks, or a month), sit down and tally those expenses. You might be flabbergasted by how much you spend at the grocery store or the dry cleaners.

Go further and break those expenses down into separate monthly categories (this is where the receipts come in). Are you really spending $80 a month on latté, $120 on fast food, $40 on frozen pizzas, $320 on frozen packaged convenience foods, and $60 on getting your nails done? Only by writing everything down—and then sitting down to analyze it—will you find out where your money is slipping away.

I'm not saying these purchases are necessarily wrong. If having attractive nails is important, that's fine. But this way you can no longer complain that you don't know where all your money goes, because you'll know.

# . 192 .

## PLUG THE HOLES

Knowledge is power. Now that you've tracked your expenses (#191), it's time to plug the holes.

Which of your expenses are at odds with your vision of a simple life? Has it always bugged you that eating fast-food produces so much waste? Try brown-bagging your lunches from home and saving the money (and the waste). Are you buying frozen convenience foods at the grocery store because you don't have time to cook? A simpler life involves making more time for you and your family so you can prepare meals from scratch.

See where I'm going with this? Tracking purchases is one of the tools for finding out what daily or weekly expenses are complicating your life. Having the numbers in black and white right in front of your eyes can be enlightening.

Once you've established where your money is going, you can begin to recognize your consumer weaknesses, your "automatic" spending (the daily latté, restaurant meals, whatever), or your splurges. You'll know how much you're paying in bills (credit cards, student loans, car payments, utilities), as well as how much you're spending on entertainment and other expenses.

Now do something about it. If it means paying off a debt, maybe you should give up the restaurant meals and eat at home for the next few months. If it's a step closer to financial freedom, maybe you should sell your car and get rid of the car payments, and buy a used vehicle for cash.

One thing's for sure, nothing will change unless *you* do.

# . 193 .

## WHEN A SALE IS NOT A SALE

Most people are reasonably intelligent. We are competent in our jobs. We get around in society. We (mostly) don't get flim-flammed by scam artists. Yet collectively we have certain inbred weaknesses regarding purchases. Advertisers have learned to tap into those weaknesses in an effort to part us from our money.

It helps to be aware of subliminal advertising. But a frequent and apparently successful tactic that we swallow is the urgent "sales" that are advertised on television, radio, and newspapers. "Our after-holiday 50 percent off sale is going on now!" the print will scream. "50 percent off all lavender-velvet frammer-jammits in stock!"

Well, if you happen to need a lavender-velvet frammer-jammit, great. But more likely than not, it's the "50 percent off" part that has your eyes sparkling. You figure it's worth going to the store to see what these frammerjammits are like. Wow, what a bargain! They're normally $100, but you—lucky devil—only have to pay $50.

Sorry to pop your bubble, but you very likely didn't need a lavender-velvet frammerjammit to start with, and now you're out fifty bucks *and* stuck with the stupid frammerjammit. And what about those extra items you never knew you needed but bought anyway because *they* were on sale?

One of my personal pet peeves in radio advertising is the fast-talking narrator whose urgent "must-do-it-now-or-we'll-be-all-sold-out!" phrasing has us reaching for our car keys. It seems that the faster and louder a narrator talks, the more "urgent" the sale is.

Sales can be useful, but only if you actually need the product. If you bought something on sale that you didn't need, you didn't "save" money, you spent it.

# .194.

## DON'T BE PENNY-WISE, POUND-FOOLISH

Do you drive ten miles out of your way to save $2 on laundry detergent? Do you spend five minutes circling the parking lot, looking for a space closer to the store's entrance? Do you believe the advertisements when they tell you you'll "save" money by purchasing a big-screen TV when they're 25 percent off?

Advertisers have led us to believe that "sales" will save us money (especially when we don't need the item to begin with). We think we're "saving" time or energy if we circle the parking lot to find a space close to the store's entrance. And of course, it's a bargain to get laundry detergent for $2 off even though it cost us $3 in gas to get there.

We might be proud of our ability to pinch pennies at the grocery store, but then we blow our "pounds" on an expensive restaurant meal.

Or consider the homeowner who is convinced that he can "save" the cost of a plumber by fixing the plumbing problem himself, even though he doesn't know one end of a wrench from another. Of course, he screws it up so badly that he has to bring the plumber in on an emergency call to undo the mess he's made.

Perhaps we avoid going to the doctor for a regular checkup in an effort to save money . . . only to discover a major health issue that could have been caught (and treated) earlier and cheaper.

So think things through before you try to "save" money or time. Sometimes you're being pound-wise . . . and sometimes you're not.

# .195.

## RECOGNIZE SUBLIMINAL ADVERTISING STRATEGIES

When I was in high school (late 70s), I saw a movie on subliminal advertising strategies. I've never forgotten it. Subliminal advertising isn't about flashing "Buy Popcorn!" in previews at movie theaters. No, it's much more blatant—or subtle—than that.

See the sexy woman on the ad for vodka? What does it imply? If you're a woman, it implies that if you drink this vodka, you'll be this sexy. If you're a man, it implies that if you drink this vodka, you'll attract women who are this sexy.

How about the cigarette ads with the rugged cowboy? The implication is that if you smoke this brand of cigarette, you'll be as manly and rugged as a cowboy, rather than smelling like an ashtray.

Beauty products? Naturally, if you use this brand of mascara your entire facial structure will alter and you'll look like a model.

Clothing? Just buy this outfit and you'll lose fifty pounds and grow five inches in height. Wow.

Recognize advertising tactics for what they are—methods to get you to buy a product. In ads, nothing is an accident. *Everything* that you see or hear is planned and executed deliberately, with the intent to convince you (consciously or unconsciously) about something. Awareness is half the battle.

Of course, none of this means that the product is necessarily bad. But awareness of subliminal advertising will help you make conscious, deliberate choices about your purchases, rather than automatically buying something because of the ad's strength of promotion.

# . 196 .

## BE SELF-SUFFICIENT

By "self-sufficient," I don't mean you need to live on a farm, raise all your own food, and work at home (though that's how some people interpret it). By self-sufficient, I mean you're not depending on someone else for your food, your housing, or your income.

Clearly this doesn't apply to minors, college-age kids, or other dependents. For those with physical or mental challenges, obviously your ability to be self-sufficient may be limited. There are times when we all have a streak of bad luck, and need to lean on someone for awhile. No problem.

But for the vast majority of us, it's time we stand on our own two feet. Quit turning to your parents every time you need money. Stop taking checks from the government. Don't assume that someone else will pick up the slack for you.

We knew some people who owned a huge home with a mortgage payment far beyond what they could afford each month. They actually began to appeal to friends and church members to "chip in" to help pay their $3,500 monthly mortgage! Needless to say, people were less than enthusiastic about this request. The couple finally wised up and sold the home, then bought a smaller place they could afford.

J.G. Holland said, "God gives every bird its food but does not throw it into the nest." No one ever said self-sufficiency would be easy. But it does wonders for your peace of mind. One less link in your dependency chain means you're that much closer to the simplicity of financial freedom.

# .197.

## TANSTAAFL

This stands for "There Ain't No Such Thing As A Free Lunch."
You can't get something for nothing. There is *always* a cost.

I recently saw an online ad that told me I could download a
beautiful undersea screensaver for "free." Wow, I thought. How
nice of them. And what a beautiful screensaver! I clicked on the
ad and found that the "only" thing I had to do to download
the screensaver was to provide my email address. Naturally, my
email address (which I prefer to keep private) would then be
sold to untold numbers of buyers, and I would be inundated
with spam. The breach of my privacy was the cost of the "free"
screensaver.

Recognize hidden costs for what they are. What are some
other "free" things we frequently encounter?

Public education is not "free." Teachers must be paid, build-
ings must be built, and books must be bought. None of these
things materialize out of thin air. They are paid for with ever-
increasing taxes.

A "free" toaster when you purchase a new car is not free.
Instead, they build the cost of the toaster into the price of the car.

A "free" puppy might not cost anything to acquire, but of
course you must provide food, shots, and a collar.

This isn't to say that these "free" items aren't worth it. You
may love your local public school, your new car (and toaster),
and the puppy. That's great. My point here is to help you recognize simple economics for what it is: simple.

# .198.

## STOP SPENDING MONEY

Spending money is such a mechanical, instinctive thing. We don't blink an eye to buy a pack of gum, or a latté, or a movie rental. But those nickels and dimes add up, sometimes to extraordinary amounts.

Try an exercise in which you spend no money whatever for two weeks. This may require some preparation (sufficient food in the house, for instance), but whenever you come across an opportunity or a desire to buy something, think instead what a free or low-cost (or homemade) alternative might be.

Do you normally buy a mocha espresso on your morning commute? Think about bringing homemade coffee in a thermos instead. Renting a video for the evening? Read a book. Buying lunch? Brownbag it.

The purpose of this exercise is to become aware of how much we spend, and on what. In *Your Money or Your Life*, Joe Dominguez and Vicki Robin make it clear how we are trading our "life energy" for things that aren't necessary. By eliminating any spending for a couple of weeks, you'll become aware of just what sorts of nonessential things you're spending your life energy on.

As an added bonus to this, trying keeping a small notebook handy, and write down what you were going to spend money on (but didn't), as well as the amount. You might be surprised how quickly it all adds up.

If you're the type who works well with tangible rewards, at the end of this exercise try banking half of the money you saved, then use the rest toward paying off a debt.

# . 199 .

## RECOGNIZE YOUR CONSUMER WEAKNESSES

I am not your typical female. Consumer items over which other women flutter leave me unmoved. Clothes, shoes, jewelry, lingerie, makeup, purses (okay, maybe a little) . . . I can take 'em or leave 'em. And then I slam into my own particular consumer weakness: books.

Books are expensive, in case you hadn't noticed. I could spend a month's salary on books in a matter of hours, with little effort. Even though I rarely buy new books (I find them at yard sales, library sales, thrift stores, etc.), there's always the lure of the Internet. I'll be browsing along and suddenly come across two or three books I just *have* to have.

It's the urgency of the situation, you see. If I don't buy the book *now*, then I'll forget where I've seen it was and will never have the pleasure of reading it. Or someone else might buy it. So I used to whip out the plastic and order up. Obviously this couldn't continue.

One of the factors of living more simply is to understand where your consumer weaknesses are. Do you spend thousands of dollars on electronics? Do you have to have a new car every year? Do you "upgrade" your home (and mortgage) every five years? Do you have to have the latest clothing fashions? Do you buy a new computer every six months? Do you redecorate your home every year?

Learn to control the urges. Then, and only then, will your finances begin to simplify.

# . 200 .

## MAKE A LIST, CHECK IT TWICE

In one of my frequent "duh" moments for my particular brand of consumer weakness (books), I started a list of "Books to Buy Someday." Now, every time I come across an interesting book, I put the title and author (and sometimes the source) on this list.

You might do the same for whatever your consumer weakness is. Shoes? Make notes in a little notepad about the style, brand, price, and location. Don't buy them on the spur of the moment; make a note of it instead. Jewelry? Same. Makeup? Ditto. Tools? Exercise equipment? Sporting goods? You get the picture.

The idea behind this is to avoid the urgent, I-have-to-buy-it-now-or-it-will-be-gone-tomorrow situations. The urge passes once the item is out of your sight. Or, if it doesn't pass, give it a few days or even a month. Whatever it takes, if you want or need it badly enough, let it "cool" for a period of time before buying it.

My list of books is eleven pages long now, and I realize that there are only a few that I would like to outright purchase. The rest I can get through my local library. It's a lot cheaper this way.

Of course, the best way to avoid temptation for your particular consumer weakness is simply to avoid being where those items are sold. If shoes are your weakness, avoid shoe departments. If it's computers, avoid computer stores. Cars? Bypass the car lots. Clothes? Stay away from the mall.

*Voilà.* Simple.

# . 201 .

## AVOID DESIGNER LABELS

Why do we buy the brands that we do? I can think of only two reasons: quality and ego.

In terms of quality, I'll admit that there are certain brands of products whose quality I like, and which I will continue to buy: Crest Toothpaste, Jergens lotion, Ivory soap, Arm & Hammer laundry detergent, Suave shampoo. Everything else we buy is a store brand product. I find no difference in quality—using our criteria—that would cause me to switch to a name brand for anything else.

How about clothes? Shoes? Stereo equipment? Cars? Electronics? Computers? Clearly there are some situations, especially regarding electronics, where quality is a consideration for certain brands. But the vast majority of purchases can be made with generic brands, or (better) bought used, and be just as good.

Anything with a designer label automatically costs money. The higher price does not, for the most part, reflect a higher quality; rather, it reflects the costs of advertising. Advertising is very expensive, and manufacturers spend millions of dollars assuring you, the consumer, that their particular product is better than the competitor's. There's nothing wrong with that. I like a free-market economy. But if you want to simplify your life, understand that what you're paying for is overhead and ego.

Try buying generic or house brands and check out their quality. It could be that all this time you've been over-paying for what is, essentially, the same quality as the name brand.

# . 202 .

## THE EGO OF LABELS

So what's the deal? Why are people, particularly women, so enamored of certain designer labels? Ego, that's why.

Okay, I'll confess: I don't care about clothes. Fashion, style, and other considerations are no longer a part of my life (yippee!) and therefore I couldn't care less what company makes my garments. Besides, I buy 99 percent of my clothes at thrift stores anyway.

But do you think that you are somehow "better" when you walk down the street sporting a designer label? Of course not. If you think that heads turn and people murmur appreciation of your superior taste and fine judgment because you've purchased something that has a label on it, I'm here to tell you otherwise. Most people are not *nearly* as impressed with designer labels as we think they should be. And, if they are, are you satisfied being judged by the brand name of the clothing you wear, rather than who is *in* the clothing?

Get over your ego. Stop feeding the gaping maws of the designer industry. Set your own style. Think for *yourself*, for cryin' out loud.

With few exceptions, I'll bet you can dress entirely appropriately for your job in non-designer labels. No one will think less of you. Or, as I've mentioned before, if they do think less of you, then they're probably too shallow to worry about. Your life will be simpler if you are not a slave to fashion and at the mercy of designers. Try it.

# .203.

## NEEDS VS. WANTS

Money is nice, isn't it? There are few people on this planet who don't think that just a little more money than they currently have would be a nice thing. My husband and I feel the same way. We are, after all, human.

We all work hard at our jobs to make money to buy things. Obviously this is as it should be. We all need food, clothes, shelter, and medicine. But when our immediate needs are met, we delve into the "wants." We put in longer hours to make more money to buy more things. We get a bigger house (and mortgage). We get a nicer car (and car payments). After all, we *deserve* them after working so hard.

I have no objection to people who move up in the world through hard work and sacrifice. But be careful lest at some point the *things* become more important than *people*.

Your longer hours at work mean you'll see less of your family. Your high credit card, mortgage, or car payment debts mean you'll never have peace of mind. In a downturn of the economy, these things become burdens.

Find a happy balance between the *needs* of your family (for your attention and physical presence) vs. your *wants* for the latest whiz-bang expensive whatever. Find a happy balance between making more money and having the free time to nurture your relationships with your family and friends. And don't forget to find some time for yourself in order to decompress.

Simplicity is knowing the balance between your needs and your wants.

# . 204 .

## STOP BEING SLAVES

Slavery is defined as being under subjugation, captivity, or under complete control or ownership. What ugly, ugly words these are. So why do you enslave yourself to creditors?

Yes, enslave. People seldom think of being in debt as being enslaved, but in many respects it is. For the most part it's voluntary, too (unlike real slavery). People swallow the line that more is better, so they dig themselves deeper into debt for stuff.

Remember that quasi-humorous bumper sticker that says "I owe, I owe, so off to work I go"? It's cute until you realize it means you will never be free. Free to cut your hours to spend more time with your family. Free to move elsewhere. Free to retire. Free to follow your dreams. You are chained, shackled, fettered, enslaved. Is this any way to live?

Whenever you think you "need" a new car, bigger house, big screen TV, or a new paint job for the living room, stop and think whether you can pay cash for it, or whether you need to "finance" it. If you need to finance it, you are probably living beyond your means. If you lose your job, you find out just how enslaved you are.

Learn to downscale your wishes and desires for *things* in order to get or stay out of debt. Those who don't owe money on credit cards, student loans, car loans, and other non-secured debt are a rarity in this country. And, oddly, you'll find that those individuals who *are* free from debt do not live an ostentatious or flamboyant lifestyle. Catch a clue here. The freedom of being debt-free is the ultimate in simplicity.

# .205.

## LEARN TO EAT LENTILS

There's an old story that goes something like this: A rich man saw a poor man eating a bowl of lentils. The rich man said, "If you learned to toady to the king, you wouldn't have to eat lentils." The poor man replied, "If you learned to eat lentils, you wouldn't have to toady to the king."

In many ways this is the essence of a simpler life. Learn to be satisfied with simple things, and you will no longer have to toady to what society might define as successful, such as a huge house, fancy cars, and other expensive goods.

Who is wealthier? The family living in the McMansion with two expensive cars in the driveway, five credit cards (maxed out), three kids in daycare, two parents each working sixty-hour weeks, and a standing prescription for ulcer medicine at the local pharmacy, or the family living in a small suburban house in a blue-collar part of town with one ten-year-old car, one credit card (paid in full each month), three kids at home with their mother, and the father working nine-to-five as a bank teller or backhoe operator?

Who is toadying to King Debt? And who is eating lentils? Besides, lentils are good for you. Lots of fiber and all that.

# . 206 .

## SIMPLICITY AND
## YOUR STANDARD OF LIVING

You may have noticed that people who are poor—truly poor—seldom talk about simplifying their lives. That's because simplicity is a concept of the wealthy.

I'm not talking about the money-wealthy, I'm talking about resource-wealthy (as most of us are in this country). Those of us who have roofs over our heads, food in our bellies, and some means of income are wealthy by comparison to many people in this world. Our physical needs are met, and therefore we have the leisure to think about our impact on the environment, society, and our children.

In the book *Gone With the Wind* by Margaret Mitchell, Scarlett makes some interesting observations when she returns to Tara after the fall of Atlanta. She recalls how in the old days (before the war) she had so many complicated problems to think about. There were issues on jealous girls, elegant clothing, hairstyles, and hundreds of other details. Yet now, when it was all gone, " . . . life was so amazingly simple. Now all that mattered was food enough to keep off starvation, clothing enough to prevent freezing, and a roof overhead . . . ." I doubt this is the kind of "simplicity" you want.

The truly poor cannot simplify. Indeed, their lives are very complex. Believe me, it's *not* simple to be dirt poor. Just ask a villager in Bangladesh. People only worry about returning to simplicity if they can afford it.

You can simplify your life without lowering your standard of living. Indeed, you can increase your standard of living, *if you redefine* what your standard of living is.

# .207.

## WHAT GOES AROUND,
## COMES AROUND

Becoming aware of the "leaks" in our finances is very enlightening, and sometimes frightening. It's all too easy to go the other direction and become obsessed with watching pennies and following a budget. You could become a miser and squeeze every penny until it shrieks. However, I believe that part of a simpler life is the joy of giving and sharing and helping.

Helping others doesn't have to be expensive. Indeed, if you have little money to give, then give something else (time, effort, a sympathetic ear, blood, or a good word).

Don't forget to be generous and charitable with your resources. Simplifying your life doesn't mean you have less to give to others. It's quite the reverse, in fact. You'll have more time to help, more money available to assist someone in need, and more energy and interest in charitable causes or situations.

A simple life includes connections with friends, church, and community that provide a cushion during times of need. The day will come when *you* need help. That day comes to everybody. Those most likely to *receive* assistance are those who *gave* assistance. Call it what you want—good karma, less time in purgatory, what goes around comes around—the idea is that generosity in one form or another is appreciated by God.

# . 208 .

## WHAT WOULD YOU DO IF YOU WON THE LOTTERY?

Your answer reveals a lot of who you are. Maybe it's because we rarely play the lottery, but I find myself fascinated by articles about what people do after they win staggering amounts of money. I frequently shake my head because it seems that people seldom spend their new-found riches in a sensible fashion.

Rather than paying off all their debts, paying off their mortgage (or buying a home for cash), and investing a large portion so they can live off the interest for the rest of their life . . . instead the Nouveau Riche start buying expensive racing boats, luxury cars, electronic equipment, fancy vacations, designer clothing, and other things. In some of the more extreme cases, the winners actually raced through the money and were broke within a year or two. It staggers the mind how someone could take the opportunity of a lifetime and blow it.

Naturally my husband and I have asked ourselves what we would do if we won the lottery. We agree that we would purchase (for cash—no mortgage!) a hundred-acre farm with a cozy old farmhouse and build up a beautiful homestead. The rest we would divvy up between investments that would provide income for the rest of our lives, funds for our children, and funds for charitable donations.

So what would *you* do if you won the lottery? If your first impulsive answer was to purchase a bunch of high-end consumer items, then this may reveal your deep desires, and those desires may end up complicating your life, not simplifying it. What'll it be?

# . 209 .

## IT'S NOT A LUXURY,
## IT'S A CHOICE

Did you know that most families where one parent stays at home with their children are *not wealthy?* Yes, really. I know this comes as a shock, but most families with one stay-at-home parent aren't rich. They work their butts off to economize in order to afford it.

For some reason, though, people look at families who have one stay-at-home parent and assume that they have the "luxury" to do that. That's completely wrong. Families who have one stay-at-home parent have put into practice what their priorities are.

Sorry, but you're not going to get a lot of support from me for career-minded parents whose priorities are their jobs rather than their children. If you have kids, it's *your responsibility to raise them*, no matter how enticing that extra paycheck is. So now the question is, how?

There are reams of literature on the details, but some of the basics are: live within your means. Move to an area where housing is cheaper. Work alternating shifts so one parent is always home. Don't accrue debt for luxury purchases (a boat, a second home, a big screen TV, etc.).

C'mon, people . . . these are *your kids*. They *need* you. They don't need luxuries if it means going without mom and dad.

This is not to make light of struggling parents everywhere. I know there are many people who have circumstances beyond their control that force them to work (death of a spouse, medical bills, etc.).

But *don't* dismiss the sacrifices that stay-at-home parents have made as the "luxury" to stay home. It's not luxury, it's sacrifice. And for some parents, it's a sacrifice worth making.

# . 210 .

## THE ECONOMICS OF A
## SECOND INCOME

Many couples claim that it's impossible to get by without two salaries. Yet if both parents work, it's critical to realize how much of the paycheck for the lower salary is consumed by additional expenses.

Daycare is the biggest expense by far, ranging from $3,000 to $14,000 per child per year depending on where you live (nannies, of course, are even more pricy).

And then there is the cost of the commute (especially with gas hovering around $3 a gallon), lunches, work clothes, dry cleaning costs, take-out foods (because you're too tired to cook) and possibly even a housekeeper (because you're too tired to clean). This can add up to many thousands of dollars per year.

Despite additional deductions, a second income can also boost you into a higher tax bracket, so even more of that paycheck is sucked away.

When all this is figured out, the actual net salary from a second income can be pennies on the dollar. When you consider the well-being of your children, and how much simpler your life would be if you raised them to be strong and moral and less affected by peer pressure, then things (hopefully) begin to fall into perspective.

The whole idea of a simple life is the get off the treadmill of spending, debt, and workplace insanities. I truly believe that life is simpler for families with one stay-at-home parent. The children benefit most of all, since children can either make your life a joy, or a living hell. It behooves you to ensure that it's the former and not the latter.

# .211.

## DON'T DIVORCE—IT'S TOO EXPENSIVE

Few things will save you more money than not parting from your spouse. Think of the child support you won't have to pay. Think of the alimony that won't be coming out of your pocket. Think of the attorney's fees and court costs and separate residences and post-divorce counseling for your children and other expenses that won't happen . . . all because you chose to honor your vows and not divorce.

Obviously this won't apply to everyone. Sometimes the marital circumstances become too heinous and the only choice is to get out. But if you're married to an ordinary decent person, *work* on making your marriage happy. Don't *work* on ways to get out of it because you're bored or annoyed or "want to find yourself."

The vast majority of divorces result from dissatisfaction with one's partner, *not* from serious problems such as abuse, addictions, or extra-marital affairs. A few years into marriage, people realize that they're facing a lifetime of the same-old, same old, and they panic and want out.

It's not an easy thing to do, but it's worth working on a marriage rather than dumping it. Divorce is messy, it's complicated, it's expensive, it's devastating, and it's traumatic. Is it worth all these negatives because your "happily ever after" turned out to be bland and monotonous?

So don't divorce. Work on your marriage. Do it for the children. In the long run, it will make your life simpler.

# .212.

## YOUR FINANCES IN A
## DOWN ECONOMY

I know a couple with massive credit card bills and one very modest income. They often pay their bills by maxing out one credit card after another. Yet they give each other lavish birthday and holiday gifts and have every up-to-date computer gadget imaginable. Then the wife will drop $50 or more a month on impulse buys because she "needs" to escape from their financial stress.

A thrifty lifestyle used to be the norm in this country. With credit unavailable or hard to get (and entirely dependent on one's projected ability to pay), people were forced to live within their means. Anything big—a house, a car, an education—was diligently saved for. People seldom knew the lure of instant gratification.

All that has changed. And now the chickens have come home to roost as our country faces economic hardship. That's why financial simplicity can contribute so strongly to peace of mind.

We have enough on our plates to worry about without having to add the worry of massive credit card bills, a massive mortgage, and other massive expenditures. Often the "massives" happen because the nickels and dimes add up: The $5 book from the grocery store three times a month; the $4 daily latté; the lavish (and usually unneeded) gifts for special occasions. Lunches and dinners out. Convenience foods. Movie rentals (or purchases). The list is endless.

Get your finances under control. Yes, it's hard. Yes, it may take years. But learn frugality as a way of life and see how much it simplifies your life.

# Nine-to-Five Simplicity

You spend anywhere from eight to twelve hours a day in your office or on the job, and that doesn't include the commute or the work you take home with you. Whether or not you enjoy your job, it is important that you do everything possible to keep things simple in the workplace. While this can include keeping your desk tidy, simplifying your professional life goes much deeper.

Today the job market is tight and it's not uncommon to be employed one day and looking for work the next. Avoiding bad work habits may be the thing that keeps you on the job, while your former co-worker is handing out résumés.

# .213.

## LEAVING STRESS AT THE OFFICE

Our behavior and attitude at work can influence not only how much we like or dislike our jobs, but it can have a major effect on our stress levels as well. A complex or contentious work environment will also influence our home life. How often do the frustrations and hassles of your job follow you home? How often (intentionally or not) have you "shared the load" with your spouse or children?

This section addresses not only your current job, but it also touches on what you may wish to do for a living beyond your present employment. It includes tips on looking ahead and finding your "right livelihood," to search out work that you may find more satisfying than what you do now.

Nothing says that your current situation must stay this way forever. If you don't like your job, you will find some ideas in this section to assist you in mapping out a future for yourself that will make your life simpler, happier, and more content.

But whatever the future holds as far as your occupation, there are things you can do *now* that will simplify your professional life.

# .214.

## YOU ARE AN INDEPENDENT CONTRACTOR

I'm going to fill you in on one of the least-understood work-related realities out there. However, you probably won't like it because it can destroy one of your most cherished self-pity mechanisms.

You are an independent contractor. When you accept a job, you enter into a voluntary and equal arrangement with another independent contractor (your employer). Both you and your employer have exactly the same goals (to make money). You both have contracted for exactly the same thing (exchanging time and skills for money).

If you understand this, you can put away your feelings of inferiority and anger and resentment about being an "employee." If you feel the arrangement is not equal, then when you have completed your contractual obligations, you have the freedom to seek new employment.

Remember, your employer *is not in business to keep you employed*, he is in business to make money. I recently heard a news story about a company that was laying off workers. These workers intended to sue in order to retain their jobs despite the fact that the company was undergoing financial difficulties. It might be hard to accept the fact that you're getting laid off when the company CEO makes a million dollars a year, but remember: you have no "right" to be employed there, and the employer has every "right" to manage his company as he sees fit. Both of you are independent contractors in exchanging time and skills for money.

Start acting independent and responsible, and see if this simplifies your life.

# .215.

## DON'T DO OFFICE POLITICS

Keep yourself sane at the office by avoiding office politics. You can start by avoiding gossip. Don't start any gossip, don't spread any gossip, and don't receive any gossip (if possible). If any gossip comes your way, zip your lips and don't pass it on.

Smile a lot. Shut your mouth a lot. If you can't say anything nice about someone . . . well, you know the rest.

Office politics thrive through word of mouth. If you hold yourself aloof from gossip, you'll be less involved with the politics, backbiting, character assassinations, and other unpleasantness that can breed whenever a bunch of people are locked together in a building for a large portion of each day.

For some reason people seem unable to simply *do their jobs* without embroiling themselves in what isn't their business. If someone is having a scandal in their personal life, and unless if affects their performance in the office, ignore it.

If someone is having a scandal within the office, you should only get involved insofar as it affects you. If you're the boss, you need to deal with it competently and professionally. If you're not the boss, only deal with it with regards to your own personal job.

Your career may be complex, but you can simplify it as much as possible by not participating in destructive or unethical behavior during the workday. Assisting in the destruction of someone's reputation, whether deserving or not, will complicate your life. Don't do it.

# .216.

## DON'T BACKSTAB

Now, of course if you become aware of a serious breach of ethics or legalities, you should bring it to your supervisor's attention through the standard channels. Don't backstab the person in question through gossip or character assassination.

I recall a situation in an office in which I once worked where an older man was making inappropriate remarks to a very young receptionist. This girl, barely out of high school, was too intimidated to confront him, and finally came to me.

I took my supervisor aside in confidence and reported the matter. The supervisor reprimanded the employee verbally. The employee apologized to both my supervisor and to the receptionist. End of problem.

How much more complex would it have been if I had taken the young receptionist's confidence and spread it all over the office? If we had all gossiped and whispered behind the man's back and chewed over the deliciously nasty recent comment he had made? If we had speculated about what kind of perversions the man was capable of? It could have gotten ugly. *And it would have proved that I wasn't trustworthy* when it came to dealing with office issues.

Sometimes your good intentions of staying out of office politics can backfire. Sometimes, because you're staying aloof, you're the one who becomes the subject of character assassination. It goes without saying, of course, that if your work environment is too toxic, then it's time to find a new job.

# .217.

## KEEP YOUR PROFESSIONALISM

I can think of few things that will knock down your professionalism faster than inappropriate behavior, dress, attitude, or grooming.

The most obvious breach of professionalism is sexual. I'm not only referring to the in-your-face aggressive behavior we can easily picture when the term "sexual harassment" is mentioned, but also the passive behavior that can sexualize a workplace.

This can include clothing that is inappropriate for a professional environment, flirting, innuendo, inappropriate emails or voicemails, and of course the *pièce de résistance*, affairs.

Keep your professional reputation intact by dressing, speaking, and behaving as if the eyes of the whole office are upon you . . . because they are. Anything you do that is out of line, anything at all, will be noted by other employees, gossiped over, stewed over, and you'll be the subject of speculation and character assassination.

Professionalism, of course, extends beyond sexual matters: If you lose your temper, if you smell bad, if you talk too loud or too much, if you gossip or indulge in office politics, if you drag your personal problems to the office, if you dress inappropriately (too sloppy, too casual, too sexy, whatever), if you use office equipment for personal purposes . . . the list goes on, but you get the picture. To act other than professionally will complicate your work environment.

You were hired to do a job, and it makes sense to not allow yourself or your attention to be diverted from achieving that goal. Keep things simple. Keep things professional.

# .218.

## DRESS SIMPLY

Do you hobble down the street in heels that are too high, skirts that are too narrow (or short, or both), weighed down with multiple jangling strands of jewelry? Maybe it's time to simplify. Simple dressing doesn't weigh you down. Streamlining your wardrobe means you have fewer options to fuss over in the mornings.

I recall the time I got my first corporate job after working as a secretary for a number of years. I took all the office clothes out of my closet, laid them on my bed, and decided that I had the wardrobe of a secretary. I was moving up in the world. It was time to dress for success, by golly.

I got my keys and credit cards and prepared to go shopping. However, I stopped and glanced one more time over the clothes laid out on the bed.

Something made me pause and look things over with a fresh eye. *You know, if I got a black velvet blazer* (fashionable at the time), *I could tie in at least six or seven of these pieces and make them look professional. If I bought another blouse or two, I could mix-and-match a lot of other parts of the wardrobe for a more professional look.*

So I went shopping, bought the select few items I felt I needed, and had my wardrobe down pat. It was simple and inexpensive.

Though there are many books available on dressing for success, reducing your wardrobe, streamlining your accessories, and decluttering your closet can go a long way toward making your morning routine simpler.

## LOOK OUTSIDE YOUR PARADIGM

"Paradigm" is one of those absurd 90's Dilbert-style buzz-words that probably should have died by now. Still, the term has its uses. A paradigm, for purposes of definition, is your established way of thinking. It's the way you do things.

To look outside your paradigm is to think outside the box, to look at things with new eyes. This is a technique stressed in the high-tech industries to help develop new products and services. It is also a necessary process for you to simplify your life.

Consider the history of the Swiss watchmakers. For years, the Swiss dominated the watchmaking industry. Their precision gears and stunning craftsmanship were works of art. They were rightly proud of their accomplishments . . . so proud that they refused to heed the news that some Japanese upstarts had the temerity to introduce an electronic watch that ran on batteries and didn't need winding.

The Swiss scoffed at the idea that these Japanese newcomers could actually think that anyone would take them seriously. The Japanese making watches? Never.

The Swiss watchmakers were unable to look outside their paradigm and see that this new concept for making watches could replace the centuries of fine craftsmanship they had achieved and they couldn't grasp the idea that anyone else could come to dominate the watchmaking industry. And now, of course, the Japanese standards for watchmaking have become the norm.

Look outside your paradigm to find ways to simplify your work life. Maybe you should consider some careers that you dismissed because they didn't pay well enough, didn't have enough glamour, didn't have enough respect, or weren't what you were "expected" to do.

# . 220 .

## WHAT DO YOU WANT TO BE
## WHEN YOU GROW UP?

If you were to look outside the box of all the expectations for a "happy" or "successful" life that have been laid on you, what would you find? As a "successful" person, you are often the product of expectations from your parents, your extended family, your teachers, your friends, your spouse, even your children.

Yes, I know you've spent many years becoming educated in your field. You might be something extremely specialized, such as a surgeon or an attorney or an airline pilot. Now pause and ask yourself if these highly respectable occupations leave you fulfilled. Yes? Good! Congratulations.

But if this question made you pause and answer "Hmm," then you need to look outside the box to see what career might fit you better.

It's tough to admit that you may have "wasted" a large number of years training for a profession that no longer makes you happy. However, it's my personal opinion that knowledge, education, and experience are never "wasted," even if you don't work in the field in which you trained. (I should know. I no longer use my graduate degree in biology because I became a stay-at-home mom and a writer instead—and I'm much happier.)

Now look at your hobbies and creative pursuits. What are your passions? How do you spend your spare time?

To do what you truly love as a profession, even if it's a demanding occupation, can bring an element of simplicity to your life because you know you're using your gifts. And getting up every morning eager to use these gifts by doing something that you love beats the alternative.

# . 221 .

## WRITE A "BUSINESS" PLAN

What's your dream? Where would you like to be in five years, ten years, twenty?

We always hear how we're supposed to write business plans for our work, but people don't seem to think about doing this for their lives. Do you want to stay in your current job, current home, and current situation forever? If so, good for you. If not, then it's time to write a business plan.

What would be your dream job? What is necessary to reach that dream? Map it out. Write down goals you can accomplish within six months, a year, two years, five years. Plan this with your spouse if you're married. Be realistic. It does no good to dream of being a prima ballerina if you're forty-five years old and fifty pounds overweight, but it doesn't preclude you from losing the fifty pounds and joining a local dance troop.

The planning is the important part. If you have concrete, visualized, obtainable steps in front of you, very little can prevent you from making strides toward your goals.

Sometimes dreams must be put aside for a time. Sometimes we have aging parents, or a handicapped child, or a severe illness to deal with. Sometimes our dreams have to be revised in accordance with new developments in our life or economic circumstances beyond our control. But that's okay. Nothing says that dreams must be static and unmovable. And sometimes dreams become reality in the strangest ways, so go with the flow.

Life is too short to be bogged down doing things we don't like. A simple life doesn't have to mean an unexciting life. Get busy and dream.

# .222.

## DON'T TAKE LEAPS OF FAITH

Let me amend that: don't take leaps of faith when it affects your family in a negative way. Aesop said, "Look before you leap."

Dave Ramsey, a financial advisor I admire, said, "Leaving one job for another is OK. The idea of deciding you just don't like something, though, and walking away from it when you've got a bunch of bills is just plain irresponsible. You don't jump off the dock until the boat is there."

While sometimes it's fun to be impulsive in life and take a leap of faith, you'd better think about who might suffer first. The time to take leaps of faith is when you're single and have no major obstacles. But when you have a family to consider, those leaps had better be well-planned and well-researched.

You have an obligation to support your children. But that doesn't mean you have an obligation to live in a huge house or drive an expensive car. Millions of people support their children with modest, wholesome, less materialistic lifestyles by doing the work they love.

Refraining from leaps of faith doesn't mean you have to stay in a dead-end job you hate. On the contrary, you are free to contemplate whatever career appeals to you. You just have to plan for it—save money, or go to school at night, or work part-time in the field that attracts you.

But don't risk your security and the safety of your family to follow *your* dream, because doing so could shatter *theirs*.

# . 223 .

## DON'T QUIT YOUR JOB, YET

Does avoiding leaps of faith mean you can't ever quit your job? Of course not. The operative word here is "yet." Rushing into unemployment will not simplify your life. Trust me, I know. We did it, and it was painful. We left our lucrative jobs in California and moved to Oregon with no employment. Desperate, we started a home woodcraft business. Ultimately it was successful for us, but it took a long time to get where we are now.

The key to changing careers, jobs, environments, or anything else, is to go slowly. This ties into writing your "business" plan (#221). Visualize what you want to do with your life, make a plan or roadmap on how to get there, and then start implementing these changes. If you can begin working toward your dream while still employed, your stress level will not be as high. You might go through a busy patch (especially if you need to go back to school, or work evenings or weekends), but unemployment won't contribute to your peace of mind.

Remember, too, that if you have a family, your highest obligation is to them. Your children are dependent upon you; they don't care if you hate your job (I'm assuming you would never be so heinous as to take out job-related frustrations on your spouse or kids). But to rush into unemployment, or to take a risk on a start-up business with no cushion of financial support, is irresponsible and detrimental to your family. No matter how distasteful your job is, at least it provides income. Count your blessings.

Now go plan for the future.

# . 224 .

## LACK OF PREPARATION
## ON YOUR PART . . .

Many years ago I worked as a legal secretary in Sacramento. We constantly needed to file paperwork with the court system in a timely fashion. It was before the days of faxes or email, so we always ran (sometimes literally) to the clerk's office to file the necessary paperwork.

Sometimes we secretaries would arrive, panting, papers clutched to our chests, mere minutes before the clerk's office closed . . . only to find a line of other secretaries in the same frazzled state. Unhurried, the clerks would use the automatic date-stamper on the paperwork until the clock hit 5 pm. Then they would close their windows regardless of who was left in line.

They didn't close their windows to be cruel (or so they said). They closed their windows because anything that was automatically date-stamped at 5:01 pm or later was considered late and therefore unacceptable to the court system. A small sign above the clerks' heads explained their philosophy: "Lack of Preparation on Your Part Does Not Constitute an Emergency on My Part." It was stressful, but after a couple of near-misses I learned to get my paperwork done in time.

The clerks worked in an unhurried manner because they *weren't* in a hurry. It wasn't *their* fault that *we* were running behind. Their jobs were stressful enough without having desperate legal secretaries demanding service beyond what the clerks were required to do.

Keep this in mind for your job. No one else is responsible for your lateness, your sloppiness, or whatever other issues you may have.

# . 225 .

## WHAT'S IMPORTANT TO YOU IS NOT AS IMPORTANT TO OTHERS

Realizing and accepting that your agenda may not match anyone else's can help simplify your job.

When we were selling our house in Oregon a few years ago, we made an appointment with a realtor. We waited and waited and waited for the realtor to show up for his appointment, growing more annoyed. He never came, and he was unreachable through his office or cell phone. Disgusted, we decided to call another agent.

The realtor contacted us the following morning and apologized. He explained that his son had a bicycle accident in which he broke his arm. The realtor had forgotten our appointment because, distraught, he was rushing his son to the emergency room. Our appointment (agenda) was not as important to the realtor as his son.

This past winter here in north Idaho was rough. We've had huge amounts of snow and frequent road closures do to white-out conditions. A neighbor who commutes to the city for her job was forced to use a large number of vacation days because she couldn't get to work. While this might seem unfair, her boss pointed out that it's not *his* fault she chose to get a job so far away from her home. He expected her to be available to do her work, and beyond a certain point she was compelled to use her vacation days for the times she was unable to show up. While our neighbor didn't necessarily *like* that decision, she was forced to admit her boss was right.

Remembering both sides of this issue can simplify your life as you realize that your agenda doesn't match anyone else's. Welcome to reality.

# . 226 .

## IMPROVE YOUR WORK ETHIC

Does it ever drive you nuts at work when people don't do their share and somehow you end up stuck with the extra? It's frustrating and unethical. People are paid to do a job. But people are also lazy. When these two conflicting factors collide, the result is that some people try to skate through their workday by doing as little as possible. Employers hate that. But . . . are *you* guilty of it, too?

The mere act of improving your work ethic—showing up on time, paying attention to details, fulfilling your job requirements, having a good attitude, and not getting involved in office politics—will set you miles above the competition.

My first job after high school was working in a fast food restaurant. My mother always told me, "Be dependable. Get to work on time and work hard." It didn't matter that it was "merely" a minimum wage job. It didn't matter that it was temporary. It didn't matter that I was leaving in three months to go to college. The point was that a job worth getting was a job worth doing well, which meant approaching it with a high work ethic. Later, my boss gave me a good reference when it came time to apply for another job, and I was able to start building a work history and résumé.

That kind of work ethic can translate into all aspects of your life—volunteer work, family responsibilities, and church obligations.

Be different. Improve your work ethic. Do your job. It may not be "simpler" but it is the ethical thing to do, and being ethical can bring satisfaction and peace of mind. In this day and age, it can also mean the difference between remaining employed and looking for work.

# .227.

## KEEP THE CLUTTER DOWN

What is your impression of a cubicle with papers shoved everywhere, piles on the floor, three dirty coffee cups (and a dried-up spill on the carpet), and an overflowing garbage can? Do you get the impression that the employee is professional and organized? Of course not.

You might be the most disorganized person on the planet, but it is important to make an effort to be tidy at the office. A neat desk, cubicle, or other workspace will improve your reputation. A messy work environment does the opposite because it is assumed that a sloppy desk translates into a sloppy work ethic or a sloppy job performance.

Your workstation should contain only the things you need for your job (with some exceptions—I'm sure everyone has a potted plant or a photo of their kids). But when you start dragging in plaques with cutesy slogans or accumulating dirty coffee cups or shoving the remains of take-out lunches in corners, then your reputation suffers, as does your productivity ("Where's that memo? *Where is it?*").

Don't try to pass off the ol' "A messy desk is a sign of genius" routine, either. And yes, I've known people who have accomplished amazing things in the midst of a chaotic workstation. However, unless your boss is remarkably understanding, you will find yourself less likely to be considered for a promotion, asked less for your opinions, and dismissed as disorganized.

By simply cleaning up your workstation, you accomplish far more than just a tidy desk. It is a simple way to improve your reputation as well.

# . 228 .

## LEAVE EARLIER

No, I don't mean leave your job earlier. I mean leave your house earlier so you can get to work on time. There are few excuses for rushing in the morning if you plan appropriately.

If traffic is an issue in getting to your job, add a margin of error into your morning routine. Arriving late due to commuting woes leaves you frazzled, breathless, and in a poor frame of mind. An extra five or ten minutes can make a huge difference in how efficient your commute is.

Many people shave their morning routine into ever-slimmer margins. Maybe they're hoping to get some more sleep, maybe they've got the chaos of getting kids ready for school. Whatever the issue, they're already late by the time they jump into their car or catch the bus. But this is unacceptable. You have an obligation to your employer who not only pays you for your time, but also needs you there so that he won't fail in *his* obligations to customers or clients.

If you have children, rushing your morning routine and being chronically stressed and late fails in your obligation to them as well. They are less prepared for school, they are stressed by your frantic dashing, and they get a poor model of the importance of meeting commitments.

Leaving earlier for work is a simple thing to do, and it will improve your outlook for the day . . . *and* that of your family.

# . 229 .

## ORGANIZE YOUR MORNING

Of course, leaving for work earlier will do no good if you don't improve your morning routine so you can get out the door in time.

It never fails to amaze me how many people feel they "must" snatch those few extra minutes of sleep. They finally roll out of bed fifteen minutes after their alarm rings, which then messes up their whole morning's schedule. Then they have to dash through feeding the kids, shove them on the school bus, rush to the car, and speed through traffic, only to arrive late.

For crying out loud, *get up earlier*. Thirty extra minutes may not make a big difference in how much sleep you get, but it could make a *huge* difference in how relaxed your morning routine is. Those extra thirty minutes may allow you enough time to pack the kids' lunches, briefly tidy the house, allow your children time for breakfast, and maybe even give you the opportunity for a quiet cup of coffee with your spouse before you head out the door.

Of course the corollary to getting up a bit earlier is to go to bed a bit earlier. The vast majority of people who stay up late do so to watch television, claiming it's their only "relaxing" time.

Is it worth "relaxing" by staying up until midnight only to start the next day in a frantic, frazzled rush to get out the door? Forego the late-night activities and hit the hay instead.

# . 230 .

## BE ON TIME

Don't be late. I'm not talking about the occasional traffic accident that snarls your normal routine. I'm talking about chronic, constant lateness. This single, simple factor will increase the respect from your boss.

You are paid to do a job, which means you are contractually obliged to show up when required. Your honor and reputation are tied to keeping the obligations that you accept. Chronic lateness is interpreted as sloppy and unorganized. Timeliness, on the other hand, is seen as having a high work ethic.

When my husband and I first started our business, we hired a temporary worker to help in the shop. Fred was a little slow in some regards—he was no mental giant—but the man had a work ethic that amazed us. In the two years we employed him, he was late once—once!—by five minutes, and he apologized over and over again for that blunder. He would barely take fifteen minutes for lunch (though he was allowed an hour). And he wouldn't stop work until the clock hit 5 p.m., not one minute earlier.

Fred eventually went on to a different job, but his work ethic so impressed us that when it came time to hire someone else, we told the temp agency, "If the new person can't be here on time, tell him not to bother coming." We were paying someone to work a certain number of hours, and had no patience for those who didn't take that commitment seriously.

Being on time is a simple and startlingly effective way to demonstrate your work ethic. Try it sometime and dazzle your boss.

# . 231 .

## BE RESPONSIBLE

Employers depend on their employees to be responsible, mature adults in the workplace, and you (as an independent contractor) are obliged to provide those attributes of responsibility and maturity. You also have every reason to expect those attributes in return from the independent contractor you are working for.

For purposes of definition, by "independent contractor" I mean you are free to voluntarily accept employment or not (see #214). You are under no obligation to take a job. However, once you do, then you have an obligation to perform that job for your boss. And when I refer to your boss as an independent contractor, I mean that he is under no obligation to hire you. If you fail in your duties, he has every reason to fire you. That's the real world.

When working for someone else, some of your responsibilities include: Dress appropriately. Maintain a professional attitude that won't embarrass your employer. Don't badmouth your company, the boss, or your fellow independent contractors (coworkers). If you have a problem, follow the approved channels to resolve it. If that doesn't work, leave and find another job.

You are responsible to honor the contract that you agreed to by giving your time and best efforts in exchange for pay. Being petty, vindictive, rude, late, and lazy are not professional attributes. Blaming others for your unfinished projects won't garner any respect from your boss. Believe me, being professional and sticking to your agreements will simplify your work life.

# .232.

## ANY JOB WORTH DOING IS WORTH DOING WELL

Do you hate your job? Well, too bad. Unless you are prepared to quit (and that is, given the current economic climate, something to consider *carefully* before doing), you are required to perform your work in the manner which is expected. So cut out the snarky attitude. Stop thinking you're too lofty and above doing something. Take pride in doing your job well, even if you hate it.

Plus, if you don't like your current employment, nothing is preventing you from searching for a better job during your spare time. But for the moment, on *this* job, do it well.

It's funny how performing well at work, regardless of how much you "like" it, can have long-term effects. This can range from a good recommendation from your current employer to skills you may have picked up that are beneficial on your next job.

And people appreciate a good attitude. I remember the garbage collector at our old home in Oregon. He was always smiling, always cheerful, and he always had a nice word to say. One day when I was nine months pregnant, I was late in bringing up the trash can. Seeing me lugging the can up our steep driveway, he jumped out of his cab, grabbed the can, and took care of it. I thanked him and promptly went into the house to call his supervisor. Anyone who can collect garbage with such aplomb and helpfulness deserved a good word.

When you can take pride in your high work ethic, your attitude improves—and a good attitude is necessary for a simpler life.

# .233.

## IDENTIFY WHAT YOU LIKE BEST

What aspect of your job do you enjoy the most? Is it the computer skills you're honing? Is it the interaction with customers? Is it the lack of interaction with others? (Some people work best alone.) Is it answering the phones? Is it troubleshooting?

Finding what part you like best can help you focus on a possible career change. For example, I worked for many years as a projects coordinator for an agricultural tech firm. My college major was zoology, so this job was not in my field of study (though otherwise it was a fine job). A very minor side aspect was assembling a monthly newsletter, for which I taught myself desktop publishing. To my surprise, desktop publishing became a cherished skill that I have carried with me into a myriad of different jobs, both professional and freelance.

My husband, who worked as an environmental engineer, took a woodworking hobby and turned it into a business that has supported us for the past eighteen years and allowed us to simplify our lives.

I know someone with superb needlework skills. She has started a specialized business providing beautifully sewn and embroidered vestments for clergy.

If you love working with people, then a sales job or a marketing job might be an excellent match. If you hate working with people, then consider what kind of employment will provide a solitary work experience.

When a job matches your personality, your life is simpler because you can look forward to work instead of dreading it.

# .234.

## LET COMPETITION BRING OUT
## THE BEST, NOT THE WORST

All of nature is competitive, and humans are no exception. We compete for everything: jobs, promotions, salaries, sales, in industry and sports. Competition is not only ingrained, it's critical for improvement in business, sports, and manufacturing. It provides a means where (usually) the best person or product wins.

Competition can also bring out a truly ugly side to people. In your efforts to win, you crush everyone in your path. You undermine others. You backstab. You sabotage. You lie. And God forbid that after all that effort, you *lose* that promotion or pay raise or new position. Then you are bitter, you sulk and pout and mutter about retribution and unfairness. You might even think about suing.

Once, while working as a legal secretary, we needed to hire some additional office help. One candidate stood out negatively because of her startling inability to type a letter or answer phones. For several days after the interview, she called four times a day to check if she was hired. When we finally told her we had selected someone else, she blew up and threatened to sue us because we didn't hire *her*.

C'mon, folks, lighten up. How you handle competition can show you to be a truly decent person, or a jerk. Think how much we admire the gracious winner . . . *and* the gracious loser.

A balanced, respectable approach toward competition is easier on your health (blood pressure and heart stress levels). Bring some simplicity to your workplace by treating competition fairly, courteously, and morally.

# . 235 .

## MANAGE YOURSELF

It doesn't matter how much you're supervised, it is your responsibility to manage *yourself* in the workplace. And it begins with the professional impression you create. You're responsible for your own appearance. Don't dress in anything high-cut, low-cut, or see-through. Don't smell bad. Don't be sloppy. Be clean, neat, and professional. Arrive on time. Don't leave early.

Your boss can't look over your shoulder every second of the day, so don't develop the attitude that you can do something inappropriate when he's not looking. Don't get me wrong, I'm not concerned with the occasional personal phone call or e-mail (though if your boss *is*, then behave yourself), but don't think that because the boss is away for the day you can put your feet up and relax.

In fact, supervisors are likely to be *more* impressed by what you accomplish in their absence than in their presence. Imagine the satisfaction of finishing a project without your micromanaging boss directing your every step. What a nice feeling to plop that report on his desk when he returns from vacation.

No matter how intensely supervised a position is, your boss will be impressed if you can perform like the professional you are. Your workplace situation can simplify if you develop a reputation for being responsible.

Besides, honing the skills of self-management can pay off later if you ever decide to start your own business or work from home, which many simplicity-seekers ultimately decide to do. If you can't supervise yourself, your work-at-home dreams are dashed from the start.

# . 236 .

## CHANGE YOUR HABITS

Somewhere I read that if you can do something for four weeks, it will become a habit. Whether it's the habit of arriving at the office on time, or keeping your workplace clean and decluttered, or turning in your reports by the deadline, or keeping a lid on your temper, whatever habit you have that has become detrimental in the workplace, change it.

Change is never easy, but it's doable. A groove is merely a path that you've worn down from constantly following the same route. Once you get out of the rut, so to speak, change becomes easier.

Change can even become self-feeding. You will receive praise or other rewards for your new and improved ways, which gives you the impetus to continue the new habit. The feedback loop helps cement the new behavior.

As painful as it is, it might be smart to sit down quietly with your boss and ask for honest feedback about whatever bad habits you might have. You might be surprised at the response. Perhaps someone has mentioned that your perfume is too strong. Or that your breath smells bad. Or you blame others when something goes wrong. Or you micromanage your staff. Or you swear too much.

Whatever the habit, take the advice to heart and work on changing it. Author Stephen Covey said, "Our character is basically a composite of our habits. Because they are consistent, often unconscious patterns, they constantly, daily express our character."

What kind of character do you want to convey? Good habits are simplifying, whether it's in the workplace or the home.

# . 237 .

## STEP OUT OF
## YOUR COMFORT ZONE

When I was fresh out of college, I worked for a few years as a legal secretary (not my field of study, but hey, I needed a job). The work was well within my comfort zone so I was fine. I was learning to be an adult in the working world.

But it gradually dawned on me that I had a problem with social situations. It was hard for me to meet new people. Anywhere that people didn't know each other but were expected to be social filled me with dread. Whenever I was thrust into these situations, even in something as mild as attending my husband's office Christmas party, I felt awkward and socially inept and clumsy (and still do.)

This wasn't a problem until I got a more professional job in which social networking was expected. I couldn't be a wallflower any more. It was tough, but I forced myself to stop propping up the wall and walk up to perfect strangers. I'd stick out my hand, introduce myself, and ask what they did for a living.

Yes, I made blunders—lots of them—but I also learned that other people are a *lot* less concerned about your blunders than you are yourself. It became easier to network (though I still don't particularly enjoy it).

So step out of your comfort zone and try something new. Only by doing this can you grow and learn and expand. Trying new things will help clarify (and even stretch) your limits. And honest self-knowledge is important in figuring out how to simplify your life.

# . 238 .

## GET ORGANIZED

Organization in the workplace starts at home (see #229, Organize Your Morning) and carries into the office. An organized person finds what he needs, when he needs it. He isn't late to meetings because he knows where the necessary files, paperwork, or contact information is located. He finishes his projects on time because he knows where all the component parts are.

That sounds nice, doesn't it?

Organizational professionals abound, so if you're completely disorganized at work you may need to call in the pros. But you might start by literally cleaning off your work surfaces and only putting back what you actively need and use. Talk to an organized coworker and ask his or her secret.

Remember, ultimately you are a business. The work you receive, and the jobs you get, are the result of your past performance and your potential customers' impressions of you. Even if you're working as a team—say, assembling hamburgers at a fast-food restaurant—then your precision and accuracy and mental organization will improve your job performance.

Like any number of other factors, your ability to be organized will draw positive notice from your supervisors, especially since it will almost automatically follow that your productivity will increase. Organization includes such actions as not postponing decisions, attending to paperwork in a timely fashion, and improving your time management.

If you're spending eight to ten hours per day (or more) at your job, it behooves you to make it as simple to perform as possible. Organization is a good place to start.

# . 239 .

## BACK UP YOUR COMPUTER

Why do you wear your seat belt? Why do you have smoke detectors in your home? Why do you vaccinate your children? These are all safeguards against accidents and diseases. So why won't you back up your computer?

In April 2007, my computer just up and died. Just bam, it was gone. Zip, zero, nada, a blank screen. Well, crud. All my writing, all my emails, all my desktop publishing projects . . . gone. *Or was it?*

You see, I had done a full-scale backup two weeks earlier. And, by the grace of God, I had backed up my most recent writing *the night before* my computer crashed. Result: my losses were minimal. If I had lost all my writing, I would be shattered. So would you if you were to lose your family photos, files, music videos, e-mails, and other personal documents.

Ever since, I've become fanatic about the subject of backing up computers. My father, a retired engineer, is sympathetic when I tell him how infrequently people back up. "Yes, and no matter how many times you tell them, they still won't do it," he warned.

External hard drives can be purchased for a fairly cheap price these days. Every Friday during your lunch hour, set your computer to back up. Before you go to bed at night, use one of those little flash drives to back up your most recent files. The next time your computer crashes—not if, but *when*—you won't lose much. Let's prove my father wrong, shall we?

# . 240 .

## LEARN TO HANDLE A DIFFICULT BOSS

If your boss is difficult to get along with, you have two choices: you can leave the company, or you can learn to live with it. And one of the most important things you can do to "live with it" is to not lose your cool. If he screams at you, don't scream back. If he is sarcastic with you, keep a lid on your own sarcasm. This is hard, I know! But maintaining your professional demeanor can't hurt. Certainly blowing your top will *not* improve things.

Another difficult concept is to not take things personally. My brother once had a hot-tempered boss who literally yelled and screamed at his employees (the employees stayed on the job because the pay was extraordinary). My brother came to realize that screaming was this man's management style and didn't take it personally. Once he learned that his boss didn't have it "out" for him, he was able to perform his job without losing his cool or getting defensive or blowing his top.

It helps if you can develop a stress outlet as well (which should *not* include smoking, drinking, drugs, shopping, or taking things out on your coworkers or family). Physical exercise is one of the best ways to combat stress, so try walking or jogging on your lunch hour.

Obviously it might come to the point where the stress level isn't worth it, in which case, you should seek a new job. But until you do, at least knowing that your boss (probably) doesn't have it out for *you personally* may help you cope.

# .241.

## DITCH THE EDUCATIONAL SNOBBERY

A drawback of immersing yourself in a high-powered career is that you associate almost exclusively with people of your own educational level. Most of the time, doctors and lawyers don't socialize with car mechanics and backhoe operators. Unfortunately this can translate into educational snobbery—the attitude that you are superior because you achieved a higher level of education.

When we were searching for our Idaho home, I spent many days in the company of a charming realtor. During the long hours in the car, she told me how she put her husband through law school, only to have him dump her after he passed the Bar Exam because—are you ready for this?—she was not of his educational level. While this may just have been his excuse so he could bed some hot young babe, it was a low blow nonetheless. She began to think of herself as inferior because she never went to college, regardless of her considerable success as a realtor.

One of the advantages of downscaling your life is that you are more likely to meet people of all educational levels. Those who have successfully simplified or those whose lives were never complex to begin with often have vast reservoirs of knowledge, creativity, and experience. I stand in awe of my neighbors' ability to make soap, fix tractors, and live cheap. They didn't go to school for this; they learned it "on the job."

So don't be snobby about your fancy degrees. In the end, they may not mean a whole lot when you simplify.

# . 242 .

## YOUR PROFESSIONAL LIFE IN
## A DOWN ECONOMY

If ever there was a time to put multiple irons in the fire, it's now. During hard times, people who are the most employable are those who are generalists, not specialists. If you're faced with unemployment, don't obsess with finding a job in your own field if you know you're capable of working somewhere else. Can you bartend while you're looking for another job as a computer programmer? Can you drive a truck while looking for another job as a hospital administrator? Can you work in a grocery store while you're looking for another job as a civil engineer?

Consider finding a part-time job using any extra talents you may have. Two or three part-time jobs may be able to approach the income you had from one full-time job. And frankly, a lot of irons in the fire mean that if you lose one job, at least you have other resources to fall back on. You've heard the term "Don't put all your eggs in one basket." Consider applying that wisdom to your employment opportunities.

And last but by NO means least, *don't quit your job.* In our current economy, it's an employer's market, not a job-seeker's market. If you want to leave your job, don't do it unless you are absolutely positive you have another secure job lined up.

# It's Easy Being Green

▼

G reen living is a popular topic these days. What-ever your political views on saving the earth, going green can also save your pocketbook if it's done intelligently. Unlike many of the "green gurus" who are trying to save the earth by selling you things you don't need, simplifying your life will automati-cally make you an environmental expert.

# . 243 .

## WHAT IS GREEN?

It's sometimes hard to distinguish between a green lifestyle and a simple lifestyle. The two are entwined to an amazing extent . . . but often not for the reasons you think.

In our rural area, most people do things that are considered "green"—they buy in bulk, they carpool on their trips to town, they don't use many disposables, they minimize their garbage, they compost, they garden, they don't use clothes dryers. Many have no mortgages.

These people have been doing this long before it became fashionable to save the earth. They do it for very practical reasons—it decreases their expenditures and increases their independence. *And* it protects them during periods of economic depression.

Not one of them puts saving the earth at the top of their list. Not one of them is overly concerned about environmental consciousness. Does this make them any less "green"? Of course not, and if you argue to the contrary, then you're supporting only the "talk" and not the "walk."

If your belief is that it's impossible to be environmentally conscious without supporting the extreme Left's socialistic philosophy, then you're mistaken. Some of the greenest people in this country are those with a fierce love of independence and a wish to be left alone.

Good stewardship of the earth just makes sense, but by looking at green issues through the lens of intelligence rather than blind worship or political power-grabbing, people can make sound choices that protect the environment, *without* a lot of hype that can lead to dangerous and socialistic trends. And ultimately, it leads to a simpler life.

# .244.

## SUPPORT GREEN LIVING, NOT THE GREEN MOVEMENT

We are urged to consider the sustainability and impact of our choices in order to think "green." I find this to be a high calling, one worthy of everyone's attention.

I support green living. I try to live by the principles of green living. It's all so sensible—and simplifying. However, I do *not* support the green *political movement* because these activists are using "green" to advance Socialism. And Socialism, as any student of history will tell you, *does not make anyone's life simple.* Socialism takes away independence. Sustainability increases independence. Which makes more sense to you?

Columnist Rebecca Hagelin writes, "If you let people control their own destinies, there's no limit to what they can achieve. But if you bind them with the straitjacket of central planning, smother their creativity with over-regulation, fence them in with high tariffs and take their hard-earned money with high taxes, you kill their dreams *even as you wreck an economy.*" [Emphasis added.]

But the march toward Socialism is subtle, and prettily wrapped up in 100 percent recycled green wrapping paper. After all, as commentator Walter Williams points out, there's less resistance if liberty is taken away a little at a time. This year, light bulbs. Next year, temperature controls in your house. After that . . . who knows?

History has demonstrated the destructive results of Socialism. Become green and independent, not part of a collectivist society. Think for yourself. Only then will your life simplify, unless, of course, you prefer the simplicity of no longer having any choices at all.

# .245.

## DO I NEED IT OR DO I WANT IT?

I frequently use the terms "need" or "necessary" in this book, and contrast the term with "wants." I do so to make a clear distinction between things of value to you and your family versus things that provide no concrete benefit or may even be detrimental to the goal of simplifying your life.

It's pretty obvious that we all need food, clothing, shelter, employment, and medical care. Quite literally, everything else in life is a "want."

But unless you're an ascetic who eschews all modern comforts and conveniences, most of our "wants" quickly become "needs." I can say that I "need" my laptop computer for my job as a writer, for example. But could I write with a pen and paper? Of course. However, it would take a lot longer and be a lot more difficult (if not impossible) to convince an editor to read my hand-written stuff. In that regard, my "want" (a laptop) is a "need" (to sell my writing).

Nor do I suggest that you should live in an undecorated shack with four chairs, a table, and little else. I don't believe it is at odds with a simple life to have some luxuries, assuming you can afford them. In our house, the walls are covered in prints (thrift store finds), shelves upon shelves of books (library sales), and recycled stereo equipment (yard sales). These things are "necessary" because they give us pleasure and enrich our lives.

The secret, I believe, is balance. Does an item actively contribute to enjoyment or will it keep your life simple? It's a question worth examining.

# . 246 .

## BE FRUGAL

How better to be "green" than to avoid overconsumption of resources? A frugal lifestyle will reduce your consumerism. Consider it a great compliment if someone calls you a tightwad. In fact, if you're the type who feels that purchasing anything used or second-hand is beneath you, you're going to have a harder time simplifying your life.

Frugality was something my husband and I were forced into early in our marriage. We had left our lucrative jobs in California and moved to Oregon, where I started graduate school in Environmental Education and my husband started our home woodcraft business. For a long time we had no income. None whatever. We lived on some modest savings until I found part-time work and my husband was able to sell some of our products.

To say our finances were shaky is a massive, enormous, colossal understatement. We scraped, literally scraped, for money. There's nothing like unemployment (coupled with a strong streak of independence) to make you examine every expenditure to see if it's necessary.

I was forced to become a student of thrift, but it wasn't until I read Amy Dacyczyn's *Tightwad Gazette* books that I realized that thrift could be a "viable alternative lifestyle." Here was a woman—with six kids, no less—who practiced the ultimate in voluntary simplicity, as a means to an end.

Frugality, like anything else, is a learned art. It takes some adjustments, both of habits and ego, but the results are incredibly simplifying. I estimate we spend less than ten cents on the dollar to what others buy new. It's rather fun to look through our house and see how much was purchased second-hand at a fraction of the retail cost.

# . 247 .

## THE FREEDOM OF THRIFT

One extra side-benefit I hadn't expected when I learned how to be frugal is the freedom it provided. I learned to stop "fighting" my frugality and instead embraced it. I even started taking pride in it.

When we first moved to Oregon without employment, we were forced into frugality whether we liked it or not. Our schedule was so busy that we didn't have the time or inclination to wander through the mall and marvel at our deprivation. After awhile, thrift became second nature.

Being thrifty is very freeing. No longer did I need to feel guilty for not, say, lavishing Christmas presents on extended family members. Unashamedly, cheerfully, I'd bake cookies or cheesecakes, and these became our gifts. Believe me, I have yet to have a friend or relative turn their nose up at three dozen homemade shortbread cookies, a fresh cheesecake, or two quarts of applesauce from our own trees. I no longer felt compelled to keep up with the Joneses.

Being frugal is fun, it's challenging, it's good for your finances and the environment, and it's good for your kids. Rather than being defensive, take pride in it. If you have an overwhelming urge to compete with the Joneses, do so by beating them in how little money you spend. When you can furnish a home, purchase stylish clothing, and feed your family healthy dinners for less than the Joneses spend on frozen pizzas every month, congratulate yourself.

# .248.

## "PRE"-CYCLE

Recycling is a worthy and correct endeavor. But those who are trying to simplify might consider going a step further: *pre*-cycle.

Pre-cycling is simply considering the "re-cycle-ability" or usefulness of something prior to purchasing. Usually this results in the item not being purchased after all, which saves you money, too. Do you really *need* a blue-satin nignog, or are you merely succumbing to the lure of advertising? Is the nignog something that you or your family will truly use and enjoy? If not, skip it.

When I was a young adult, my cousin and I had a "girl's day out" in San Francisco. We came across a street vendor who was selling Alpaca rugs. Alpaca, in case you don't know, have some amazingly soft, beautiful fur. Giddy with excitement of a day in the city, we each bought one.

Well, that gorgeous rug hung around for *years*. My cousin uses hers, but the only thing I used my rug for was to serve as a prop to photograph our girls bare side up when they were infants. Finally, after two decades of pushing and storing and having this rug taking up close space, we sold it.

I should never have bought it to start with. If I'd known about pre-cycling back then, I wouldn't have. Ah well, live and learn. Now someone else is getting some use out of it.

# . 249 .

## SHOP THRIFT STORES

For those who love to shop, you could do worse than thrift stores. For instance, we tend to favor the big oversized rural landscape prints in gilded frames that were popular in the 1950s. We sure as heck aren't going to find them at Macy's, so every time we visit a second-hand store, the first place we search is their pictures department.

Sure, you are unlikely to find designer furnishings at a thrift store. But who cares? Who wants stuff just like everyone else's?

You'd be amazed what you can find. We've found furniture, household furnishings, dishes, kitchen implements, bath towels (do your towels *have* to be the same color?), sheets, sporting equipment, books, lamps, bikes, backpacks, dufflebags, toys . . . the list goes on and on.

And clothes, of course. With the exception of socks and underwear, we buy 99 percent of our clothes second-hand. Don't turn up your nose; a well-stocked thrift store has a stylish, handsome assortment of all the clothes your family will ever need.

I once saw an extremely chic woman in the grocery store. She was a professional who had obviously just gotten off work and she was wearing a skirt that I positively drooled over. I asked her where she'd gotten it. She leaned close, smiled, and said, "Goodwill. I buy all my clothes at Goodwill."

Trust me: no one but you will ever know where you bought your clothes. Besides, it's a great way to help save the planet. It's the ultimate in recycling.

# . 250 .

## SOME BENEFITS OF SECOND-HAND

Lack of packaging. Ever see those toys that are wired to the package with forty-eight twist-ties, as well as sharp-edged plastic shells that can only be blasted off with dynamite? Well, the good news about buying used is that packaging is seldom an issue. Bring your own bags and it's not an issue at all.

Variety. Fabulous variety. It's like a treasure hunt—you never know what things you'll find. If you're on the "lookout" for an item, give it a few months and you'll doubtless find exactly what you need. I needed a couple of sturdy wicker laundry baskets once, and within three weeks I had them. It's the same with furniture.

Necessities are cheap. If you are perpetually on a budget like we are, this is an important factor. When winter comes, we all troop to the thrift stores to stock up on winter boots, coats, snow pants, and other things the kids have outgrown. We restock our supply of hats, gloves, mittens, and scarves. Come summer, we reverse our purchases and stock up on shorts, T-shirts, bathing suits, sneakers, and anything else kids seem to outgrow overnight.

Because of the low prices, we can often indulge in things that we would seldom purchase otherwise because the cost of new items is too high. Nearly every time I go through the register at our favorite thrift store with mountains of clothing and other items for a grand total of twenty bucks, I marvel to the clerks why *anyone* would shop anywhere else.

# . 251 .

## DON'T DIVORCE—IT'S BAD FOR
## THE ENVIRONMENT

In December 2007, news hit the media about how bad divorce is for the environment. Yes, really. It was a serious study and, in my opinion, deserves serious consideration because no one had (apparently) thought of it before.

Divorced couples go their separate ways and establish two separate households. Two homes. Two sets of washers and driers. Two microwaves. Two dishwashers. Two hot water heaters. Two times the amount of electricity. You get the idea. Naturally all this extra consumption can't be good for the environment . . . and oh yeah, it isn't exactly a bed of roses for your kids either.

Jianguo Liu, an ecologist at Michigan State University, analyzed the environmental impact of divorce. "A married household actually uses resources more efficiently than a divorced household," he said.

Dr. Liu said people seem surprised by his findings at first, and then consider it simple. "A lot of things become simple after the research is done," he said. He adds, "People have been talking about how to protect the environment and combat climate change, but divorce is an overlooked factor that needs to be considered."

Most people don't marry badly. They marry decent, ordinary, flawed human beings and then forget to "treat kindly" (#50). But divorce is one of the most complicating things you can do in your life. The impact on children can be even worse. And now we have word that divorce is bad for the environment, too.

Sounds like a no-brainer to me. Stay married. Work hard to keep your spouse happy. Keep your life simple.

# . 252 .

## DON'T BE TAKEN IN BY IMMEDIACY

A responsible citizen looks intelligently at environmental issues before deciding what kind of action to take. The trouble starts when our politically charged media begins to shout "Fire!" in a crowded theater. There is a stampede, and people get hurt.

What often results is legislation to "fix" a problem, and this legislation is usually poorly thought out (such as banning incandescent light bulbs in favor of compact fluorescent bulbs, which many people feel to be dangerous due to the mercury content).

Every day the media is littering the airwaves with news of environmental "emergencies." And many people are quick to swallow the news without truly considering whether or not the issue is truly an emergency. They applaud government intervention in the form of additional regulations or outright bans without considering whether the solution is better than the problem.

While it's annoying to have government-backed regulations controlling our options, it all starts because people listen to the hype rather than taking the time to think things through in a rational manner. For some reason, environmental issues seem to be very susceptible to this illogical application of hype rather than sense, resulting in complicated new requirements and excessive taxation on issues that may not have been all that important in the first place.

# . 253 .

## GET ORGANIZED

Entire industries have sprung up in the past decade dedicated to helping people get organized. Now we have consultants, television shows, Websites, and store chains selling every conceivable organizing gizmo . . . it seems that our population is suddenly incapable of living an organized life. Yet the national "crisis" of disorganization can largely be attributed to one single issue: *we have too much stuff.*

No, I'm not suggesting that we empty our homes to the point where we would rival the average household possessions of a citizen of Bangladesh, but stop buying *stuff.* You have enough already.

Organization becomes a snap when you reduce the sheer quantity of *stuff* in your house. William Morris said in 1880, "If you want a golden rule that will fit everybody, this is it: Have nothing in your houses that you do not know to be useful or believe to be beautiful."

Look around your home. What haven't you used in over a year? How many clothes do you have bulging out of your closets? Count the number of knickknacks and collectibles. Consider the sporting equipment you no longer use, the kitchen gadgets you never touch. Do you really *need* or *want* all of this stuff?

Simplicity implies a certain calm order in your home. Once you get rid of what you don't need, or what you don't find beautiful, organization will almost take care of itself without the need to purchase more *stuff* in the form of organizers that allow you to cram in even more stuff.

# .254.

## ONE IN, ONE (OR TWO) OUT

Some people swear by this rule, though with two kids and a busy life I tend not to follow it. (We rely on the occasional massive purge instead.) The idea is that for everything you bring *into* your home (toys, knick-knacks, books, clothing, etc.), designate one (or two) things to take *out*. This rule makes sense and, properly followed, it works wonders to control the clutter and chaos that so many people have in their home.

I know, the logical conclusion of this concept is that eventually nothing is left and your house is empty. Obviously you have to stop when you've reached a point where you're happy with the amount of your possessions.

This is a good rule to teach your children because it helps them let things go. If they want a new toy, ask if they're willing to put two of their current toys in the Goodwill box, and then follow through. (I'm assuming you demonstrate this yourself, of course.)

Set up a give-away box (make it large!) in an out-of-the-way place (washroom, garage, etc.). Try not to use the basement or attic because it's too hard to transfer the contents of the box to Goodwill when the time comes.

This might also help you decide *before* you purchase something whether you're willing to also get rid of something you already own. If you're contemplating the purchase of a new pair of shoes, are you willing to give up one (or two) of your existing pairs? It doesn't necessarily have to be the same thing. Perhaps you can purge your purse collection instead, or thin the number of sweaters your own.

Finally, the "one in, one out" rule is simple to do, which is always an advantage.

# .255.

## LOOK TO THE ELDERS

If you want some fabulous advice on how to live a frugal, thrifty life, talk to someone who has lived through the Great Depression. That decade-long school of hard knocks taught harsh lessons in how to "use it up, wear it out, make it do, or do without." Can you think of a better recipe for conserving resources, reducing consumerism, recycling, or general thriftiness?

Besides giving an older person a thrill (for having a chance to share memories), you might learn a thing or two about how people coped when most of our modern, high-tech, energy-consuming conveniences weren't available. What kinds of foods did they eat? How did they prepare it? How did they make clothing out of flour sacks? (My mother wore flour-sack dresses when she was a girl.)

In the casual abundance of our current times, most people of my generation or younger don't have any clue of how hard it was to live through the Depression. Occasionally you read about people whose hoarding behavior has filled an entire house, garage, and barn with pure junk. For many, that instinct began in their formative years when even a single sheet of paper was precious beyond words. Looked at in that light, hoarding is an understandable obsession.

But in our modern, wired, hooked-in, throwaway world, we cannot grasp a time when anything and everything wasn't easily available.

Look to the Elders to teach you some principles of frugality. You might learn a thing or two, even if you never have to make a dress out of a flour sack. And who knows? The stuff you learn may become critically important.

# .256.

## RACKING UP THE CREDIT CARD TO SAVE THE PLANET

Many of us grew up laughing at our grandmothers for rinsing aluminum foil, unwrapping Christmas presents with surgical precision, and saving jars for other uses. How silly. How extreme! Instead, they should recycle those jars and then spend $29.95 on a made-from-80 percent post-consumer recycled-materials jar to hold their "other uses."

I mean, really, why reuse paper grocery bags when Grandma could purchase 100 percent organically-grown green cotton eco-bags to hold her groceries? They're more chic, too.

As for reusing that old Christmas paper, aren't our grandmothers aware that there are handsome 100 percent recycled wrapping paper products they could purchase, which have the added benefit of saving the planet?

Why go through all the trouble of making compost out of grass clippings and leaves when she can purchase 100 percent organic compost at the garden center?

Why buy mismatched glassware at the thrift store when she could purchase beautiful 100 percent recycled glassware online and have it shipped directly to her door?

For heaven's sake, Grandma even insists on making this yucky avocado-based facial beauty mask instead of sensibly purchasing cruelty-free organic beauty products. C'mon, Grandma! Get with it!

See where I'm going here? Maybe, just maybe, our grandmothers' Depression-bred thriftiness out-"greens" our current efforts to save the planet through our credit card purchases.

Simplicity and environmentalism are intertwined to an amazing degree. Don't try to save the planet by using your credit card; try using your brain instead.

# . 257 .

## EXAMPLES OF GREEN SILLINESS

Is it better to buy a $100 pair of pre-distressed, organically-grown cotton jeans that have been transported all the way across the country, or a $5 pair of jeans from Goodwill that look much the same? Which option is "greener"?

Is it better to purchase paper products made from exotic animal dung (no kidding) in order to provide cottage industries to rural natives, thus encouraging them to spare the animals? Or is it "greener" to save your money (and the transportation costs necessary to move these products across the oceans to your mailbox) and deny these entrepreneurial opportunities to third-world people try to raise their standard of living?

Is it better to buy a $475 air purifier (unless you have a medical reason) that sucks power, or is it better to simply open the window? (If you can't open the window, maybe you should move to someplace where you can!)

I don't know. I can't answer these questions for you. But I do know that anyone can slap a "green" label on a product these days, triple the price, and people will pay it, regardless of how truly "green" it is or what resources it takes to make that product available to you.

I'm not saying these products aren't useful or don't provide the benefits they claim. However, people often blindly purchase these things, thinking they're protecting the environment, without considering that it may be "greener" not to make such purchases at all.

Don't let a green label fool you into thinking that you're saving the planet when, in fact, you may be buying yet more stuff that you do not need.

# . 258 .

## RURAL LIFE ISN'T SIMPLE

Some people feel the urge to simplify their lives and save the planet by plunging into what they think will be a rural, sustainable, green lifestyle. I understand that urge. I've felt it since I was a child. It's why I now find myself on a rural homestead, living a practical and green lifestyle.

But I will be the absolute first to admit that this lifestyle isn't for everyone. This thought occurred to me as I bent at a forty-five degree angle into a howling snowstorm, dragging an old tarp filled with hay, skidding it over the snow in order to feed our herd of Dexter cattle. The cattle provide us with milk, meat, manure (for the garden and orchard) and income. They have to be fed, regardless of the weather.

Afterward, I stomped the snow off my (second-hand) boots and warmed up in front of the woodstove (which is our only source of heat) filled with wood my husband and I cut and split. Feel like joining us?

Until you actually experience the "simple" life, it's only too easy to imagine the cozy winter evenings in front of a crackling woodstove; the gentle sounds of your own organically-raised animals; the beautiful garden filled with lush vegetables ready to be picked. The trouble is, all that requires *work*.

Sometimes I'm just too tired to feel "green." Or simple. Our lives are filled with work, our leisure seems too brief, and sometimes I don't really feel like saving the planet. Not today, thanks. Got too much to do. But would I change it? No.

# . 259 .

## BEWARE "THE VILLAGE"

We are urged to turn to "the village" in order to better raise our children, live a greener lifestyle, and otherwise behave in a decent and respectable manner. The trouble is, the term "village" has been twisted and bloated beyond its intelligent origin.

The "village" used to be just that . . . a village. You lived among a group of neighbors, most of whom had similar lifestyles, attitudes, religious views, and other societal norms. Everyone knew everyone else. If little Charlie Jones was caught throwing rocks at the Smith's windows, the Browns or the Moores could collar Charlie, march him home, tell his dad (of *course* Charlie had a dad!), and little Charlie wouldn't be able to sit for a week. That's a village.

Now we are told we must accept a different kind of "village." We must blindly follow mandates from distant capitals made by people whose primary goals are to make your life more complex (have you read the tax code recently?) at the point of a gun (see what happens if you refuse to pay your property taxes).

We are told that it takes a village to raise our kids. You, the dim-witted parent, can't be trusted to educate or discipline your own kids, so "the village" will do it for you.

And you, the dim-witted consumer, can't be trusted to be green enough, so "the village" will force greenness upon you by dictating your home lighting and heating options, among other things.

You are far better off creating your own "village" by forming ties with friends, neighbors, relatives, and church. Strengthening these ties will give you the sense of community you seek. It is also a healthier "village" for children.

The village of old was your friend. The new "village" is not. Beware the village.

# . 260 .

## ABSURD JUXTAPOSITIONING

I have a strong interest in interior design (though I confess I don't have much talent for it). This past Christmas I saw a magazine in our grocery store that featured homes of a particular style that I admire, so I purchased the issue, especially because the magazine featured advice on how to have a green Christmas. What an interesting juxtaposition I found.

The magazine did indeed have lengthy articles full of advice on how to keep Christmas less commercial and more green, right alongside page after page after page of advertisements from architectural firms who will build ten-thousand-square-foot upscale homes. Oh, but of course these homes are "green." Sure.

I'm sorry, and maybe I'm too dim to grasp it, but how can a ten-thousand-square-foot home be "green"? I don't care what materials were used to build it. It could be made of 100 percent recycled beer cans for all I care, *but it's still too big.*

I have no interest in living in a mansion (think of all those bathrooms to clean!), but I confess a voyeuristic interest in their interior design. However, to place photos of these upscale homes right next to articles on how to have a "green" Christmas was . . . well, ludicrous.

Massive homes use resources on a similarly massive scale. More water. More electricity. More natural gas or heating oil. More landscaping. More, more, more.

If you want to *really* be green, don't buy a mansion. Buy a modest home suited to your family's size and needs. You'll use a lot fewer resources and pay a lower mortgage.

# . 261 .

## TEST YOUR CARBON FOOTPRINT

I don't think much about the "carbon credit" stuff that's become so popular lately. To me it smacks of purchasing indulgences, or of using money to assuage guilt for a ridiculously resource-rich lifestyle. It's also become too much of a status symbol. But finding out your carbon footprint can be quite useful to determine where the "holes" are in your quest for a simpler life.

If you type "carbon footprint quiz" into a search engine, you'll find dozens of tests you can take. These quizzes aren't always accurate. We get reamed, for instance, because we eat meat. Nothing in these quizzes accounts for the fact that we own twenty acres and raise our own organic grass-fed beef (as well as harvest our own milk). Still, by most websites, our carbon footprint is about one-quarter the U.S. average of 20 tons a year. Most environmentalists say the worldwide average needs to be reduced to 2 tons in order to combat climate change.

Regardless of what kind of primitive and austere lifestyle you would be living at a target level of 2 tons of carbon per year, I feel that taking your carbon footprint can be highly instructive.

Did you score high in the "home" energy use section? Maybe it's because your home is too big. Did the "car" section smack you? Perhaps you have too many cars, or your commute is too long. How about food? Perhaps you're purchasing too many convenience foods or fast food.

These are useful tools to determine what areas in your life are too complex, and how you might simplify them.

# . 262 .

## EXAMINE SOME "SURVIVALIST" ISSUES

Like any movement, survivalism has its extremists. However, there are some fair things to consider among survivalists that include both green issues and simple living issues.

If there are disruptions in power, water, transportation, or food, what will you do? Anything from natural disasters to terrorist activities can ruin anyone's good day. But if you have the means to eat, drink, stay warm, and see at night, then you're doing pretty well.

It makes sense to keep some kerosene and kerosene lamps on hand, to have a woodstove and a supply of wood (don't forget matches!), and to have food and water stored up (including for your animals). Unfortunately this can't apply to everyone. It's one thing to have a woodstove and a couple cords of wood outside your door if you live in rural north Idaho; it's another thing entirely if you're in a high-rise New York City apartment.

Still, do what you can. Put aside some nonperishable foods and a few gallons of water per person. Have some oil lamps or candles, and some matches, so you can see at night. Be prepared to hunker down for awhile if something happens.

If the lights go out in a wild storm and stay off for a week, don't you think it would be simpler if you are warm, well-fed, and can while away the dark evenings by doing puzzles or reading out loud to your kids?

Knowing you're prepared to outlast a time of trouble will help you sleep better. You'll have the peace of mind that is the goal of simplicity.

# .263.

## THE CREATOR, NOT THE CREATED

The poet Robert Browning said, "Of what I call God, And fools call Nature." It always amazes me how people can take a natural ecosystem—the planet Earth—and chose it as an object of worship.

I see absolutely no conflict between green living and a religious life. I'm quite certain that God takes pleasure in the responsible stewardship of our planet. I'm equally certain that He would frown upon rampant pollution and littering. But to transfer our worship from God to a complex ball of rock, dirt, and gases makes no sense. When we do that, we lose our perspective on being green. It becomes the end (worship) rather than the means (stewardship).

Because of my love of nature, I got my bachelor's degree in zoology and a master's degree in environmental education. We chose a lifestyle some would call "green" to live cheek-by-jowl with the environment. We try to raise much of our food, and we are raising our children to enjoy the outdoors. Believe me, I am second to none in my admiration for the wonders of the natural world. But I do not bow down and pray to rocks, fields, and mountains. I might as well bow down to my shoes, my oatmeal, and my soap. I would get about as much response as well.

From the earliest days, man has searched for the face of God in nature, and I truly believe that it's possible to find Him among the rocks, fields, and mountains. Just be sure to direct your prayers to the Creator, not the created.

# . 264 .

## THE DEPRIVED CHILD

Did you know that there is a new phenomenon known as nature-deficit disorder? While not exactly tongue-in-cheek, and most certainly not recognized as a medically-valid disorder, the premise is outlined in Richard Louv's book, *The Last Child in the Woods*. The idea is that our children are growing increasingly disconnected from the natural world, and this separation leads to a slew of maladies, from hyperactivity to attention-deficit disorder to obesity.

My husband and I have been asked, with a straight face, how we could be so cruel as to deprive our children of cultural benefits (museums, zoos, concerts, etc.) by isolating them in the wilds of rural Idaho. But because of our "cruelty," our kids are experiencing things that were common-place a hundred years ago but are rare now.

We've all heard the stories about toddlers who scream in fear when their bare feet touch grass. We hear about over-zealous parents who have an excessive fear of exposing their children to "germs" without consideration that exposure to natural germs from playing in the mud, climbing trees, or building forts can improve a child's immune system. We hear about kids in intensely urban environments who have never seen the stars because the city lights are so bright. I'm sorry, but to me *that* sounds like deprivation.

Not everyone can, or wants to, live a rural life. But don't forget that the farther you get from nature, the less you can benefit from it. Children, especially, need a touch of dirt to grow up healthy. Try not to deprive your child. They need nature.

# . 265 .

## WHO ARE YOU IMPRESSING?

The incomparable Will Rogers once said, "Too many people spend money they haven't earned, to buy things they don't want, to impress people they don't like." Sound familiar?

We buy things to fulfill social obligations with little regard as to whether the things are worth having. Frequently they are not.

This can apply to "green" purchases as well as conventional purchases. Do you really *need* a fruit basket made from recycled chopsticks, or are you buying it because you're trying to impress people with your environmental consciousness?

A quick search on the Internet will reveal loads of eco-gifts made from recycled materials. Many of them are creative uses for stuff that would otherwise end up in the landfill. However, there was not one product—not one—that was *necessary*.

And green items are expensive. I saw, with mouth agape, a towel rack made from recycled metal that cost—drum roll, please—an astounding $250. I guess all the "recycled" towel racks available at thrift stores aren't "green" enough.

If you feel compelled to give a gift to someone made from a recycled bicycle chain, then go for it, I suppose. But what if the recipient doesn't *need* the item any more than you did? Oh, I'm sure they'll "ooh" and "ahh" over your environmental awareness. But you see what I mean? You impressed them, that's all. You haven't done anything for the environment. And the recipient will probably end up getting rid of it eventually.

So watch your purchases. Perhaps it's greener to only purchase what you or someone else truly needs.

# . 266 .

## PICK UP TRASH

My husband and I live on a twenty-acre farm in north Idaho among some of the most stunning natural beauty imaginable. We never cease to marvel at the view of mountains and prairie and to enjoy the wildflowers and birds.

So why do we keep finding discarded beer cans by the side of our two-mile dirt road? It's because we know someone who lives nearby who doesn't think about the consequences of littering. He just tosses his cans. And his cigarette butts. And his candy wrappers.

Some people are like that. They can litter stunning scenery with aplomb. Who knows why they do it? Perhaps they're just lazy. Perhaps it's a habit. Perhaps they think that one more beer can, cigarette butt, or candy wrapper won't make a difference.

What should we do about this? Sure, we could stomp over and dump all the beer cans at the guy's front door. Or we could lobby our local government to stiffen the littering laws, then turn the guy in. Or we could get into a heated argument with the fellow and thus ensure bad neighborly relations for the next decade. Or we could just pick up the beer cans.

You will never solve the littering problem by any means other than to pick up the litter. *Everyone*, even the litterers, knows that littering is bad. If someone is going to be a slob, there's not a lot you can do about it unless it's rampant and witnessed. Sometimes it's better—and simpler—just to pick up the trash.

# . 267 .

## DON'T UPGRADE

In our throwaway world, people have become very cavalier about getting rid of perfectly useful things in order to grasp at the latest, shiniest, glossiest, more high-tech versions.

Most of the time, people don't get rid of things because they're worn out or broken. They get rid of things because they're tired of them or they lust after the latest model. People want something new, so they'll trade in their three-year-old car for one that's shinier. They'll upgrade to the next-most-powerful computer. They'll buy a whole new wardrobe when fashion decrees hemlines should be shorter by two inches. They'll switch to HDTV even though their television works fine. They'll sell their home in order to get a bigger house in a trendier neighborhood. Even a perfectly-working cell phone gets chucked for the newest model that takes photos, folds laundry, and cooks dinner.

This tendency to get rid of perfectly useful things in order to "upgrade" is endless. It leads to dissatisfaction with everything we own. We're always comparing our possessions to our neighbors or coworkers and come away feeling inadequate. Besides, almost *everything* has an upgraded version, so when do you stop? When do you realize it is simpler and greener not to be obsessed with upgrades?

Get over your ego and hang onto things longer. If *you* don't make a huge issue out of your older car or your beautiful but second-hand garments, I can assure you no one *else* will either. Maybe you can even hang onto your home long enough to (gasp) pay off the mortgage.

# . 268 .

## FIND ALTERNATIVES TO
## DISPOSABLES

Single-use things tend to bug me. Sure, not everything has a reusable version (toilet paper comes to mind), but there are lots of things available that can provide a more permanent alternative to your disposable item.

During cold season or sniffly winter weather, we're crazy over bandanas, which we use as handkerchiefs (we also use them as sweat bands during hot summer days). And we prefer windup or rechargeable flashlights over battery-powered flashlights.

When my girls were babies, I loved using cloth diapers (contrary to popular belief, you *don't* have to swish them in the toilet to rinse them). In addition to being a lot cheaper and more comfortable than disposable diapers, they make excellent rags after they're too shabby for their original purpose.

I dislike those chintzy plastic utensils for picnics or camping events. For about the same price, you can get loads of unmatched metal utensils at thrift stores that can be used again and again. As an added benefit, when kids need a beat-up spoon or fork to use in the sandbox, you won't have to spare any of your good kitchen set.

Look around your house and note what disposable things you use. See if you can find a sensible alternative. Cloth napkins instead of paper. Rewritable CDs instead of single-use. Ceramic mugs instead of Styrofoam cups. There are even reusable forms of feminine hygiene products and printer ink cartridges.

It makes sound economic sense—and green sense, too—to reduce the number of disposables in your life. Think creatively and see what you come up with.

# .269.

## DON'T WASTE FOOD

Dr. Tim Jones, Professor of Applied Anthropology at the University of Arizona, spent ten years studying patterns of waste among Americans. He found that Americans throw away shocking amounts of food—half of America's food never gets eaten. Half. Yet, oddly, most people when polled say that they waste virtually nothing.

He points out that since most of us are no longer involved in the direct production of our own food (we just buy it from the store), this diminishes its value in our eyes. He also points out how a surprising number of people believe that food actually goes "bad" at the end of dinner, rather than realizing that leftovers can be saved for future meals.

If your family says, "Ew, yuck," when you try to serve them leftovers, it's likely that they got that attitude from you. Stop it.

Reuse leftovers creatively. Some people freeze scraps until they have enough to make a hearty soup. We are not big soup eaters in our house, so I make a lot of "leftover pies" by tossing meat, vegetables, beans, and rice into a piecrust. Leftovers also make superb bag lunches for work. Most offices have a microwave and small refrigerator. Bring some of last night's dinner and enjoy a hot, delicious meal at the office.

Far be it for me to sound like your mother and say, "Clean your plate. There are children starving in India," but maybe mom had a point. Stop wasting food and watch your grocery bills go down.

# . 270 .

## TEACH YOUR CHILDREN NOT TO BE CONSUMERS

We've all heard the stories of how young children develop precocious brand loyalty. ("No! I don't want *those* vitamins, I want *these* vitamins!") Oh great, the next generation is already becoming enslaved to Madison Avenue, thus embarking on a lifetime of consumer dissatisfaction.

Don't buy your younger children designer clothing or toys or they'll learn to expect only the very best. For older children, teach them to distinguish between needs and wants by making them pay the difference.

For instance, we buy all our sneakers at thrift stores for $3 a pair. The ones we purchase are always sturdy, little worn, and in excellent shape. Besides the fact that the price is right, we feel better knowing that our purchases are "greener" because they are second-hand. However, recently my older daughter wanted Pirates of the Caribbean sneakers for $30. We told her sure as long as she was willing to cough up the extra $27.

She wasn't, of course. It took only a brief moment for her to understand the differences between *need* (shoes that fit her feet) and *want* (designer sneakers that might impress her friends).

If she *had* decided to chip in the $27, then she would have learned how ephemeral such satisfaction is. She outgrew the thrift-store sneakers in a few months, and frankly I doubted any of her friends would have noticed her designer sneakers unless she made pains to point them out.

Life is simpler and greener if your kids aren't obsessed with labels.

# . 271 .

## DON'T SCARE YOUR CHILDREN

In an effort to impress upon their children the need for environmental awareness, some parents end up terrifying their kids. Children are told that everything is toxic, poisonous, dangerous, or damaging to the earth—clothing, food, toys, blankets and sheets, cleaning products, etc. The implied message is, "We're all gonna die, and soon."

Some of the more extreme rhetoric will say that humans are evil and should be eradicated from the planet. What will children conclude from this? That they should never have been born? What do you suppose that does to a child's psyche?

If you want to feed your child only organically-grown foods and clothe them only in organically-grown cottons, that's fine. However, try not to terrify your poor kids to the point where everything they do or see is evil, wrong, or dangerous.

Kids tend to internalize things to an alarming extent. If they come to believe that all the air they breathe or the water they drink or the toys they play with are poisonous, they're likely to become depressed, anxious, or paranoid.

I think it is far more sensible to teach children not to be avid consumers, not to be wasteful, and to involve them directly in food production (this can include cooking from scratch as well as growing a garden or raising livestock).

But scaring the bejeebers out of the poor kids (or worse, implying they should never have been born) is at best counterproductive, and at worst downright evil.

For a simpler life, raise balanced children with a healthy attitude of stewardship toward the earth.

# . 272 .

## RETHINK YOUR LANDSCAPING

Many years ago, I was visiting a friend who lived in a tightly packed subdivision. While chatting over tea, I idly watched as a woman emerged from the house across the street, picked up a single leaf from her immaculate lawn, and retreated back inside. I blinked in surprise and asked my friend what that was about. My friend made an exasperated noise.

"She's obsessed with the perfect lawn," she told me. "Every blade of grass has to be the same height. Weeds aren't permitted. Every time a leaf falls from the tree, she goes outside to pick it up. See the neighbor's maple tree? Sometimes the wind will blow leaves onto her lawn, and she tries to sue the neighbors to cut the tree down. She's not, er, well-liked around here."

I'll grant this woman's behavior was eccentric, but many of us fall on a continuum of wanting the perfect lawn. This is contrary to a simple, green life.

I happen to be a "lawn" person. They're so wonderful for romping with kids. If you want a lawn, though, it behooves you to plant tough grass suited to your particular environment (i.e., drought-tolerant grass if you're in a low-rain area). Stop with the herbicides already. Don't worry about a few weeds (or get out there with a trowel if they really bug you–it's good exercise, too). Use a push-mower. Let cut grass lie–it's good mulch. Use native plants.

Be simple in your landscaping so you can apply the time and energy you might otherwise devote to your lawn into more sensible and important things.

# . 273 .

## GREEN LIVING IN A DOWN ECONOMY

If you're sensible about it, there is no finer way to save the earth than by picking and choosing those things that will save you money at the same time. Take line-drying your clothes, for example. You always hear people nagging you about the high cost of running your dryer, but I can testify that it's true. In the summer, we line-dry our clothes. In the winter, we use wooden clothes racks (keep an eye out for them in thrift stores and yard sales). Not using a clothes dryer will save you literally hundreds and hundreds of dollars a year in electricity or propane.

Look around you and come up with other ideas as to ways to trim expenses and go green at the same time. Buy used clothing. Purchase non-disposable versions of products. Choose to walk, bike, or take public transportation to work. All of these things will contribute toward reducing your carbon footprint, yes, but more important for your immediate focus, these things will save you tremendous amounts of money in either the short-term or the long-term. And right now, with the bad economy and many jobs disappearing, saving money and marshalling your financial resources should be among your top priorities.

Done intelligently, living green is a superb way to save money and simplify your life. And if nothing else, it will let you be one up on the Greenies.

# Time Off for Good Behavior

▼

After a hard day (or a long year) at the office, or a rough time taking care of the kids, everyone needs a break. It's time for the pause that refreshes, to get rid of the ball and chain of worry and stress. In other words, it's time for some simple recreation.

# .274.

## WHAT IS SIMPLE RECREATION?

In this context, "recreation" refers to anything you do in your free time. Vacations, holidays, travel, time at home, leisure, hobbies, sports, visiting with friends, and volunteer work. These things may or may not contribute to a simpler life.

If you cram your afternoon schedule with so many activities that you or your children have no time to relax and decompress, what have you gained? If you try so hard to have a "perfect" Christmas that everyone ends up in tears or furiously angry, why do you do it? If you travel to exotic destinations with one empty suitcase merely to fill it with junk that you buy, why are you cluttering your home? If you're so stressed about a "perfect" house that you can't bear unexpected company for fear that they'll see a mess, then what happens to your friendships? Are you watching so much television that you barely have time for anything or anyone else? If you pack three giant suitcases for a trip and end up using only a quarter of the things you've brought, what have you gained (except a sore back)?

The whole purpose of simplifying your recreation is to make your life quieter, more peaceful, more welcoming, and more relaxing. A walk in the woods, a visit to an art museum, playing a board game with the kids, and puttering in your garden is likely to leave you refreshed, not stressed.

# .275.

## WHAT IS RECREATION?

The term *recreation* is frequently misunderstood. Without getting too New Age-ish, to recreate is to re-*create*. To create yourself anew, rather than stressing yourself by trying to cram too much vacation into too few days.

Doing stuff that leaves you more tired and stressed than when you started is absurd. When you re-create, the result should be a feeling of being refreshed and renewed, which in turn allows you to cope with daily pressures and stresses.

Everyone needs down time or decompression time. No one can run on adrenaline forever without developing serious health complications. These days, people justify their actions by saying that since they *work* hard, they should *play* hard, too. They spend their free time seeking thrills and chills without considering that thrills and chills aren't really conducive to re-creation.

I'm not saying that strenuous activities like sports, hiking, or even hang gliding (if that's your bag) aren't recreational. But if that's *all* you do—if you get up in the morning and recreate your brains out, and then fall into bed exhausted—exactly how have you de-stressed?

To simplify your life is to re-create yourself with less stress, less tension, and less anxiety. You can't relax if you never stop. If you only have two precious weeks a year for vacation, maybe you should rethink the idea of a frenzied see-fourteen-countries-in-fourteen-days type of trip. You're more likely to come home exhausted, in which case what have you accomplished?

For those who seek to simplify, it behooves them to seek out recreational activities that do just that.

# .276.

## ENTERTAIN YOURSELF

Milton said, "Solitude is sometimes best society." Spend time with yourself and by yourself. Don't try to keep yourself occupied with frantic activity or socialization.

If you're not used to solitude, it might take a little work. At first glance, the concept might even be a little scary, not to mention boring. After all, how do you compare the excitement of a good sports bar, a nice restaurant, a nightclub, or a movie, to an evening on the couch with a book?

But entertaining yourself is a good habit to cultivate. It's a rare talent in this world of hustle and bustle. A simpler life is not a life of constant, frenzied activity. It is a life in which you can achieve the goal of slowing down, of balance, and of occasional solitude. Besides, it's less expensive.

So stay home. Type a letter to a friend. Read. Listen to music. Play a game with your kids. Talk with your spouse. Bake something elaborate. Balance your checkbook.

Discover that being alone doesn't mean you're lonely. You might find that the superficial acquaintance you have with yourself can blossom into a real and significant friendship.

Staying home might also be a good time to think about your goals (#221) or start working from home (#342) or pursue your creative interest (#290). At any rate, entertaining yourself at home is a talent that is necessary to a simpler life. Give it a try—you might find you like it. And you might find you like yourself, too.

# . 277 .

## EXPECT UNEXPECTED COMPANY

I have found it helpful to have "instant" meals in case of unexpected company.

One time I got a call out of the blue from an old friend. She and her husband and her in-laws were traveling and would be passing near our home. Could they stop in and say hello? Of course, I said yes. In fact, I invited the whole group to dinner.

My friend protested, saying that there would be four adults and one child. I said no problem. I hung up the phone and walked over to the pantry where I had several quarts of lentil soup I'd canned the previous year. I cleaned up the house, made a salad and some garlic bread, heated the soup, and we all had a lovely visit.

Some simplicity books urge you to give up your social contacts and to take a break from your constant social turmoil. This might be a good idea, *if* your social whirl is *driving* you rather than being *led* by you.

Since we live in a rural area, social contacts are less frequent and therefore more welcome. I like having people feel they can drop by, especially if they're the forgiving sort and don't mind that I haven't vacuumed or that the kitchen is a mess. Therefore, I find it useful to have some meals that can be prepared quickly. It cuts the stress level and I can stop obsessing over what kind of elegant dinner I should make. That way my friends know they are always welcome. Even for dinner.

Remember, humans are social creatures. Don't allow yourself to become isolated.

# . 278 .

## REDUCE YOUR OUTSIDE ACTIVITIES

Parents saddle children with every conceivable activity. We cram so many extracurricular pursuits into our kids' lives that the children end up stressed and exhausted. Why do we do this?

Guilt. Obligation. A passing interest by the child in horse-back riding or karate. An interest that the parent never had a chance to explore as a child. ("If my parents could have afforded lessons, I'd be a world-class skier by now.")

In an effort to provide their children with "advantages," some parents consider the sheer number of a child's lessons and activities to be a symbol of success. "Well, *my* child does Taekwondo, soccer, baseball, piano, tennis, art, *and* acting lessons!" We are expected to offer our kids all the "benefits" we can afford. Meanwhile, little Johnny is tottering under the burden, depressed and stressed and snappish.

It's the rare child who longs for a schedule so full of activities that he has no "down" time. Children need the opportunity to do nothing. They need the chance to curl up in a corner with a book, or dream, or build things with wood or Legos, or draw, or jump in mud puddles, or climb trees, or whatever they like to do in their free (yes, free!) time. (For the record, I think of TV watching as "captive," not "free" time. Besides, it does nothing for their imagination.)

Limiting yourself to one outside activity per child will greatly simplify your life—not only the lives of your kids, but also the lives of the parents who have to chauffer them around.

# . 279 .

## ESTABLISH TRADITIONS

The year before I got married, my brother gave me a Christmas present consisting of a series of cheap ceramic mugs shaped like animals. I'm sure he didn't expect me to actually *use* these mugs; they were more like a gag gift.

Well, they've become a mainstay ritual in our house. Every night, as we put the children down to bed, my husband selects one of the mugs, fills it with water, and covers it with a towel. Then he gives the kids clues on what type of animal it is. They get a drink after they guess the "surprise cup." As a side benefit, the kids have learned some biology facts. Giraffe have seven cervical vertebrae, just like most other mammals. Cheetahs are the fastest land mammal. They've also learned the differences between Indian and African elephants.

Even at the age of fifteen, my older daughter still dotes on this ritual. Over the years some of the mugs have broken—always traumatic—and occasionally we'll pick up a new one to surprise them. But this silly ritual is something our girls will remember long after my husband and I are gone.

Children thrive on rituals. Having something predictable in their lives gives them a sense of control and stability. Rituals can be as profound as daily or weekly religious observances, or as lighthearted as "surprise cups."

The more rituals you have that your children enjoy, the more secure their world is.

# .280.

## IS NIRVANA DOING NOTHING?

Amy Dacyczyn (author of *The Tightwad Gazette*) made an astute observation: that the act of *doing* things is more fun than doing *nothing*. Many simplicity guides list a goal of "doing nothing" as a symbol of having achieved the simple life. In fact, the simple life requires work—lots of it. The difference is that it is work we love to do. Or for some of the work at least, we love *having done* it (it would be a stretch to say that I *love* mucking out the barn, for instance, but you get my drift).

Ms. Dacyczyn quotes playwright George Bernard Shaw, who said, "The secret of being miserable is to have the leisure to bother about whether you are happy or not." Perhaps that's where the "good old days" myth comes from: our forefathers were busy and productive all the time, and so they didn't have the leisure to sit around and realize that, perhaps, they should be miserable.

I don't believe that the ultimate goal in a "simple life" is to strive toward the chance to do nothing. I believe it means you've reached a stage where the things you do are so enjoyable that doing "nothing" is boring by comparison, and that the number of things you must do is reduced to the number of things you can do well, and with all your heart.

This is your chance to look at what you hate doing in your life. Perhaps you hate your commute. Or your job, or being in debt. Now work to change those things you hate so you can have a life you love.

# . 281 .

## VOLUNTEER?

If you've read as many simplicity books as I have, you come away with the impression that volunteering is the be-all and end-all of life. Many books suggest that we should simplify with the purpose of volunteering our time to help others. I'm a homeschooling mother of two teens. We also have a farm and a home business in which we work every single day. How on earth am I supposed to devote umpteen hours to volunteering? And volunteering for whom? To make things worse, I live in a deeply rural area, and the nearest organized charities are at least an hour's drive away.

It all got very complex and guilt-ridden. I mean, volunteering is certainly a noble thing to do, so the fact that I wasn't devoting ten or fifteen hours a week to some worthwhile organization left me feeling shamefaced and uncomfortable.

Also, truthfully, one of the reasons I wasn't actively volunteering was that I didn't want to be at the "mercy" of charitable organizations in case they ask more and more and more of me until I burn out.

But it turns out that I *do* volunteer, and I'll bet you do, too. Take an assessment and see what you do for others. Are you teaching a young bride how to cook from scratch? Are you showing a new coworker around town? Are you checking in on the neighbor who broke his leg? Do you have the latchkey kid up the street stay with you until his parents get home every evening? Do you feed your neighbor's dog while he's gone overnight?

Volunteer work is a much simpler, effortless thing if it's doing something you feel strongly about. You're left feeling warm and fuzzy and so are those you've helped.

# . 282 .

## VOLUNTEER FOR WHAT'S
## NEAR AND DEAR

If you are reluctant to work for a large, established charitable organization, you can still donate your time and effort. Look around and see what little things can be done to make the world a better place.

I gradually recognized that I do more volunteer work than I thought—none of it "organized" and all of it so enjoyable that I hadn't even realized I was volunteering. Here's my list. It might help you start yours.

I bring an elderly lady to church and home again, and check in on her periodically to make sure she has enough groceries. I do newsletters for my writer's group and our church. I help our local library with fundraising events. Our family helps pack and distribute Christmas baskets every year for the needy in our area. My husband built a stage curtain for the local high school's theater department. We help our neighbors. I give blood.

See how it works? Until I stopped to think about it, I didn't even realize any of this was "volunteering." Yet it is, without any of the guilt or stress that I tend to associate with charitable organizations. I'm *not* saying you should avoid organized charitable groups, I'm just saying it doesn't work for me.

Volunteering is part of the "think globally, act locally" concept. Helping those close to you brings you closer to your community. The idea behind volunteering is to get our focus off the "me" mentality that sometimes takes over. What a great idea.

# . 283 .

## JUST SAY NO

People have the hardest time saying "no" to things. This *so* complicates our lives.

Can you serve on this committee? Sure. Can you make thirty yarn dolls for the crafts fair? No problem. Can you take on this extra project? You bet. Can you start picking up my kids after school? Certainly. Can you make costumes for the school play? Absolutely. Can you put in some overtime at work? Of course.

This is in addition to whatever professional and personal responsibilities you already have. Suddenly your life is so full that you can barely think.

Why do we *do* this to ourselves? Why can't we turn people down? It's because we don't want to disappoint. Because we don't want to decrease anyone's good opinion of us. Because we're too nice. Because we feel guilty.

The truth of the matter is that saying *no* is painful. To avoid the pain, we'll say *yes* and then find that the pain we experience later on is even worse.

But here's some news: they'll get over it. Someone else can serve on the committee, make thirty yarn dolls, take on the extra project, pick up the kids, make costumes, and put in overtime.

Okay, not always. Kids can't stay after school alone. Working overtime may not be an option. But if you have to work overtime or pick up someone's kids after school, at least you haven't committed yourself to making thirty yarn dolls for the crafts fair *and* serving on a committee. Sometimes you have to pick your battles.

# . 284 .

## THE CASE AGAINST TELEVISION

We all know the facts and figures about children watching too much television. But what about adults? I see no recreational advantage to zoning out in front of the boob tube for hours on end to "relax." At the end of your viewing, you are not re-*created* or refreshed or renewed. Yes, of course, there are fascinating programs on television (the History Channel, for instance), but is it *really* worth having a faceless box sucking up all your free time?

It is also a poor example to the rest of your family. Do you yell at the kids to keep the noise down because it interferes with your soap opera or sporting event? If so, you have your priorities *seriously* mixed up. Turn off the TV and spend time interacting with your family.

I'm not a Luddite who is against any and all technological entertainment. We have a TV (though no TV reception) and we watch movies. We have the Internet and spend time on the computer. The secret is to find a balance. You might be diligent about not using the TV or computer as a babysitter but how about for yourself? What are you *avoiding* by watching TV or surfing the Internet?

Anytime you are staring at a computer screen or television, you are avoiding face-to-face contact with your family and you feel irritated when you're interrupted by a child or spouse needing attention. Believe me, I understand. But your family life—and your decompression time—will benefit and simplify enormously when you choose healthier forms of recreation.

# .285.

## READ

Ah, reading: The King of Entertainment. Reading is simple to do. It can be done in short bursts. It requires no special equipment (except, as you reach my age, reading glasses). It can be done on a subway or on a lazy afternoon in a hammock. It can help put you to sleep (no drugs!) and it gives your mind something to do as you wake up with a cup of coffee. And of course, the greatest benefit is that it makes your brain work in a way that is impossible while watching television.

Books are cheap or free. You can explore untold quantities of fascinating subjects—history, science, mystery, romance, adventure—wherever your tastes lead you.

If you "hate" reading, it's probably because (a) you were not exposed to reading as entertainment when you were a child, or (b) you were forced to read things you didn't like in school. Now's your chance to overcome this early bias and discover the absolute, utter joy, of reading.

But it takes practice. Like anything else, reading is an acquired taste. Some people acquire that taste very young, but others don't discover it until adulthood when they are no longer forced to read what doesn't interest them.

You might start by investigating a favorite subject—antique cars, Egyptian pyramids, dragons. Whatever it is, you'll find someone, somewhere, has written a book about it. Try your local library.

Once you acquire the habit of reading, the whole world opens up, and your recreation time can become delightfully simple.

# .286.

## WALK

There is nothing like walking as a truly simple recreational option. Aside from the fact that walking is probably *the* best overall exercise you can do, it has the added advantage of being automatic. Anyone who is able-bodied can walk without a lot of concentration or preparation.

Walking is free. It requires no special equipment except comfortable shoes (I use $3 sneakers from Goodwill). You get the physical benefits, of course, but you also get the psychological benefits of fresh air and sunshine. You see new sights that you wouldn't see from a car (the birds twittering in the bushes; a new flower pushing up from the earth; the way the sun sparkles through the trees). You can say hello and be friendly with passers-by.

It allows time for unfocused thought—a truly re-*creational* benefit. It gets you places. You can do it with others, including your children (though you'll be walking slow, which has its own advantages).

It also allows conversations to flourish in ways that might otherwise be too intimidating if you are face-to-face. A friend tells me that she's had all the "facts of life" discussions with her young teenage daughter exclusively while they were walking together because the daughter was less embarrassed and had something to "do" while talking.

Walking is a chance for my husband and I reconnect after a busy day, even if we've spent the busy day working together. Kids cherish walking time with their parents.

Walking is a truly simple way to re-create. Consider adding a half-hour walk to your daily schedule and see if you don't come back more relaxed.

# .287.

## CULTIVATE YOUR MIND

Your body needs exercise to keep healthy. So does your mind. But it's so easy, after we are released from our formal schooling (be it high school, college, or graduate school), to forget to keep learning.

Studies continue to be published which show that continued learning means a longer and more active life. And it's so easy! Learning does not mean studying dusty books on long-dead philosophers (unless, like me, you like that kind of stuff). Simply think about the things you enjoy, and learn more about them.

You say the only thing you enjoy is television? Fine. Read a book about your favorite actor. Find out how a television show is made. Try writing a script or a screenplay. It is the *act* of learning something new that is important.

I'm always fascinated by people who, through no formal training but merely by following an interest, have become recognized experts in their hobbies or areas of passion: Car repair. Bird behavior. Growing dahlias. Making wine. Renaissance history. Sign language.

Continued cultivation of your mind is also an excellent example to your children. If you homeschool (as we do), it becomes additional learning opportunities for your kids as well.

So learn a poem. Read a speech from Shakespeare. Memorize pi to the twentieth decimal place (just for the heck of it). Listen to a CD of Beethoven. Look up the name of Australia's prime minister.

Learning something new keeps us young. Or at least, young at heart.

# .288.

## NEVER STOP LEARNING

Research has shown that an active mind can stave off Alzheimer's disease. A quest to keep learning makes you a more vital, interesting individual. Continued learning makes for a multi-layered, happy person. Even Cicero, way back in the first century B.C., recognized the importance of continued learning.

Just for kicks, try stepping outside your comfort zone and learning something completely new like Japanese poetry, the proper way to grow roses, Babylonian pottery, obsessed book collectors through history, UFOs, the biography of Stalin, or making soufflés.

My husband has a fascination for reading about Christian theology. He may not agree with everything he reads, but so what? It makes him think and it strengthens his beliefs.

I've become fascinated by the Harvard classics and have begun a slow and laborious reading of the collected works. So what if I was bored by Adam Smith's *Wealth of Nations*? I found myself unexpectedly interested in Socrates and the Greek Dramas. My mind is broadened and expanded.

My kids groan every time they ask a question and I reach for an encyclopedia. But now they know where Suriname is located and who invented the cotton gin.

You might ask, of what use is random knowledge of Babylonian pottery or Japanese poetry? I guess you could argue of what use is a rose. Knowledge is the beauty of a rose . . . for your mind.

Besides, if nothing else, this stuff gives you something to think about on your walks.

# . 289 .

## SLEEP

The ability to get a good night's sleep is an indicator of how well you're doing in your quest to simplify. If you're busy until midnight every day and then have to get up by 6 a.m., you haven't managed to dial back your life yet. This assumes that your lack of sleep isn't caused by a medical reason (illness) or a mechanical reason (lousy mattress).

There are many studies demonstrating the importance of sleep in both mental and physical health. To attain a simple life, it's essential that you limit the number of outside activities or other stresses that may be reducing the number of hours you're sleeping.

If you're married, and for a better night's sleep, try cuddling. If it's too hot, throw off some blankets and keep cuddling. If it's too cold, cuddling is even better. My husband agrees that nothing gives peace of mind better than spooning or being spooned. It brings you closer to your spouse as well.

Many years ago when I worked the swing-shift, I'd crawl into bed exhausted around 4 a.m. My body was tired but my mind wouldn't shut down. The only way I could get to sleep was to cuddle up with my husband. Soon my mind *and* body were relaxed.

Examine what it is in your present life that is causing your sleep pattern to be interrupted (if it is) and then do what you can to change it.

# . 290 .

## FIND A CREATIVE OUTLET

Everyone needs a stress reliever, an activity or hobby or diversion they enjoy.

Learn a musical instrument. Learn a foreign language. Learn Irish dancing. Fix up antique cars. Quilt. Grow prize roses. Write poetry. Do jigsaw puzzles. Write. Do photography. Do woodworking. Dance ballet. Create gourmet desserts. Knit spectacular sweaters. Find your own creative passion.

I'm not saying you have to be *expert* in your passion or hobby. You just have to *enjoy* it. You can take five minutes a day to throw a few more pieces on your jigsaw puzzle, or learn another French verb, or install the hose on your 1949 Ford. There is also a sense of pride that comes with having a creative outlet, a feeling of accomplishment, and an enrichment of self-esteem.

I once knew a mail carrier who was getting up there in age. One day the subject of retirement came up. "I'll never retire," he said. "I have no hobbies, so if I retired I would be dead in a year because I would have nothing to do."

I found that sad. Not that he took pride in his job (which he did), but that he would be lost *without* it. Hobbies and interests outside one's employment broaden the mind.

Relieving stress through a creative outlet may not overtly simplify your life, but it can make you capable of handling stress more easily. And *that* is important in simplifying.

# .291.

## GARDEN

I recommend gardening even though I have a black thumb (as my husband can testify). The ability to grow plants is possible whether you're on a farm in north Idaho or in a high-rise apartment in New York City.

There must be something genetic about humans wanting to get their hands dirty. Gardening may not provide much of a workout for the body, but it sometimes surpasses walking or bicycling in providing a sense of accomplishment. I may not be good at growing plants, but I still like to try.

You may never know whether your inner-office memo on ball-bearings had any real benefit for your job or your company; but that small pot of flowers on your desk or that huge vegetable garden in your backyard is something that *you* brought to fruition. How cool is that?

Plants cannot be "hurried" into growing faster. By their very nature, they force you to slow down to their pace, which is not a bad benefit in this hurry-up world we've created.

Plants are suited to nearly every possible living situation imaginable. They are tolerant and forgiving of blunders (guilty!). All they ask is a bit of sunshine (direct or indirect), some water, and a bit of fertilizer. What's not to love?

The poinsettia that a friend gave me three years ago is thriving. I'm so proud. And I've even gotten to the point where my tomatoes yield so much fruit that I'm busy canning for weeks.

Simplicity is enjoying the modest things in life, like watching a plant grow.

# .292.

## TALK

Consider a nice conversation as recreation. I'm not talking about gossiping or discussing dire financial or political woes, but the simple act of giving and telling stories.

Humankind throughout history has used the spoken word as a means of sharing information and drawing closer to one another. For women, conversations are a release. They can share emotions ("Yuck," says my husband) and vent about troubles.

Men converse too, my husband hastily adds. If two men are sitting on a dock fishing, then the *sitting* is recreation, and the *fishing* is recreation, but so is the manly camaraderie. Men also share feelings, but unlike women, they share by exchanging mental pictures. They might do this by bringing up mutual past experiences or describe in detail their latest hunting trip. Men are visual, and visual talk is how they converse.

Many women complain that their husbands don't talk to them. Perhaps it's because the women expect the men to act like other women, and when they don't, the women become annoyed. Treat your man like a man, and you'll talk together just fine.

To jumpstart a conversation with your man, never *ever* say, "We need to talk." Men interpret this—quite accurately—as a forthcoming criticism or a discussion on "feelings" (which they hate). Instead, invite your spouse on a nice brisk walk and see what lovely conversations result.

Regardless of what form it takes, talking is a wonderfully simplifying thing to do if it's not used to batter or hammer someone down.

# . 293 .

## STOP RECREATIONAL SHOPPING

Okay, I'll admit, recreational shopping has never "done it" for me, which is a good thing because I can think of few things that are less conducive to simplifying.

Recently, while attending an out-of-town function, I had several hours to kill until the event opened up. So I wandered into a large shopping center. I spent *hours* combing the aisles. Occasionally I'd look at an item, think "Gosh, that would look great in my house," and move on. When I finally killed enough time, the sum total of my purchases consisted of a tube of lip balm, which I'd needed for awhile anyway.

Think of the money I didn't spend. Think of the waste or garbage or packaging I didn't produce.

Recreational shopping is virtually anathema to the simple life. It promotes dissatisfaction for what you already possess. It puts you in debt. In consumes time and resources. It sets a bad example for your children.

Obviously if you're in need of something, then it behooves you to shop around until you find the best deal (and "shopping around" in this case can mean scanning the pennysaver ads, hunting thrift stores, or searching yard sales). But recreational shopping—going to the mall not because you *need* something, but because you like looking at stuff—is bound to backfire by cluttering up your life with unwanted or unneeded stuff.

Simplicity implies a freedom from unwanted things. Recreational shopping should be one of the first activities to go.

# . 294 .

## TONE DOWN THE VACATIONS

Have you ever wondered about the futility of trying to cram a year's worth of relaxation into two frantic weeks of vacation? It rarely works. You return to your job exhausted (mentally and physically) only to come face-to-face with piles of paperwork at your office. Sometimes it seems easier not to take a vacation at all.

And you're right. It might be easier *not* to take a two-week vacation. One of the growing trends in the workplace is to spread out vacation days to make a bunch of mini-vacations in the form of three or four-day weekends. You might take a short trip, or hang around at home, or make a holiday break a bit longer. What a great idea!

This also allows you more frequent breaks to look forward to. You might be so intensely focused on your two precious weeks of vacation at the end of June that when it comes, you're disappointed if everything isn't perfect. And then, at the beginning of July, you realize with a groan that you have a whole year to get through before you have another precious two weeks of freedom. But by spreading out your vacation days, you get more breaks. Breaks are good.

Tone down your expectations of what a "vacation" implies. Rather than thinking of something grand, elaborate, and expensive, why not stay close to home? Do things that will allow your brain and body to unwind. You'll return to work more relaxed, especially since you know you can take another "vacation" in about a month.

# . 295 .

## DON'T TRY TO "OUT-VACATION" THE JONESES

Like everything else, vacations have become something to brag about. Anything you can do, I can do better.

Did you spend two weeks backpacking through Yellowstone? Well, I spent two weeks backpacking through the Alps. Did you go on a luxury cruise to Alaska? Well, I went on a luxury cruise to Alaska *and* Mexico.

Who cares what the Joneses do? Go where you want and do what you want on your vacation. Glitzy isn't always better. Don't let competition be your travel agent.

Vacations are to relax, to regroup, and to refresh you in body and soul. If you're eaten up with a spirit of competition, what have you achieved? Nothing except a lot of debt and perhaps a lot of stress.

Naturally this does not mean you should *never* splurge on a fancy vacation. My parents, after many years of wishing, finally went on a cruise to Alaska and saw glaciers. They were thrilled by the experience of being on a cruise ship and seeing stunning scenery. They hope to go again. But they didn't go on a cruise to show off or brag; they did it because they *wanted* to (and they could afford it now that they've finished raising their family).

If hanging around your backyard is what you *really* want to do this vacation, more power to you! And if the Joneses smirk over their latest trip to Europe, just smile a secret smile and imagine what their credit card bill looks like compared to yours.

# .296.

## DON'T OVERPACK

When you take a trip, it's a common tendency to overpack. I've actually heard it said that there are two types of travelers: those who pack light, and those who *wish* they had packed light.

Whether it's a reluctance to wear the same set of clothes more than once, or an attempt to anticipate every possible situation that might require a different outfit, the average traveler ends up lugging multiple suitcases, dealing with the hassle of lost luggage, and trying to cram too large a bag into the overhead compartment.

Ever notice those efficient-looking flight attendants in airports? In their smart uniforms and single small overnight case, they look like the well-organized traveler's dream. Yeah sure, you say; the flight attendants wear a uniform and probably won't be gone more than one or two nights.

But think about your last trip. How much of what you brought did you actually use? And how much *less* could you have brought by re-wearing a few outfits?

For clothing, assume that you'll get at least three days' use out of each set (not necessarily three days in a row, either) and see how many fewer sets of clothes you need. When I know I'll be traveling, I start a list as far in advance as possible so I don't forget anything important. One time I forgot my eyeglasses (what a disaster!) so now I even list my glasses.

Streamline your travel requirements. Get multiple uses out of everything you bring. Your trips will be much simpler. And since airlines are now charging for additional baggage, you'll save money as well.

# . 297 .

## VACATION AT HOME

A growing trend among busy employees is to take a series of mini-vacations rather than one long two or three-week hiatus. Not only does this minimize the shock factor when you return to work, but it spreads the enjoyment throughout the year. By combining vacation days with existing holidays (Memorial Day weekend or Thanksgiving), then you can have a luxurious stretch of days off without a lot of the stress and hassle of a formal vacation.

And home is the logical place to go. Staycation, anyone? A home vacation gives you a chance to catch up on things. Maybe you have a huge improvement project you could concentrate on. Maybe you could finally take the kids to the park or the museum like you've been promising. Maybe you could explore some of the local sights that you keep meaning to get to but never have. Whatever you chose to do, you're likely to spend less money, use less gas, and enjoy yourself more if you stay close to home.

For the ten years we lived in Oregon, we lived only a few miles away from a regional tourist attraction. It wasn't until just before moving to Idaho that we visited it (finally!) and discovered that we should have gone far sooner. How sad for us. Dollars to donuts you have lots of things in your immediate area you haven't seen yet either.

Don't forget to cultivate your home life so that staying home is pure joy. A home that is decluttered, moderately tidy, and not filled with arguments and strife is hard to beat as a vacation destination.

# .298.

## DITCH THE SOUVENIRS

It always amazes me how people can travel to an exotic destination surrounded by beautiful scenery and fascinating people and magnificent culture and incredible history and do nothing but *shop*. And many souvenirs are meant for other people, thus cluttering up *their* home as well as yours.

The trouble with souvenirs is that they are purchased on impulse and seldom used or looked at again. Perhaps you're taking a grand vacation to an exotic place and want to buy something to remember it by. You come home and proudly display your exotic knick-knack(s) around the house.

And then you take another trip and buy more. And more. And more. The more you travel, the more souvenirs you accumulate. A souvenir that would otherwise be lovely and noticeable when framed by *space* becomes merely one item amongst a vast collection, no longer noticeable. All these things must be displayed (taking up valuable room in your home), dusted, cared for, and perhaps even insured.

Sometimes—and here's irony for you—travelers become so caught up in *buying* on their vacations that they barely see the beautiful sights and exotic culture they may have longed to experience.

Shift your priorities. Travel to *see* and *experience* things, not *buy* things. If you want something to help you recall a beautiful place, try purchasing postcards to place in a photo album. Or take lots of pictures. Photos (whether postcards or with your digital) are probably the most practical souvenir your can have, plus friends can "see" the place as well. Ditch the souvenirs. It will make your traveling, your luggage, your finances, and your home simpler.

# . 299 .

## DON'T BUY ONLINE

Okay, before you have a conniption, let me explain. The ability to shop from the comfort of your own home has completely altered the retail landscape in this country. Now you don't even have to change out of your pajamas or comb your hair or drive to the mall to blow your credit limit. You can do all your shopping from your bed if you wish.

Shopping, always a popular recreational activity, has taken on a new dimension with the Internet. You can be even more impulsive. You can fill your house with junk without even leaving it. You can buy that combination waffle iron-trouser press that you didn't even know existed. It's only a click away.

Obviously the Internet is a huge help if you're specifically shopping for an item. The Internet allows you to compare prices and brands or get reviews. But my point is that online shopping has made it much easier to clutter your home and get into debt with items you don't need and didn't know existed until you happened upon them, and but now can't live without. Impulse buying (online or otherwise) is contrary to a simpler life.

Before you click on that "add to cart" button, bookmark the site and let your impulse cool for a day or two. Maybe a week. It's like any other purchase. Let it sit for awhile and see if you still want it, if it's within your budget, if you need it, and if it's conducive to simplifying.

# . 300 .

## WASTING AWAY AGAIN IN TV-VILLE

One day my husband came into my office with a calculator in hand. "I don't think I'm figuring this correctly," he said. "I *have* to be wrong. But according to my calculations, if you watch two hours of television a day . . . ." He began punching calculator buttons again. "Then that's 730 hours a year . . . divide by 24 . . . that's thirty solid twenty-four-hour days of doing nothing but watching television!"

We calculated and recalculated those numbers and kept coming up with the same thing. If you watch only two hours of television a day, seven days a week, then you have wasted *one entire month* out of your year doing nothing but sitting on your butt in front of the boob tube. Wasting away again in la-la-land.

Worse, the Nielsen Company reports that the average American watches, not two hours a day of television, but *four* hours. That's *two solid months* a year.

If this describes you, then don't you *ever* dare whine again about how you don't have enough time to start a home business, or fix up the house, spend time with your kids, get an extra job to pay off debt, or anything else to simplify your life. Ever.

Those two (or four) hours a day could be spent cooking a nice meal, or playing Monopoly with your children, or doing the legwork for a home business, or scouting around for a less-expensive home to reduce your mortgage payments, or doing any number of things that are useful toward the goal of simplicity.

# . 301 .

## ENJOY THE HOLIDAYS

I don't much mind the "commercialism" of Christmas. I think it's rather grand that a whole nation can turn itself over to general merry-making for a month. I love seeing the lights, the smiles of strangers, the bell-ringers for the Salvation Army, the splendid decorations. Of course, our family has always been mindful of the "reason for the season," so that makes it special for us.

Collins Publishers' wonderful book, *Christmas in America*, said it best in the Introduction: "Just when the air turns frosty and the days shrink into darkness, the Christmas season arrives in America. It begins at Thanksgiving—with families, feasts and football. Then, during the next six weeks we shop and decorate, worship and make merry. Our hearts warm in the winter cold. We find compassion for strangers, and we remember there are miracles. Pious or festive or both, we join together in an extraordinary national festival."

Christmas is the one time of year when even the busiest families make a special effort at togetherness. If you were to ask your children what their favorite part of Christmas is, most kids would probably say something like, "Baking Christmas cookies." "singing carols," "decorating the tree," or "eating popcorn in front of the fireplace."

While presents are nice, it shouldn't be the focal point. What children remember most about the holidays is the amount of *time* you spent with them. Did you take a couple of hours to bake cookies? Did you walk in the woods to find things for a wreath? Did you attend a candlelit service at church?

Scale back your outside commitments so you can enjoy the holidays.

# . 302 .

## SIMPLIFY CHRISTMAS

Your holidays should be enjoyable, but for too many people, the whole focus of Christmas is presents. I would never suggest ruining yourself financially for the sake of buying *stuff*. When I suggest making merry, I'm thinking more along the lines of modest gifts and lots of family time.

You can make Christmas cookies. You can toast in the New Year with homemade Irish cream. You can watch the kids play games with the Nativity figures. You can pull your tree through the snow and then set it up in solemn splendor in the living room. You can put the gifts teasingly under the tree for the kids to shake and probe. You can go to the candlelit service on Christmas Eve. You can play a CD of holiday music. Yes, to me there's nothing like Christmas.

I am also aware that there are lots of people who go way overboard in the gift department, perhaps forgetting that it's just a small part of the overall enjoyment of the holiday. The average family spends $500 every year on gifts. Many people don't pay off their Christmas credit card purchases until *July*.

There is an excellent book called *Unplug the Christmas Machine* by Jo Robinson and Jean Staeheli that highlights a lot of the folly people fall into during the Christmas holidays. It also has some wonderful advice and tips on how to get off the holiday merry-go-round and make things simpler, easier, and more enjoyable for everyone.

This year, simplify your life by keeping your celebrations simple and joyous.

# . 303 .

## RECREATION IN A DOWN ECONOMY

The two most obvious things to emphasize when considering recreation in a down economy are (a) cost, and (b) stress.

There's a reason "staycations" have become popular in the last few years: they're cheap. I applaud those who decide to discover the many undiscovered treasures in their immediate vicinity which they've never had time to explore before. Others still travel, but they'll camp instead of staying in expensive hotels; or pack food instead of eating out; or use other money-saving ideas.

But vacations can be stressful as well. Those who seek out the chills-and-thrills method of "recreation" are unlikely to be calm and relaxed at the end of their vacation. Those who try to cram untold "experiences" into too short of a time are likely to be worn out by the time they're done.

But it's not just your once-a-year, two-week vacation to think about; it's also your day-to-day activities. Consider making your home the center of your recreational activities. Host a weekly potluck with neighbors or friends. Have a movie night. Rediscover the joys of a good book before a snapping fireplace.

In other words, make sure your recreational activities aren't contributing toward a worsening of your circumstances in a bad economy. Keep your recreational activities cheap and peaceful.

# Nothing New Under the Sun

▼

All humans like to think we live in unique times. Our problems, our politics, our dramas, our economic woes . . . they are exclusive to us and have never been experienced before.

Or have they? The words of the ancients prove there's nothing new under the sun—and we can learn from their words of wisdom.

# .304.

## NOTHING NEW UNDER THE SUN

Somewhere around 1908, the president of Harvard University, Dr. Charles W. Eliot, made a rather bold statement. He said in a speech that the elements of a complete education "could be obtained by spending fifteen minutes a day reading from a collection of books that could fit on a five-foot shelf." (I believe in the original speech he said a three-foot shelf, then later changed his mind.) The implication was that it wasn't necessary to go to college to get a well-rounded education; it could be done at home by reading great works of literature.

The publisher Collier & Son challenged him to put his money where his mouth was, and by 1909, Dr. Eliot had compiled the works that were published into a fifty-one volume set collectively known as the Harvard Classics.

I have become enamored of these books and am slowly acquiring the set. In reading them (and I'm only just starting!), the amazing thing is that they provide wisdom for what to us seem like extremely modern problems. Drowning in debt? Experiencing marital strife? Have problem children or an unsatisfying job? In poor health? Concerned about the environment? It's all here among the pages of the Harvard Classics.

Even back then, the great thinkers and philosophers were advising people to simplify their lives.

# .305.

## THE "SIX MISTAKES OF MAN"

Marcus Tullius Cicero was a great Roman lawyer, political figure, orator, and philosopher. Among his many wise sayings, he put together something called the "Six Mistakes of Man." These are:

1. The delusion that individual advancement is made by crushing others;
2. The tendency to worry about things that cannot be changed or corrected;
3. Insisting that a thing is impossible because we cannot accomplish it;
4. Refusing to set aside trivial preferences;
5. Neglecting development and refinement of the mind and not acquiring the habit of reading and studying; and
6. Attempting to compel other persons to believe and live as we do.

Seldom have I seen a more accurate and succinct collection of the pitfalls of human thought and behavior.

Are you guilty of any of these mistakes? How much do we complicate our lives by trying to force our ambitions and agendas on those around us? How much do we let our minds stagnate, or fill them only with fluff and gossip? How frequently do we mire ourselves down with ridiculously detailed or trivial things? How often do we not strive for impossible things because it hasn't been done in the past? How do we hurt those around us in our quest for success or money?

Keep in mind, by the way, that Cicero lived in the first century B.C. As I said, there is nothing new under the sun.

# .306.

## CRUSH! KILL! DESTROY!

The first of Cicero's "Six Mistakes of Man" is the delusion that individual advancement is made by crushing others. Remember those semi-funny greeting cards congratulating someone on their recent promotion and offering them your back to step on next time? Yeah, we all give a rueful chuckle because it's so often true.

You want that promotion. It will give you power, money, prestige, or other benefits that you didn't have before. And you don't care how many people you have to crush (your kids, your spouse, you coworkers) to get it.

But in all honesty, what do you gain? What is power without self-control, or money without true friendships, or prestige built not on respect but on fear?

It is often true that individual advancement is impossible without "beating out" someone else. We all compete, whether it's in sports, the workplace, or love. Every time you land a new job, you "crushed" others who also applied for the job. This in and of itself is not bad.

So what to do? Be gracious, that's what. Don't gloat, don't lord it over someone, don't be a jerk. Be humble.

Remember the kid's movie *Cars*? In the end, Lightning McQueen lost the race (on purpose) but gained fame. The antagonist won the race, waited for the accolades, and found himself universally loathed because he was a jerk.

This isn't to imply you can't advance yourself. The key, I believe, is to be as gracious and honorable a winner as you are a loser. *That's* what people admire.

# . 307 .

## DON'T WORRY ABOUT THINGS THAT CANNOT BE CHANGED

The second of "Cicero's Six Mistakes of Man" is the tendency to worry about things that cannot be changed or corrected. Why spend energy on worrying over what cannot be changed? Acceptance is a much more peaceful, simple solution. This is not to imply that acceptance is *easy*, but in the end, acceptance is more peaceful than fighting.

Is your mother a difficult person? Stop trying to change her. Accept her for what she is. Then, and only then, can you decide whether she is worth keeping in your life.

Do you desperately want a new car but can't afford it? Rather than trying to live beyond your means or envying your neighbor' new car, accept the fact that this is not your time to buy a car.

Do you have a medical condition that is not curable? Accept it. It's simpler than fighting it. I read a news story once about a woman who had endured almost two hundred operations in her life due to a horrific childhood accident. She knew she could stay in bed and cry every day if she wanted to, because she hurt all the time. But she made the choice to be positive, not bitter.

Some things, as terrible as they may be, cannot be changed. It simplifies your life if you can accept them. Then be grateful for the gifts you have.

# . 308 .

## ACCOMPLISH THE IMPOSSIBLE

This is the third of Cicero's "Six Mistakes of Man": the tendency to insist that a thing is impossible because we cannot accomplish it.

Did you know that, sometime around the early 1900s, the U.S. government nearly closed the Patent Office because it was thought that nothing new could possibly be invented? Considering the technological and medical breakthroughs we've had in the past hundred years, such an idea now seems ludicrous. But back then, any of the marvels we now take for granted were considered impossible.

Just because *you* can't do something doesn't mean someone else isn't striving for the very thing you dismiss as impossible. Personally, I find this a delightful idea. Think about European society a thousand years ago, at the height of the medieval period. The science of medicine was virtually nonexistent. Technology was often limited to simple machines (inclined plane, lever and fulcrum, etc.). Think how far we've come in terms of medical and scientific knowledge.

Now think about what our lives might be like a thousand years *from* now. Will illness be snuffed out? Will the moon or Mars be populated? Will the earth be polluted beyond belief, or more pristine than we can imagine? Will nations cease hostilities, or will war be a way of life? Who can tell?

On a less celestial level, think about your own dreams and goals. Why does it seem impossible to simplify now? And what can you do to make the impossible possible? If you start to think outside the box and establish concrete goals to simplify your life, who knows what you might accomplish?

# .309.

## SET ASIDE TRIVIAL PREFERENCES

This is the fourth of Cicero's "Six Mistakes of Man": refusing to set aside trivial preferences. By trivial preferences, Cicero was referring to the ability to pick your battles. Is it worth arguing over the fact that you love coffee and I love tea? Is it worth coming to blows over which sports team is better? "My daddy is stronger than your daddy" is a cliché from childhood, but what adult versions do we argue about now?

Do you long to throw a punch at someone who "took" your parking place? Do you remain steamed all day because of someone's stupid remark? Do you fume over your coworker's stubborn refusal to see the merit in your argument over which beer is best? How does this profit you? What have you gained?

I've met people who actually take it as a personal affront when things don't go their way or someone's opinion differs. I've seen them turn red, clench their fists, and grit their teeth during a discussion involving sports or music.

You could stay angry all your life if you get bent out of shape over such trivial stuff. The pressure that builds up over refusing to set aside trivial preferences can result in health issues like stress, high blood pressure, and even strokes.

So pick your battles. Decide what is *truly* important to argue or fight over. Agree to disagree about the trivial things. And most of all, accept the fact that people are different. What an amazingly simplifying thing to do.

# . 310 .

## KEEP LEARNING

This is the fifth of Cicero's "Six Mistakes of Man": neglecting development and refinement of the mind and not acquiring the habit of reading and studying. Even as far back as the first century B.C., philosophers observed that relatively few people continue their education beyond what they need simply to get a job or to function in life.

Today as a nation we find ourselves obsessed by the shenanigans of pop stars and Hollywood dribble. Matters of science, of medicine, of technology, of human interest, of humor, of music, of science, of politics, of literature . . . all these are put aside so we can follow some Hollywood twit's personal meltdown.

The world is so full of beautiful things. Take the time to learn about them. Besides, now that you're all grown up, here's a nifty concept: you don't have to learn or study anything that doesn't interest you. If you have no interest in learning about Italian nobility during the Renaissance, then read up on the history of baseball or the workings of antique tractors, or dip into a good novel.

Learning is not a goal; it's a journey. The more you exercise your mental legs, the farther and faster you'll travel. There is even evidence that an active mental life can stave off Alzheimer's disease. That's not a bad result of reading a few books or expounding on the balance of Cabernet Sauvignon versus Pinot Noir, or the merits of a Chevy truck vs. a Ford.

A mind is a terrible thing to waste. What have you done for yours lately?

# .311.

## WE'RE ALL DIFFERENT—
## DEAL WITH IT

This is the sixth and last of Cicero's "Six Mistakes of Man": attempting to compel other persons to believe and live as we do. And boy did Cicero know what he was talking about. I guess even two thousand years ago, people were trying to force others to think and act like themselves.

But it's not possible. No one will ever convince me that football is worth watching. Nor will I ever be able to persuade you that classical music is the only thing that should come over your radio. My husband is positive that a 1949 Ford 8N tractor should be in everyone's garage. A friend of mine is certain that gothic romances are the epitome of literature. Some people actually think modern art looks nice. And my kids used to believe Polly Pockets ruled the world.

We can make ourselves miserable trying to force others to believe or act or think as we do. The key word here is *forced* or *compelled*. You can do your best to convince me that football is wonderful, and I'll listen politely (for awhile, anyway). But if you try to *force* me to watch a game, then prepare for fireworks. Or at least a good pout.

It is a much simpler idea to agree to disagree on certain things, and leave it at that, don't you agree? Now pardon me while I turn up the radio. They're playing Vivaldi's *Four Seasons*.

# .312.

## DON'T COMPLICATE THINGS

Confucius (about 500 B.C.) was a Chinese philosopher of rare brilliance and unusual clarity. Among his many pearls of wisdom he said, "Life is really simple, but we insist on making it complicated."

Probably one of the most effective things you can do to simplify your life is to learn what complicates it. Sometimes we pass our life in a state of numb acceptance. If we face traffic during our morning commute, we shrug and accept it. Of course, it's better than *fighting* it but what if we didn't have to deal with traffic at all? Have you thought about that?

Some complicating things cannot be changed or cured. Untimely deaths, devastating illnesses, natural disasters—there is a long list of things that cannot be cured and can only be endured. But there are also many things *within your control* that add stress to your life. Is your commute too long? Do you hate your job? Are your children getting out of control? Are you watching too much television? Do you have an addiction? Are you eating too much fast food or junk food? Is your home too cluttered?

Many of these are things we do to ourselves. It is precisely the stuff we do to ourselves that we have to ability to change. Identify what your complications are, *then take the necessary steps to reduce or eliminate them.* A simple life is a life with as few complications as possible. Only when we *realize* what complicates our lives can we start to untangle those complications.

# .313.

## HE WHO IS CONTENT

Epictetus was a Greek philosopher, born as a slave around 50 A.D. and later freed. He became an authority on the Stoic movement and a believer that man should cultivate complete independence of external circumstances (I gather this belief resulted from enduring torture inflicted by an earlier master). His *Golden Sayings* are fascinating reading, from which I've culled those that are pertinent to simplicity.

Asked, "Who is the rich man?" Epictetus replied, "He who is content." This one is hard to argue with. I think the constant lust for *more* is a form of poverty: more possessions, more power, more money, and more prestige. To want *more* of something means you think you don't have enough of it yet. I understand that attitude with true privation (starvation, thirst, etc.), but most of us aren't in that state.

At the end of your life, you could have three homes, six cars, and a constant desire for still *more*. How does this compare with the person who was satisfied with a modest lifestyle and the love, respect, and friendship of others?

Until you can be content with what you have, you will never be rich, nor will your life be simple. Ever. Contentment, however, begins within you. Until you learn contentment for the blessings you have, you will remain frustrated and grasping.

I don't believe contentment is at odds with ambition. If we didn't have goals to strive for or ideals to reach for, our lives would be pretty flat and boring. But let's keep the ambitions modest, shall we?

# .314.

## BODY AND SOUL

Epictetus also said, "At feasts, remember that you are entertaining two guests, body and soul. What you give to the body, you presently lose; what you give to the soul, you keep for ever."

I thought this was pretty neat. Epictetus recognized that we are composed of both the mortal and the immortal. It got me to thinking, what kind of soul do you want to present at the pearly gates when it's your turn to go? Is it a soul that has striven for higher things—knowledge, learning, kindness, and generosity? Or is it a soul shriveled with meanness, tainted by broken vows and infidelity, and shrunken by a constant lust for power or riches? It's clear that these are eternal questions since Epictetus pondered them nearly two millennia ago.

If you don't believe in life after death (and that would be a pity), then at least consider this: Who do you want holding your hand as you die? Your loving spouse, children, and dear friends? Or your accountant, lawyer, or other hired assistant?

Your soul needs nourishment. If you nourish it with love, friendship, dignity, humor, worship, joy, and simplicity, think how healthy it will be! If you nourish your soul with hatred, violence, anger, stinginess, impatience, lust, envy, and any other vice you'd care to mention, then you're going to have one very sick soul. Choose wisely.

# .315.

## STAND UP

Marcus Aurelius was emperor of Rome from 161 through 180 A.D. Like most Roman emperors, his reign was marked by much cruelty and warfare; however unlike many emperors, he had a philosophic bent and apparently some interest in the welfare of his subjects (when it suited him).

Among his *Meditations* appear such gems as: "Be cheerful also, and seek not external help nor the tranquility which others give. A man then must stand erect, not be kept erect by others." We have a modern way of saying this: learn to stand on your own two feet.

As we mature into adults, it behooves us to become independent. Unless we have a situation in which we are compelled to be dependent, learn the joys of standing on your own two feet. Simplicity implies a certain degree of self-sufficiency and autonomy.

This has a practical as well as a philosophic side. On a practical side, it is sensible to cultivate skills that are useful in the job market. Can you type? Answer phones? Compose letters? Speak in public? Follow directions? Give directions? Speak two languages? These are all examples of useful skills for standing on your own two feet.

The philosophic side of the equation is how much confidence you'll gain by your new skills and abilities. Confidence can simplify your life in a million ways, including the confidence to take chances on things that will, well, simplify your life.

Think about it this way: can your life ever be *truly simple* if you allow yourself to be dependent and at the mercy of others?

# .316.

## WHAT YOU ARE IS WHAT YOU DO

This is related to another What You Are (#25), only this time Marcus Aurelius said it almost two thousand years ago: "Such as are thy habitual thoughts, such also will be the character of thy mind; for the soul is dyed by the thoughts."

Over and over through history, philosophers and thinkers have noted the discrepancy in people who *say* they are one thing but *do* something else. It is said that you can judge a man's character by the company he keeps. "Company" can refer not only to friends, but to hobbies, actions, words, employment, and anything else that can demonstrate what you're really like.

What kind of friends do you keep? What kind of hobbies do you enjoy? What kind of job do you have? And, here's a thought, does any of this conflict with what you feel or say you *are*?

Your actions reflect what you truly are like inside, despite what you may protest to the contrary. (Think of your average politician.) There is no escaping the evidence. If you *say* you are one thing, but you *do* the other, which do you think will be believed?

It's the same with your thoughts. Aurelius said that the soul is dyed by the thoughts. If your thoughts are negative and destructive, your soul will be, too. Is this what you want out of life?

Make sure your thoughts and actions are in line with your beliefs, as difficult as this may be to achieve. Only by doing this can you be at peace with yourself.

# .317.

## BE READY TO LET IT GO

This wisdom also comes from Marcus Aurelius in the second century A.D.: "Receive wealth or prosperity without arrogance; and be ready to let it go."

Remember the movie *Trading Places?* Dan Aykroyd was a wealthy young stockbroker whose education and position led him to believe he was better than others. On a bet from his boss, his position was taken away and his assets were frozen. Suddenly he was down and out. Dan was arrogant in his wealth, and he wasn't ready to let it go (until the end of the movie, of course).

In J.R.R. Tolkien's *The Lord of the Rings*, the character Aragorn says, "One who cannot cast away a treasure at need is in fetters."

It's easy to lose wealth or prosperity. All it takes is being downsized and suddenly we're out of work. In these uncertain financial times, it's not hard to imagine what it would be like to lose our prosperity.

Our lives are simpler if we remember that any blessings of wealth that come our way are just that—blessings. You may have worked hard to gain them, but they can be swept aside by events beyond your control. Appreciate these blessings without arrogance.

What are you arrogant in? Are you arrogant about your wealth? Your beautiful home? Your education? Your small carbon footprint? Your degree of spirituality?

Our blessings should not be sources of comparison to others. Don't turn your blessings into arrogance because then you won't be ready to let them go.

# .318.

## THIRTEEN VIRTUES

Ben Franklin was famous for his pithy sayings and one-liners. What is less well-known are the thirteen virtues by which he tried to abide (some with less than perfect success). These are:

1. Temperance: Eat not to dullness; drink not to elevation.
2. Silence: Speak not but what may benefit others or yourself; avoid trifling conversation.
3. Order: Let all your things have their places; let each part of your business have its time.
4. Resolution: Resolve to perform what you ought; perform without fail what you resolve.
5. Frugality: Make no expense but to do good to others or yourself; i.e., waste nothing.
6. Industry: Lose no time; be always employed in something useful; cut off all unnecessary actions.
7. Sincerity: Use no hurtful deceit; think innocently and justly, and, if you speak, speak accordingly.
8. Justice: Wrong none by doing injuries, or omitting the benefits that are your duty.
9. Moderation: Avoid extremes; forbear resenting injuries so much as you think they deserve.
10. Cleanliness: Tolerate no uncleanliness in body, clothes, or habitation.
11. Tranquility: Be not disturbed at trifles, or at accidents common or unavoidable.
12. Chastity: Rarely use venery but for health or offspring, never to dullness, weakness, or the injury of your own or another's peace or reputation.
13. Humility: Imitate Jesus and Socrates.

This is a pretty rough list! Even Franklin admitted that his goal, at best, was to conquer them one at a time. History will bear that Franklin may not have succeeded on all of them (chastity comes to mind). Still, these virtues are worth thinking about because there is no doubt that application of all of them would simplify one's life immeasurably.

# .319.

## YOU GET MORE, YOU WANT MORE

John Woolman was a Quaker living in the American colonies in the mid-1700s. His *Journal* records the efforts he made to raise awareness of the evils of slavery as well as a myriad of daily concerns from life in the eighteenth century.

Quakers are traditionally a simple people, dressing and speaking plainly. Many of their principles are worth studying today for people trying to simplify their lives. Among some of Woolman's observations was that " . . . with an increase of wealth the desire of wealth increase(s)." In other words, people are never satisfied. And Woolman made this astute notation around 1743, thus proving that human nature stays the same.

We've all heard stories about people who upgrade their computers every six months or keep buying larger homes despite their small family size. I'm not saying that you should never upgrade your home furnishings or indulge in some technological marvel (if you can afford it). But must you have the latest, fastest, glitziest, most fashionable, and most expensive items all the time?

We always strive for the next biggest and better version of (pick one) a big screen TV, cell phone, iPod, boat, or car. We are never satisfied. But as Woolman observed, this is a vicious circle. "Where the heart was set on greatness, success in business did not satisfy the craving." We always want more, more, more.

Until this craving can be stopped, it's hard to achieve a simpler life.

# .320.

## HURRY UP!

John Woolman had some trenchant remarks on our tendency to go too fast. "So great is the hurry in the spirit of this world, that in aiming to do business quickly and to gain wealth the creation at this day doth loudly groan."

The context for this remark was in noting how stagecoaches could often achieve a hundred miles in a twenty-four hour period, a stunning speed for the time. Unfortunately, the cost of this speed was frequently the death or blindness of the horses, as well as the suffering and sometimes freezing to death of the post-boys. All because people were in a hurry.

My goodness, what would Woolman say today? With e-mails, faxes, jet planes, and overnight delivery, we can't imagine a time when things moved as slowly as a hundred miles a day. If they don't get caught, some drivers can now do a hundred miles in an *hour*. And for what? What have we achieved in terms of personal happiness and (dare I say it) simplicity, by going faster and faster? What modern-day horses and post-boys are we sacrificing to get somewhere more quickly?

When we hurry so much, our health suffers. Our children suffer. Our spouse suffers. Our friendships suffer. Humans need down time, a time to decompress and toss off the "hurries" of the day. Be sure to slow down and give yourself that time. Life is simpler that way.

# .321.

## AIN'T GOT TIME

William Penn is best known as the founder of Pennsylvania. In his *Fruits of Solitude* (written in the late 1600s), he offers many clear insights on various subjects ranging from knowledge and wit, to popularity and ostentation. His writings make fascinating reading and are chock-full of gems.

Even back three hundred and fifty years ago, people were aware of how precious time is. "There is nothing of which we are apt to be so lavish as of Time, and about which we ought to be more solicitous," writes Penn. "Time is what we want most, but what, alas! we use worst."

It is probably because of your lack of time that you were drawn to this book. Time is increasingly precious in this busy world, and it is what people most long to acquire. Time with your children, time with your spouse, time for leisure and relaxation.

Yet the things we do to "make" time are ultimately counter-productive. We buy fast-food or convenience food because we have no time to cook. We insist that "quality" time with our children is sufficient because we don't have enough time for "quantity" time. We have less time at home because we spend more time working to pay off the credit card debt. It seems kind of screwy, doesn't it?

The things that are most precious to you—your family, your friends, and your faith—are what you should prioritize your time around. Otherwise, as Penn concludes, "God will certainly most strictly reckon with us, when Time shall be no more."

# . 322 .

## YOU'RE NOT THE BOSS

The higher they stand, the further they fall. Those who are in the highest positions of power and authority, who love to yank our lives around, who insist upon control, are the ones most in need of reigning in, it seems. Is this person you?

"He would have others obey him, even his own kind," says William Penn. "But he will not obey God, that is so much above him, and who made him."

Yes, you may have authority over others. You might be a politician, or a supervisor, or a CEO, or someone else in a position of power. Good for you! *Someone* has to do it. But trouble begins when those in authority forget that they, too, have to report to a Higher Authority. That's when their power and authority goes to their head, and they try to assume the god-like mantle of a dictator. And most dictators love to throw their weight around and make the lives of everyone else miserable.

Some kinds of dictatorships are necessary. I think every parent, for example, should be a benevolent dictator in his own home (see #61). But for goodness' sake, don't forget that you're *not* the Big Boss.

"In his prayers," says Penn, "he says, Thy Will be done: But means his own: At least acts so."

Keep humble within your authority. Recognize your own limitations and failings. It will not only simplify *your* life, but it will simplify the lives of those under you.

# . 323 .

## HERE'S MUD IN YOUR EYE

"We are apt to be very pert at censuring others, where we will not endure advice our selves," advises William Penn. "And nothing shews our Weakness more than to be so sharp-sighted at spying other Men's Faults, and so purblind about our own."

Our pastor once used a similar line in a sermon: "We judge others for their flaws, and ourselves for our virtues." It's *so* easy to see what's wrong with others. It's a lot harder to see what's wrong with us. This is one of the places where women have a blind spot—everything that is wrong in a marriage is *always* our husbands' fault, and *nothing* is our fault. Sound familiar?

Maybe it's time to stop looking at the sawdust in your brother's (or husband's) eye, and take out the plank in your own. Could your marriage be happier if you were more considerate, more loving, more intimate, and more complimentary? Could your marriage be happier if you learned the art of holding your tongue? This isn't to suggest that we forgive evil behavior in others. It's merely to point out that we may not be as much the innocent bystander in our relationships as we would like to believe.

Of course this goes much further than just our marriages. We are quick to criticize coworkers, service workers, church members—anybody—rather than recognize that we ourselves might be the problem. But if we can recognize and fix our own weaknesses before asking others to do the same, it might make our lives simpler.

# .324.

## TEACH YOUR CHILDREN WELL

Remember the old song by the Byrds called "Teach Your Children"? Long before the 1960s, William Penn said: "Men are generally more careful of the Breed of their Horses and Dogs than of their Children."

It starts with choosing a spouse who would make a good parent. I actually knew someone who married a man on his way to jail for a double murder. But regardless who you chose to make children with, you should raise those children with more care and attention than you would give your job, your pick-up truck, your house, or your boat (our modern day "horses" and "dogs").

It baffles me when people choose to work longer hours than necessary, for instance, to buy a huge house, a new truck, or a boat, and in doing so deprive children of time and attention. Do you brush your kids off when they ask you to read a story? Do you plop them in front of the television to get them off your back? Do you skip their school plays, teacher's conferences, or sports activities because you're too busy?

Penn also said, "We are too careless of Posterity; not considering that as they are, so the next Generation will be."

What are you teaching your kids? That *money* and *possessions* are more important than *they* are? Our children are the most important things in our lives. They are dependent upon us to train them up to become loving, productive adults. Ultimately our lives are simpler if we can raise our children to be good people.

# .325.

## REVENGE IS A WASTE OF TIME

The great essayist and philosopher Francis Bacon in his *Essays: Civil and Moral* (published in 1625) said, "This is certain, that a man that studieth revenge keeps his own wounds green, which otherwise would heal and do well."

How true! If we dwell on wrong-doing, if we make a career out of being a victim, if we refuse to let go of the past, then our wounds stay green instead of healing. I prefer the much nicer "The best revenge is success."

When we burn for vengeance against someone, it consumes us. Everything becomes colored by our victimhood. We see injustice everywhere. We spend countless hours planning nasty things against the perpetrator. However, if we want true vengeance, we can't let ourselves be contaminated.

I am not making light of whatever terrible thing you may have suffered, nor am I implying that crimes shouldn't go unpunished. If, as a child, you suffered sexual abuse at the hands of an adult, then it's hard to let something like that go. Prosecute the person if possible, but then get on with life. Prove yourself better than the scum who did such awful things. Rise above. Vow never to let such a thing happen to *your* children. Succeed. Therein lay your best revenge.

To dwell on the past is useless. The only thing within our power is to improve the future. Our lives are simpler when we accept with serenity that which we cannot change (the past), and have the courage to change what we can (our future).

# . 326 .

## DIFFERENT DRUMMERS

Henry David Thoreau is considered by many the father of the simplicity movement, largely based upon his two-year excursion to Walden Pond starting in 1845. From the first time I read *Walden*, I had a bit of a problem with Henry. I felt it profoundly odd that someone would take the time to baptize his bricks or have intimate relations with his beans. Thoreau was a man incapable of understanding the joys of domesticity, the satisfaction from income-producing labor or, frankly, the need in society for the farms and industries of which he was so disdainful. Nonetheless, he had many interesting things to say in his essays, particularly the chapter on "Economy" where most of his quotes on simplicity are found.

For example, my husband and I take comfort in this quote: "Why should we be in such desperate haste to succeed, and in such desperate enterprises? If a man does not keep pace with his companions, perhaps it is because he hears a different drummer." Having marched to the beat of our own drum for over eighteen years now, we understand.

This ties in with "March to the Beat of Your Own Drum" (#13). It urges people not to be so consumed with what society dictates as "successful." If your calling in life is to stay home with your kids, or start your own woodcraft business, or otherwise buck the trend of what is termed *successful*, then more power to you. Life is simpler when we go with our strengths, our passions, and our callings.

# . 327 .

## LIVE CHEAP

With all of the costs of living we have today—taxes, mortgage, health insurance, food, bills, and more—it seems staggeringly naïve to read Thoreau's quote: "For more than five years I maintained myself thus solely by the labour of my hands, and I found, that by working about six weeks in a year, I could meet all the expenses of living."

I don't know about you, but my first thought on reading this is: "Yeah, but here's a guy with no wife, no kids, no home, no bills, no mortgage, and apparently no *life*. What does *he* know?" It's hard to compare the cost of living in 1840 with 2011, but as with most things, Thoreau had a point.

If you moved to a small house in a cheap part of the country, got rid of all but one old car, paid off every penny of debt, reduced your services to the essentials only (i.e., no cable, no internet, no dry cleaners, no take-out foods, no music lessons for your kids), then you, too, could live quite cheaply. You might even be able to make it through the year on six weeks' worth of income.

Okay, maybe not quite. But my point is that we all tend to work long hours in high-stress jobs to pay for things that not only aren't essential, but are often harmful to our peace and sanity. Our lives could be vastly simplified if we just redefined what *essential* means.

# .328.

## HOW TO BE RICH

Thoreau said, "A man is rich in proportion to the number of things which he can afford to let alone." Like many of Thoreau's better quotes, this strikes me as eminently sensible. In some respects it's similar to "Eat Lentils" (#205).

It's even similar to the premise of Thomas Stanley's book, *The Millionaire Next Door*, in which the author examines the financial practices of the very wealthy. The idea is that wealth is tied to the ability *not to spend money.*

I know somebody who is wealthy, due in large part to his financial restraint. He buys a car and drives it for twenty or more years. He bought a modest house in a hot real estate market (before it became hot) and paid off the mortgage as rapidly as possible. He also owns four other properties, all paid for in full. His daily purchases are modest, his luxuries are few, yet he lives a satisfying life. He's also very, very rich. If the economy tanked tomorrow, he'd be fine.

Now consider the ostentatiously "rich" person who insists on luxury autos upgraded every two years, a five-thousand-square-foot McMansion, designer clothes, the hottest electronics, and the staggering debt. What would happen to this person if the economy tanked tomorrow?

Dave Ramsey, the financial advisor, says that without debt, your income is the biggest wealth-producing tool you have. Use it to become rich by learning what you can afford to let alone.

# . 329 .

## PLAIN AND SIMPLE

The Chinese philosopher Lao-tzu (who lived in the 6th-century B.C.) had a spiffy idea: "Manifest plainness, embrace simplicity, reduce selfishness, have few desires." That sums things up nicely, doesn't it? Even back 2,500 years ago, philosophers were offering the *same advice that we give today* on how to simplify. When will we learn?

Manifest plainness. Yep, forego the hottest fashions, the newest electronic gadgets, and the designer houses. Consider the beauty of a home uncluttered by unnecessary possessions. Think of the money you'll save.

Embrace simplicity. It is superior to complexity. Enough said.

Reduce selfishness. Isn't life simpler when you are loving and giving with your spouse, your family, your friends, and your community?

Have few desires. As Thoreau noted, freedom from the desire for *more* can radically simplify our lives. We can become richer in the things that count.

It's all so . . . simple.

What strikes me as profound is how these ideas have been around for literally thousands of years and yet we *still* need to hear them because we *still* insist on messing up. We still don't "get" that fewer desires, less selfishness, plain possessions, and sensible choices are the keys to simplicity.

We know this. Then why do we complicate things? It's because deep down we don't want to give up our nice clothes, big house, generous paycheck, or other manifestations of our ego. We don't want to become less selfish. We don't want to reduce our desires. Therefore our lives aren't simple.

# .330.

## CUT YOUR KNOTS

Remember the story of the Gordian knot? According to legend, Alexander the Great solved the problem of untying the impossibly complex knot by merely cutting it in two with his sword.

The Swiss philosopher Henri Frederic Amiel (1821–1881) said, "A man must be able to cut a knot, for everything cannot be untied; he must know how to disengage what is essential from the detail in which it is enwrapped, for everything cannot be equally considered; in a word, he must be able to simplify his duties, his business and his life."

Seldom have I come across a quote more suited to our current, everyday, busy, stressful lives. Sometimes we just have to cut a knot or two, rather than trying to untie what may be an impossibly complex situation.

My husband and I "cut our knots" when we quit our jobs, left the city, and bought a shack on acreage in semi-rural Oregon back in 1992. At the time, we had no other responsibilities, no kids, so it was a risk we felt we could take. What we didn't anticipate were the subsequent years of poverty as we struggled to keep our home business aloft. Some might call it simplicity at the stroke of a sword, though being poor is not simple.

But was it worth it? Of course! How else would we have solved the complex knot of trying to adopt a more rural lifestyle?

Consider your knots carefully. It they can't be untied, it might be best to sever them.

# .331.

## STOP FRITTERING

Thoreau said, "Our life is frittered away by detail . . . Simplify, simplify."

How many of us bog ourselves down and fritter away our lives by detail? What type of bath towels should I buy, and can I get them in just the right shade of aqua to match the linoleum? If I take this street instead of that street, will I shave three minutes off my morning commute? Should I stop at McDonald's or Wendy's for lunch? Do these pants make my butt look fat? Should I perm or dye? Cash or charge? Paper or plastic?

So much of our precious lives are sucked up by the myriad of unimportant details associated with modern living. Evidently the same thing was happening in Thoreau's day, no matter how much we think of those times as "simpler."

If you let go of the details that suck you down, you have time to focus on the stuff that's important. If you quit obsessing over your wardrobe, you'll have more time to spend with your kids. If you stop trying to impress people with your possessions, you'll save a lot of money. If you cease worrying about whether you're living up to someone else's expectations (your parents, your teachers, your boss) then you're freer to explore your own interests.

When Thoreau urged us to "Simplify!" he wasn't referring to the *feng shui* of your living room. He was warning us about wasting the precious limited hours of our lives by worrying about nonsense that is truly unimportant.

# .332.

## BE CREATIVE

Creativity is a highly underrated aspect of simplicity. Each and every one of us has different circumstances in our lives. We have different family situations, jobs, homes, and locations. We come from different backgrounds, we have different beliefs and opinions, and we have different skills and abilities.

No simplicity book can address *all* issues for *all* readers. It's impossible. Therefore, we have to be creative. We need to make sensible, intelligent choices to figure out how to simplify our own particular situation.

Here's an example I've always admired. Everyone knows that single moms often put their young children in daycare because they must work. Yet I've heard instances where several moms will pool their resources, rent a house together, and then pay one of the women to be the designated stay-at-home "mom," who then cares for all the other children. How clever is that? While this may not work for you, it's an example of thinking creatively to come up with a solution that simplified lives.

What parts of your life need simplifying? Perhaps your marriage is rock-solid but your commute is terrible? Perhaps your kids are running wild but you love your home? Perhaps your finances are stable but you haven't set foot inside a church in decades? Perhaps your carbon footprint is nearly zero but you and your spouse fight all the time?

Whatever it is, examine the problem and apply creativity to solve it. We can all simplify to one degree or another. It's our job to figure out how.

# . 333 .

## WHO OWNS WHOM?

So much of simplicity comes down to figuring out who owns whom. Do you own things, or do they own you? This reminds me of the old joke about the definition of a boat: A boat is a hole in the water surrounded by fiberglass into which you pour money. Not really funny, is it?

We are tied to our homes, our cars, our boats, our vacation homes, our second cars, and our extreme toys. We want more—a bigger house, a fancier car, the latest fashion, upgraded computers, and high-end electronics. Our ego forces us to keep up with the Joneses.

We work long hours and expend our life's energy to afford these things. We can't let them go. They own us. So we stick our kids in daycare and stay away from home for longer hours to pay for the things which own us.

*Boston Globe* columnist Ellen Goodman said, "Normal is getting dressed in clothes that you buy for work, driving through traffic in a car that you are still paying for, in order to get to the job that you need so you can pay for the clothes, car, and the house that you leave empty all day in order to afford to live in it."

Gosh, what a depressing reality. So fix it. Stop being a slave to your possessions, your ego, and societal expectations. *Let it go.* Free yourself to simplify in order to spend time with the things that are truly important: family, friends, and faith.

# .334.

## ANCIENT WISDOM FOR
## A DOWN ECONOMY

Imagine what Henry David Thoreau would say if he were suddenly set down in modern-day times.

Thoreau had a high opinion of independence, both from government intrusion and from dependency on others for one's livelihood. While he sometimes mocked the farms and factories around him that provided his neighbors with employment, he spent his working years as a teacher, a tutor, or as a laborer in his family's pencil factory. Yet he longed for a farm which would provide both income from his own labors, and the solitude he craved.

So it is interesting to speculate what Thoreau would think if he saw us today. How would he view our longing for continued material acquisitions? For our tendency to cluster in cities with populations in the millions? For our increasing distance from our food sources and our roots in the earth? And all this from our ability to function as independent beings? What would he say about our rate of government taxation, regulation, and control? It staggers the mind.

To live simply is to incorporate many of the ideals of which Thoreau and other philosophers wrote. Contrary to popular belief, it is still possible to live simply in today's world. You don't even have to leave the city to do it.

Here's what Thoreau said: Don't be in such desperate haste to succeed. March to your own drum. Leave cheaply. Learn what things you can let alone. That way you no longer have to lead a life of quiet desperation.

# Radical Simplicity

▼

Sometimes the basic, ordinary, everyday stuff just doesn't cut the mustard. For some people, the only way to simplify their lives is to get radical. For those who have lost their jobs, are facing foreclosure, or contemplating bankruptcy . . . there may be no option but to radically simplify. Here are some ideas.

# . 335 .

## WHAT IS RADICAL SIMPLICITY?

Radical simplicity is just that: radical. It's a number of suggestions that go against the grain and the instinct of our modern society. These tips are designed to help you look outside the box of your current busy lifestyle.

Some of these suggestions are difficult and require a total rearrangement of your life. Some can be done no matter where you live or what your circumstances are. Some of the ideas are complex and some are even controversial, especially in this day and age. But the level of complexity or controversy doesn't mean the result isn't worth it.

The idea behind radical simplicity is to *look beyond the instinctive defensiveness* that may arise as you read the suggestions. Give some of the ideas serious thought. What would happen if you did, say, fire the nanny or get rid of your television? What if you dumped the high-mortgage home and moved someplace smaller? Would the quality of your life and the lives of your family members improve by implementing any of these ideas? It's easy to dismiss these suggestions as unrealistic or impossible. However, it might be that you don't want to take a chance and actually give the idea a try.

If you have managed to master nearly all the other suggestions in this book, you'll find your life has been simplified dramatically. If you continue and try some of the following, you might find yourself surprised at the measure of peace and stability in a hitherto complex life.

# . 336 .

## BE CAREFUL WHAT YOU WISH FOR

As much as you hate your job, your commute, your neighborhood, or other aspects of a complex life, you have to admit it has one overwhelming benefit: it's familiar. As difficult as it is to be in debt, to have a contentious relationship with your spouse, or to have unruly children, at least it's well-known territory. We know how to get from one day to the next without really having to think about it too much or work at it too hard. All we have to do is tread the same, familiar, habitual rut.

But when you become free, you are removed from the old familiar, comfortable ways. Maybe you decided to take the plunge and open your own home business. Or perhaps you moved away from your cramped city apartment into a sprawling old farmhouse on twenty acres. Or possibly you gave up your second income to stay home with your kids. Maybe you thought you would start treating your spouse better.

Whatever you do to simplify your life, prepare for a shock. It won't be easy. Things will go wrong. You will second-guess yourself. What have you *done?* You didn't expect it to *be* this way!

Freedom is never quite what you expect. You are now responsible for yourself, rather than having someone else do it all for you. It's a lot of work, and maybe you're not sure you like it.

But assuming you've made sound, well-prepared choices, something wondrous may happen, given time. The shock will wear off, and you will find yourself thrilled with your new, simpler life.

# .337.

## YOUR PRESENT
## IS NOT YOUR FUTURE

We often think what is happening right now will last forever. But it doesn't. To everything there is a season. Things change.

When parents see a small child going through a "stage," they know that the child will grow and mature and eventually leave that stage behind. Well, the same thing happens in life. We go through "stages." Trouble arises when we have a desire that is in conflict with our current circumstances, and we don't see why we shouldn't fulfill that wish *now*.

Perhaps you and your spouse had a baby much sooner than you anticipated, before you had a chance to finish college or just as you landed the world's best job. It behooves you to take the long view of things. Your baby is better off being raised by you rather than being put in daycare. Put off college or the job and raise your baby.

Plans must alter with life's realities. What is the most moral, the most God-pleasing, the most rational choice you can make in your current circumstance? Is it to put aside a vacation to Europe in order to care for an aging parent? Is it to put off retirement to raise your grandchild?

What decision *will make you admire yourself* later on? If you could project yourself twenty years into the future and look back at your decision, would you be pleased with your choice? If your conscience is clear when you've made your decision, you know you've just simplified things by doing the *right* thing.

# .338.

## CHANGE YOUR PARADIGM
## OF VALUE

Are you ashamed to call yourself a seamstress instead of a CEO? A stay-at-home mom instead of a career woman? A backhoe operator instead of a lawyer? A housekeeper instead of an advertising executive?

A byproduct of simplifying your life is to change your definition of "value." If you've done some of the more radical things in this book such as turning a hobby into a business or moving to the country, you may no longer be surrounded by CEOs and lawyers and other high-profile career people. Instead, you may be surrounded by truck drivers, waitresses, and highway workers. These people will have values, education, and experiences that are different than yours and in many cases *may completely dwarf yours.*

I stand in awe of my thrifty neighbors' abilities to butcher their own livestock, make their own soap, and bake their own hamburger buns. My husband, who has worked outdoors all his life, learns new things all the time from our outdoorsy friends.

Each of these people has a Ph.D. in their life experience and *you* are the new intern in the "office." When your tractor breaks down, when you have to cut down that huge dead tree, when you want to bake a loaf of bread that doesn't turn out hard as a brick, your new friends and neighbors are the experts you'll consult.

Don't make the mistake of looking down at a mechanic or seamstress or store clerk. When you simplify your life, you learn to value *everyone's* contributions to society.

# .339.

## TURN YOUR NECESSITY INTO A VIRTUE

When you simplify your life, you probably won't be earning as much money. You will need to pare down your expenses and your purchases. You may be giving up a prestigious job and day-long shopping expeditions. Some people see this as the ultimate deprivation.

We are trained and tricked and shamed every day, in every possible media source, to see ourselves as failures if we don't have that big house, new SUV, iPod, designer running shoes, jewelry, and a new boat every summer. It's insidious and wrong.

But you don't have to fall for it. You no longer have to play the sucker to these hucksters. Imagine being able to say to someone, "Nice house! It's a lot bigger than mine," knowing that yours is paid for. Imagine the melting sensation you feel when your teenaged son or daughter gives you a hug for no particular reason with the words "I love you" attached.

Be proud of your new frugality. Brag about how little money you spent this week. Let your gifts be homemade and simple (hint: cookies are *always* a hit), and don't let anyone's curled lip or lifted eyebrow deter you. Their opinion doesn't matter. You're on a mission, by golly, and you're doing the right thing.

And remember to sprinkle your pity with understanding for all those poor saps still caught up with the consumer culture. Some people just don't get it. But someday, with your example, they just may.

# . 340 .

## PREPARE TO LOSE YOUR FRIENDS

One unanticipated side-effect of simplifying is that you may lose friends. In turning your necessities into virtues, the reaction of your friends might range from utter bafflement to outright hostility. After all, who are *you* to suddenly develop this holier-than-thou attitude about staying home with your kids or refusing to go further into debt? It might be that your new attitude and behavior is pricking something deep in their subconscious, and they may react with defensiveness.

Friends who loved coming to your catered holiday soirées may not appreciate an invitation to a potluck.

Friends who enjoyed visiting your McMansion or going on a cruise on your yacht may not appreciate your new suburban home and rowboat.

The next time you go on a shopping spree with your friends, they may be a little put off when you roll into the Goodwill parking lot.

Some of your friends might be upset when they come to your place for coffee and cake, and your well-behaved kids are doing their homeschool studies.

Some of your coworkers might be miffed when you refuse to join the juicy gossip circle discussing the new secretary and her boss.

So prepare to lose some friends. But that's okay. Nothing says that friendship is static. Your new-found simplicity may honestly baffle some, but others will applaud you on your way and may even join you. And the ones who join you, and the new friends you'll find on your journey, will be *true* friends, not fair-weather ones.

# .341.

## DITCH THE COMMUTE

Commuting is one of the most frequently mentioned "complexifiers" in peoples' lives. Unfortunately, ditching your commute is not easy. It's do-able, but not easy.

You could move closer to your place of work. If you work in an expensive city, though, you may not be able to afford this. Or, if you try, you can work longer hours to pay for your new home, which hardly simplifies things.

You could take a job closer to where you live. However, you're not likely to find a job that pays as well as where you're working now. That's why, at the moment, your commute is "worth" it.

If your company has a branch location in a smaller city or town farther away from your current location, you could take a position there and move closer to your new job. This might mean a cut in pay or a cut in "prestige," but it would also reduce your commute (and likely reduce your living expenses as well).

You could telecommute. You could start your own business and work at home or in a nearby location. You could work part-time.

This would be a good moment to look outside your paradigm (#219) and see the options and possibilities that you haven't considered before. This may include a radical change of career or a radical move to a different city or state.

Ditching the commute, once you've accomplished it, will free up umpteen hours of the day. Your life will be simpler.

# . 342 .

## WORK AT HOME

Ah, now we come to the ultimate simple living dream: to work at home. Think of it. No commute, no awful co-workers, no boss looking over your shoulder. You get to sleep in, you get more time with your family, you can work in your pajamas, you get to set your own hours. Life doesn't get much sweeter—or simpler—than that.

I have good news and bad news: it's all of this, and more. That's the good news. The bad news is that often you have to work your fanny off to make enough money to support your family.

Working at home is not something I suggest you do immediately. Do your homework, treat it like a business, and make sensible and realistic plans. Probably one of the most prudent ways to start a home business is to do so in your spare time, working evenings and weekends.

Or you might make arrangements with your current (or a new) employer to do your job at home. Perhaps you can "commute" via modem, or only come into the office once or twice a week.

This is another place to look outside your paradigm (#219). Do you want to stay within your current field, or do you want to try something new? There are many books out there that can help you decide a potential home business. What you do is entirely up to your interests, abilities, and dedication.

Don't go into this thinking it will be easy or quick. It can, however, be worth it.

# .343.

## FIRE THE NANNY

Fire the nanny. Dump the daycare. Bounce the babysitter. Stay home and raise your own kids. Do whatever it takes, even if it requires a significant sacrifice, for one parent to be home with your children.

How? Well, you might try moving to a cheaper house. Sell the overpriced SUV. Stagger your work hours. Stop eating out. Budget your money. Ditch the debt. Stop living beyond your means. Whatever it takes, *raise your own kids*.

Your children are a creation shaped by your love and care. They are your gift to the world, and the lasting echo of *you* after you're gone. Raising your own kids is your duty and obligation and responsibility. It is also your greatest joy. Your children deserve it and you'll feel better for doing it.

The reason this concept is under "Radical Simplicity" is that it won't sync with a lot of today's modern, hip, career-oriented people. If you're someone with high career ambitions, then I won't be able to convince you that staying home with your kids will simplify your life. Instead, you'll have to utilize some of the other suggestions in this book to make your schedule less hectic and allow you to have as much time as possible with your children. If you're a single parent, then your life is automatically more complex, and firing the nanny or dumping the daycare may not be an option at the moment.

But if your secret dream is to be a stay-at-home parent, then do whatever it takes to make that step.

# .344.

## HOMESCHOOL

How, you may ask, will homeschooling simplify your life? Won't teaching your own kids make things more complex?

In the short term, perhaps. It takes awhile to settle into your particular teaching style. Sometimes it takes kids awhile to "decompress" from a school environment. There may be conflict, there may be tears, there may be frustration while everyone adjusts.

However, consider the long-term benefits: your children won't be affected by negative socialization at school. Drugs, teen sex, gang influences, inappropriate fashions, and the blurring of the simple concepts of "right" and "wrong" are much less likely to happen at home. Your children are more likely to maintain the values you cherish and not adopt the questionable values of a massive peer system. Because of this, you are unlikely to experience as many adolescent problems with attitude, rebellion, depression, and angst common among public school teens. Now that's simplicity.

Admittedly, this "simplification" idea isn't for everyone. It requires a serious commitment. But it's worth considering, especially if you have questions about the quality or influence of the schools in your area. If your child has a particular talent—music or dance or a sport—homeschooling gives you flexibility to address that talent.

For a nice overview of homeschooling, read *Homeschooling for Excellence* by David and Micki Colfax. Also look at the Homeschool Legal Defense Association's Webpage for a list of the legal requirements in every state (www.hslda.org).

# .345.

## WORK PART TIME

Gerald Celente, founder of the Trends Research Institute, said, "We hear the same refrain all the time from people: I have no life. I get up in the morning, daycare, eldercare, a forty-minute commute to work. I have to work late. I get home at night, there's laundry, bills to pay, jam something into the microwave oven. I'm exhausted, I go to sleep, I wake up and the routine begins all over again. This is what life has become in America."

One of the techniques people frequently use to simplify their lives is to work part time. I can already hear the howls of protest. How can I work part time when I have a house payment and a car payment and student loans and credit card bills?

Okay, obviously you can't work part time if you're staggering under all that debt. Refer to #186 and get out of debt. Yes, it may take you several years, but at the end you'll be debt-free and then you'll have more options, such as part-time employment.

Working part time will mean more than just paying off your bills. It also means you've scaled back your life in terms of possessions and acquisitions. It means you've learned how to be thrifty and frugal. It means you've learned that there is more to life than just work. It means you value your time and family more than your career, more than possessions, more than empty status. That's a lot to think about.

# .346.

## GET A DIVORCE

I hope I've made it clear in the course of this book that I do not believe divorce is something people should undergo lightly. I strongly believe in marital commitment, duty, obligation, and vows. But I also realize there may come a time when it's better to divorce.

Physical or sexual abuse, addictions such as drinking or drugs, multiple affairs . . . these are things that breach the marital vows. If you've already changed yourself and you've tried to change your spouse—if you've tried counseling, therapy, and pleading to no avail—if the loss exceeds the profit in your marriage, you might consider divorce.

There are some things that cannot be changed in a person. If you *chose poorly* in the first place when selecting your spouse, consider simplifying your life by divorcing him or her, especially if you or your children's lives are in danger (due to beatings, rape, etc.).

I hear about women who have the courage to leave an abusive relationship and seek a battered women's shelter . . . only to later return to the abuser. So be sensible. If you or your children are suffering at the hands of your spouse, for their sake it's wiser to leave. You don't want your children growing up witnessing an abusive life and then assuming that's normal, because then the cycle tends to continue. The children might grow up and either become abusers or marry abusers.

So consider a divorce. And then make sure you choose more wisely in the future.

# .347.

## GET RID OF THE TV

Untold precious hours of our time are wasted by staring at a black box in a dark room at a machine that invades our thoughts and our souls. We voluntarily witness things we claim we're against—violence and sexual innuendo and bad language and the degeneration of family values. This isn't a hard one; just stop it.

Remember if you watch two hours a day of television, that amounts to thirty twenty-four hour days (an entire month) wasted every year (see #300, Wasting Away Again in TV-Ville). Those two hours a day add up to over 700 hours a year, folks. That's a month of twenty-four hour days or—get this—three months of nine-to-five days. You want to finally start that home business? There's your first three months without having to give up your day job . . . all by saying good-bye to the boob tube.

Take those hours and apply them to something useful and productive. Spend time with your kids. Make a nice dinner. Learn a new skill. Help a friend. Call your mother. Volunteer somewhere. The possibilities are endless.

I have no patience whatsoever with people who claim to have "no time," but then plant their butts in front of the TV for two hours a day or more. That kind of excuse just doesn't fly.

If you know you need to take action, consider being radical and give your TV away so you won't be tempted. Learn to fill those empty hours. Once you get over the shock, you might find yourself free at last . . . free to seek the simplicity you claim you want.

# . 348 .

## DIAL DOWN TO DIAL UP

Congratulations! You've radically simplified your life by killing your TV. You now have more hours to put to better use. Hmmm. Maybe you should tell all your friends about the new, simpler you. There are tons of chat rooms online dealing with simplicity—now you have the time to join a few of them. You can do some online shopping. Check out profiles on some social networking pages. Watch a movie online. Perhaps (don't tell anyone!) take a peek at some "adult" Websites.

It does no good to sanctimoniously kill your TV if you become hooked on the Internet instead. You can waste time just as efficiently, and ignore your family just as much, with a computer as with a television.

The Internet is the greatest marvel of our age. You can get information, entertainment, and even gain employment online without ever getting out of your chair at home. It can help solve educational questions (we homeschool) and offer support for everything from losing weight to handling rare diseases.

It also offers temptations our society has never faced before— online gambling, chat rooms where we can "meet" people of the opposite gender, pornography, endless products to buy with the mere click of a mouse. Has this simplified your life?

If your online time is effecting your goals for simplifying, considering dialing down to dial-up. Dial-up Internet service still allows you to get online to read the news and check your emails, without offering the instant, easy, and rapid temptation of delving into risky behaviors.

# .349.

## DIVIDE THE LABOR

Just a thought: let the man of the family earn the income.

Ooh, told you this was radical.

Most men feel more "manly" if they are the breadwinners. This isn't politically correct, true, *but it's genetic*. Men are hardwired to want to protect and provide for their families. While some men are (ahem) less "wired" than others, they are the exception rather than the rule.

Most women are hard-wired to nurture a home and family. Today's culture has denigrated that instinct and made it something to be ashamed of. Women (or men, for that matter) who choose to stay home, raise their kids, and maintain a loving, welcoming house are laughed at and accused of wasting their intelligence and education.

But, as with getting over your ego (#5), and by not worrying about what others think (#12), you might try it and find that the stress in your life may decrease tremendously.

This is not intended to put down or negate the tremendous strides women have made in the last three decades toward equality in the workplace. If you have no kids, then you're free to climb the corporate ladder all the way to the top, if you wish, and I'm glad we women have the greater opportunity to do so. I've worked in a corporate environment. I enjoyed the bustle of the working world. Been there, done that.

But when children come, the simplest thing to do is raise them yourself. Divide the labor. It's much easier in the end.

# . 350 .

## MAKING A LIVING WORTHWHILE

For working mothers, career success frequently goes hand-in-glove with guilt. The guilt of not giving your family your whole attention, the guilt of putting your kids in daycare, the guilt of not putting home-cooked meals on the table . . . it goes on and on, and it's never-ending. Besides, isn't there a secret, often-denied part of you that just wants to give up the corporate mentality and stay home with your kids?

This confirms the hard-wired nature of men and women. Again, don't get me wrong, there are times and places for women to work outside the home, and I've done it. But in our situation, I'm glad that we've made the *sacrifices* and *choices* for me to be home.

But of course, I still work. We have a home business, and I work in the shop part-time. I also do desktop publishing and writing on the side to bring in additional income. But my primary focus is raising our kids and running the home, something I am proud to do.

With one person "making the living" and the other person "making the living worthwhile," beautiful things can happen. The division of labor frees up the worry for each partner. Assuming it's a traditional division, the man knows his home and children are in excellent hands, and the woman doesn't need to stress about work, commuting, daycare, and who's going to cook dinner.

And the children thrive. Absolutely thrive. Their lives are simpler, and so are yours.

# .351.

## PRACTICE YOUR FAITH

Remember how Ebenezer Scrooge vowed to keep Christmas in his heart all year long? Well, he had a point.

Practicing your faith is a wonderfully simplifying thing to do. I don't mean just going to church or reading your Bible or other outward manifestations. No, I mean keeping Christmas in your heart all year.

It might mean doing something nice for someone . . . secretly (because so often we look for others to praise our charitable acts). It might mean giving something of yourself—your time, your money, your blood, your sympathetic shoulder, whatever—without expecting anything in return. It might mean making this world just a little bit better every day by smiling at a stranger, or helping the little old lady across the street, or opening the door for someone.

William Penn, the founder of Pennsylvania, said, "God is better served in resisting a Temptation to Evil, than in many formal Prayers." Did you resist the urge the shout at the driver who cut you off in traffic? Did you take a deep breath rather than holler at your kid for spilling milk? Did you resist the temptation to turn your husband down because you weren't "in the mood," because you knew lovemaking would make him happy? Did you resist the temptation to buy something expensive because your credit card is maxed out and you're on a budget?

Little things done with a full heart are immensely satisfying. Remember how Jesus enjoined us to treat others as we would like to be treated? What a spiffy idea.

So why is this under Radical Simplicity? Because we so seldom do it.

# . 352 .

## MOVE TO THE COUNTRY

When people hear "simple living," they often think "country living." It is automatically assumed that living in the country is simpler than living in the city. Sometimes it is.

Country living provides vistas of great beauty, clean air and water, birdsongs, helpful neighbors, peace and quiet, closeness to nature, and lots and lots of elbow room.

People as diverse as William Penn ("The Country Life is to be preferr'd; for there we see the Works of God; but in Cities little else but the Works of Men: And the one makes a better Subject for our Contemplation than the other . . . ") and Aesop (remember the City Mouse and the Country Mouse?) have espoused rural life as superior to urban life. It all depends on what you want. Go back and examine your business plan (#221) and see if "living in the country" is part of your goals.

It was for us. We wanted to be in a place where our family could raise livestock, have a garden, and grow fruit trees. These are obligations that may not necessarily simplify your life (did you know that cows need to be milked *every single day?*), but they are obligations that bring joy and a feeling of independence to us. To that end, our homestead simplifies our lives. We are living our dream, but here's the thing: it's *our* dream. It may not be *yours*.

So don't move to the country unless you really, really want to. But for those who do, your lives may be simpler and happier for it.

# . 353 .

## DON'T MOVE TO THE COUNTRY

Warning: moving to the country will *not* simplify your life if you hate country living. As Doris Janzen Longacre said, "The trouble with simple living is that, though it can be joyful, rich, and creative, it isn't simple." It is a true irony that attaining a rural life can be a very complicated thing.

Country living involves mud, snow, unpaved roads, and no Starbucks. Stores are few and far between and sometimes not well stocked. Communities are small and insular and anything you do will be noted and observed and gossiped over.

If you hate mud and isolation, if you can't live without your latté, if you would curl up and die without public transportation, then don't move to the country no matter how idyllic people tell you it is. It's only idyllic if you're disposed to that kind of environment to begin with.

If shoveling animal manure or getting your hands dirty in the garden or dealing with yet *another* broken fence or being stranded by a snowstorm or having neighbors butcher their livestock in their yard or hearing gunshots during hunting season would get on your nerves, then don't move to the country.

If you feel like you might miss the amenities of the city, then you'll probably be happier staying where you are. Don't add stress to your life by moving someplace you'll end up hating.

To each his own, of course. But be honest with yourself about what avenue would suit you best, because to deliberately plant yourself where it's tough to bloom is not a simple matter.

# .354.

## MOVE TO A PLACE
## WITH LIKE-MINDED PEOPLE

If moving to a different town or even state is in your plans for a simpler life, take warning: make sure you investigate your destination area to see if you're among like-minded people.

Beyond the usual red-state-blue-state demographics, it is wise to be aware that there are certain places where the political or social climate may not be to your liking. If you have strong political beliefs, for instance, and you move to an area where the majority of people are at the opposite end of the spectrum, you're going to be miserable.

Be sure to research your target location thoroughly. Subscribe to the local newspapers. Visit. Rent for awhile, if you can.

There is joy in finding yourself among others who share your values. When we moved to Idaho, for instance, we found to our delight that we were among neighbors who cherish independence, family values, and thrift just as we do.

We know of a couple who purchased property recently in our area. They had wildly different viewpoints from those of their immediate neighbors. Wildly different. I met them once or twice and they seemed like nice folks, but I sensed trouble ahead because of their different attitudes and viewpoints. In our brief conversations, they immediately launched into their personal philosophies in a rather belligerent, defensive manner . . . almost as if they sensed they were different. I don't know all the details, but their property was up for sale again within a year.

Relocation is much simpler if you know you'll be welcomed in your new neighborhood.

# . 355 .

## PREPARE TO EVACUATE

In 1982, home from college for the summer, I watched as a wildfire roared toward my parent's house in California. We prepared to evacuate as we saw the blaze creep closer and closer. Overhead, helicopters and tanker jets dropped loads of water and fire retardant. The blaze burned 25,000 acres and dozens and dozens of homes. Thankfully, my parent's house was spared.

There are very few places in this country that don't get some sort of natural disaster. The southeastern states get hurricanes. The midwest gets tornadoes. The east gets ice storms. So be prepared.

Hurricanes Katrina and Rita illustrated that the government cannot provide individual assistance on a timely basis. It behooves us to depend upon ourselves, as much as possible, when an emergency hits.

There are times when you need to flee your home in a hurry, usually because of an oncoming natural disaster. For this you will need grab-and-go kits containing a minimum amount of food, water, clothing, and medicines for your family members. These are pre-packed in backpacks or dufflebags for literally grabbing and leaving. Depending on how much time you have to prepare (ranging from days for hurricanes to no time at all for earthquakes), you may want to include copies of critical documents, precious photographs, and your pets.

You cannot prepare for everything. But it's never, ever a bad idea to have something prepared to make you and your family marginally comfortable for a period of a few days, in case you are forced from your home.

# . 356 .

## PREPARE TO HUNKER DOWN

Not all emergencies require fleeing. Sometimes you need to hunker down in your home for an extended period of time without the possibility of leaving. Getting snowed in by a massive storm or isolated by an ice storm are examples of this type of emergency. Your preparations can be a little more extensive since you'll be at home.

Always have some food on hand. This does not mean *frozen* foods. If you have no electricity, your frozen foods will defrost and rot. You need water, enough for each member of your family plus your pets. You need a light source (candles or kerosene lamps plus matches). And you may need a heat source and cooking method that won't kill you from carbon monoxide poisoning.

Here in rural north Idaho, several miles off-road, we never know when we'll be snowed in. As I write this, we just finished a week-long stint of not being able to leave the house because of the high snow drifts across the road.

That's okay. We have our woodstove, we have oil lamps in case the power goes out, we have schoolbooks to continue the girls' education. We have plenty of food and water. We had no problems at all in dealing with the weather.

An added advantage of preparing to hunker down is that you become less of a burden on those whose job it is to rescue people. If you have no need to request help from emergency services personnel, then they (and you) are free to help those in more dire straights. Help others by helping yourself.

# .357.

## SELL YOUR HOUSE

Is your mortgage killing you? Are you staggering under monthly payments that are so high you're lying awake at night, worrying? Are you wondering why you ever thought a large home was necessary to your happiness and success? Could it be that you fell for the line that society fed us, that more is better?

Is it worth it? Is it honestly, truly worth it to own such a huge home? Do you really think you'll ever pay it off, or will you be enslaved to mortgage payments for the rest of your life? Is owning a huge home *conducive to a simple life?*

Unless you have an extraordinarily large family, I honestly cannot think of a single good reason to own a McMansion except status and ego. And now, too many are suffering as a result of unemployment or underwater mortgages.

I understand that with a depressed housing market, selling your home for what you believe is a fair value may be tough. But if you can't pay your bills, selling for less than it's worth will at least get you out from under the mortgage.

On the other hand, if you're underwater—meaning your home isn't even worth what you owe—than your options are more limited. It's time to consult a financial expert to examine your options and then act within what is ethical, moral, and legal.

The decision to sell one's home is hard. Our home is, after all, the place where we've spent years living and raising our families. But sometimes to simplify, you have to surrender.

# .358.

## SELL YOUR CAR

Along the lines of Sell Your House (#357), it might be worth thinking about selling your car, too. No, I'm not advocating going entirely without a car, although it's possible if you live in a city with suitable public transportation. Most of us need a car to go about our daily business. But nothing says we need a car that costs more than many homes in rural parts of the country.

I've heard radio ads where you "only" have to pay $499 a month for (gasp!) forty-eight months. Wow! What a deal! You get caught up with status, ego, and salesman pressure and drive away in a brand-new SUV.

And for the next four years you will be shelling out five hundred smackers a month for something that lost literally one-third of its value the moment you drove it off the car lot. How sensible is that?

I've read frequent advice that says if you *really* want to be under the onus of car payments, then pay yourself that $500 a month for a trial period to see what the car payments are like. If you can easily afford them, then great—you've just saved a spiffy down payment. But if, at the end of that trial period, you find the payments are taking a huge bite out of your household budget, then you're better off not buying that new car.

For around $5,000 (give or take), you can get a handsome, safe, two-year-old vehicle and drive it for fifteen years.

# .359.

## LEARN A SURVIVAL SKILL

No, I don't mean you should learn how to start a fire with a bow-and-drill (though it couldn't hurt). I mean you should learn a skill that will allow you to live a different life than you now have. If something is forced upon you (such as unemployment) then you'll do better if you have a skill that can be broadly applied in a wide variety of settings. Consider such skills as woodworking, mechanical skills, sewing, cooking, typing, answering phones, metalworking, construction, plumbing, electrical wiring, housecleaning, waitressing, medical transcription, elder care...and the list goes on.

Learn something that you can fall back on if you lose your job. It's better to have a wide range of skills you can apply to new employment. Or, if you chose a radically simpler life with fewer economic needs, you might enjoy doing this skill more than your previous job.

My father used to tell us kids that we could major in whatever we wished in college, as long as we had an employable skill. My skill was typing. Over the years, I've worked as a legal secretary, as a projects coordinator, a transcriptionist, a writer, and I've done desktop publishing—all related to my ability to type.

My husband's skill is woodworking. In fact, he left a lucrative career as an environmental engineering geologist to become a woodworker, and never looked back.

Who knows, your skill could lead to a new vocation . . . or at least a more constructive hobby than watching sitcoms.

# . 360 .

## TURN YOUR HOBBY INTO
## A BUSINESS

Having successfully turned a hobby into a business, I have both praise and warnings for going this route.

For praise, I can attest that few things give more satisfaction than taking something you love to do and earning a living with it. We make our income almost exclusively from our home woodcraft business, and it never fails to amaze us that we can do this.

But coupled with the praise come many warnings. Not every hobby translates well into a business. If your hobby is writing poetry, you are unlikely to sell enough poems to support your family. If your hobby is canning, you probably aren't going to be able to sell your canned items. If your hobby is embroidery or doing crossword puzzles, these obviously aren't likely to bring in much money.

The often-repeated (and unfortunately true) advice is to *find a niche and fill it.* If your hobby is to make a product or offer a service that people want to buy, you have a much better chance of turning your hobby into a business.

My strongest advice is to approach the idea of turning a hobby into a business seriously and with sound business sense. And trust me on this, do *not* quit your day job in the touching hope that your new business will immediately succeed and replace your nine-to-five income. Businesses take time to build. Even an in-demand product is unlikely to replace your nine-to-five income immediately. Play it safe and keep your day job until your new business is up and running. Remember, unemployment is not simple.

# .361.

## DON'T HAVE KIDS

Until you're married, that is.

According to Blake Bailey of the National Center for Policy Analysis, about thirty-one million Americans live in households below the poverty level. He says, "Poverty is more than a lack of income. *It is also the consequence of specific behaviors and decisions.* The 2001 Census data clearly show that dropping out of high school, staying single, having children without a spouse, working only part time or not working at all substantially increase the chances of long-term poverty. *Certain behaviors are a recipe for success.* Among those who finish high school, get married, have children only within a marriage and go to work, the odds of long-term poverty are virtually nil." [Emphasis added.]

Get the gist here? These are all *choices.* These are things that are (mostly) within your control. Don't have children until you've finished (at least) high school and gotten married, in that order. By having children out of wedlock, you may be dooming yourself and your family to financial struggles that you might never experience if you were married.

And of course, stay married. If you've "chosen wisely" (#50) when picking a spouse, and if you treat your spouse kindly, then your chances of remaining married are excellent. This translates into much happier, more secure kids, and less chance of living below the poverty line.

Don't doom yourself or your future children to a lifetime of hardship. Take Blake Bailey's words to heart and do the simple steps necessary to keep yourself out of poverty.

# . 362 .

## TAKE A RADICAL VACATION

Everyone has different ideas on what constitutes a simpler life. If you have dreams to move to a small town, turn your hobby into a business, live in a cabin in the woods, or other radically different ideas . . . now's the time to try it.

Sage advice from realtors before you move is to research your target location carefully. This advice can extend toward simplicity as well. If you have a notion about what radical change will simplify your life, give it a test run before you dive in.

So take a week off and try it. Stay in a cabin in the woods with no electricity. Visit that small town and spend time eavesdropping in the café. Live on a farm for a week and see how you like mucking out the barn. Try spending forty hours churning out three hundred pieces of the product you know will make you a millionaire working from home.

Yes, I know, doing something for a mere week hardly illustrates the whole story. You're only dipping your toes in. But if you find yourself unable to enjoy even this brief attempt, then it's likely that this aspect of simplifying may not be for you.

Gauge the reaction of your family members, too. If you and your spouse adored the week in the woods but your kids were going out of their mind with boredom, then it might cause a lot of trouble if you up and move to the woods. Young children can adapt; older children have a harder time.

If nothing else, you'll have done a reality check on your dreams and gained some insight about what it might take to radically simplify.

# . 363 .

## RADICAL DEFINITIONS

It's hard to always know which behaviors or values will lead to a simpler life. Today's culture and media don't do us any favors. The old-fashioned values are now considered just that: out of date, kind of quaint, and rather silly.

The words that used to define certain acceptable modes of behavior and morality have been weakened, watered down, or even completely flipped around. *Rights* are no longer God-given and government-secured. Now the term refers to anything you want that someone else is disinclined to give you. *Change* is a goal, rather than a process. It's not a *tax*, it's a contribution. *Volunteering* may be made mandatory (go figure) in order to earn a diploma or get your paycheck.

So, radically, I suggest that you begin to *really* think about the things you hear on the news, or on the street, or from your friends. Start recognizing that the words you hear may not be what the speaker means. Their concept of *choice* may not include *your* choice. Their beliefs about *obligation* may mean not what you will accept, but what they wish to assign to you. And their definition of *duty* might only apply to their political philosophy or organization, not your duty to your family, friends, and God.

Knowing the difference between the old meanings and definitions of these important words may not in itself simplify your life. But correctly understanding someone else's intentions for you and your family can.

Things that are old-fashioned may not be merely quaint or silly as well as out of date. They may hold the key for moving toward a simpler life.

# . 364 .

## SELL YOUR POSSESSIONS

These days it's best to be quick on your feet. You never know when you'll face a job loss, transfer, or even eviction which may require you to move in a hurry. How much better if you're not loaded with so many possessions that you're glued to one place?

I have some friends who, due to a series of job losses and other economic issues, moved six times in two years. By the time they settled more or less permanently, their possessions had been pared down to what could be moved easily. Even their living room furniture was made of wicker with handsome cushions, which were lightweight and easy to move. They could, quite literally, pack everything in their home and load it onto a moving van within a day.

It's worth noting that this family is relieved to be settled at last, but they have resisted the urge to reacquire the possessions they once had. This streamlined lifestyle has allowed them to buy a smaller (meaning, less expensive) home, one well within their budget. Though the circumstances under which they jettisoned so many things were difficult, the result has been a blessing.

You don't have to go quite to this extreme, but consider the advantages of a severe paring down of your possessions. What kind of valuables do you own which, let's face it, you don't use or appreciate? Can you put them up for sale on eBay and earn a little extra money? Could you have a yard sale and bring in some cash?

Less is more, as the simplicity gurus are fond of saying. In an uncertain economy, this could well be true.

# .365.

## LIFE WAS NOT SIMPLER IN
## THE GOOD OLD DAYS

This is a misconception that never fails to send me into peals of laughter. Simpler? In the good old days? *What* good old days? You mean the ones with shorter life expectancies, primitive medical care, the danger of childbirth, blatant racism, no child labor laws, unclean drinking water, no refrigeration, no household appliances, sixteen-hour workdays, questionable hygiene, washboards, wood cookstoves, once-a-week baths, once-a-week clean clothes, corsets, no voting rights for women, and *polio*?

But there *were* some better things in the "good old days." There was more family togetherness because there were no distractions from television and computers. There were more creative toys that fostered children's imaginations because there were no electronic toys. Kids were better behaved because they were better disciplined. People took more personal responsibility rather than looking to the government for handouts. The government took less of our money. There was less focus on "me" and more focus on community—not the phony "community" of chat rooms, but real people.

Here's the good news: if you truly simplify your life, you can have your cake and eat it, too. You can have all the good parts of the "good old days" while retaining all the modern wonders we take for granted.

If you raise your children simply, if you discipline them and give them lots of your time and attention, if you cut back your consumerism and television viewing and focus on what's truly important in life . . . then the good old days won't be "old." They'll be here. And now.

Now *that's* simple living. Good luck on your journey.

## SEND ME YOUR THOUGHTS

HAVE YOU SIMPLIFIED your life? Are you working toward your dream? What techniques have you used to achieve a richer, more meaningful life? I would love to hear your reader feedback.

Please send your comments to: patrice@patricelewis.com

# RECOMMENDED READING LIST

Aslett, Don; Clutter's Last Stand.  Marsh Creek Press, 2005

Aslett, Don; Not for Packrats Only.  Marsh Creek Press, 1991

Colfax, David and Micki; Homeschooling for Excellence. Grand Central Publishing, 1988

Edell, Dean; Eat, Drink and Be Merry.  Harper Paperbacks, 2000

Ramsey, Dave; The Total Money Makeover.  Thomas Nelson, 2009

Rawles, James Wesley; How to Survive the End of the World as We Know It.  Plume, 2009

Robin, Vicki, Joe Dominguez, Monique Tilford; Your Money or Your Life.  Penguin 2008

Robinson, Jo and Jean Staeheli; Unplug the Christmas Machine.  Harper Paperbacks, 1991

Sears, William and Martha; The Baby Book.  Little, Brown and Company, 2003

Stanley, Thomas; The Millionaire Next Door.  Taylor Trade Publishing, 2010

Thoreau, Henry David; Walden.  Beacon Press, 2004

Venker, Suzanne; 7 Myths of Working Mothers.  Spence Publishing Company, 2008

Wilder, Laura Ingalls; Little House in the Big Woods.  Harper Collins, 2004

Winn, Marie; The Plug-In Drug.  Penguin, 1985

The Bible